Mary Barnard,
American Imagist

Portrait of Mary Barnard, from the Mary Barnard Papers in the Yale Collection of American Literature. Courtesy of Elizabeth J. Bell.

Mary Barnard,

American Imagist

Sarah Barnsley

State University of New York Press

Front cover: Portrait of Mary Barnard, from the Mary Barnard Papers in the Yale Collection of American Literature. Courtesy of Elizabeth J. Bell.

Back cover: Untitled watercolor by Mary Barnard, from the Mary Barnard Papers. Courtesy of Elizabeth J. Bell.

Published by
State University of New York Press, Albany

Printed in the United States of America

For information, contact
State University of New York Press, Albany, NY
www.sunypress.edu

Production, Laurie D. Searl
Marketing, Anne M. Valentine

Library of Congress Cataloging-in-Publication Data

Barnsley, Sarah, 1974–
Mary Barnard, American Imagist / Sarah Barnsley.
pages cm
Includes bibliographical references and index.
ISBN 978-1-4384-4855-8 (hc : alk. paper) 978-1-4384-4856-5 (pb : alk. paper)
1. Barnard, Mary—Criticism and interpretation. 2. American poetry—20th century—History and criticism. 3. Modernism (Literature)—United States. I. Title.

PS3503.A5825Z54 2013
811'.54—dc23 2012049543

10 9 8 7 6 5 4 3 2 1

for Louise and Zachary

Contents

ILLUSTRATIONS

Acknowledgments

This book would not have happened without the immeasurable support shown by Elizabeth J. Bell, literary executor for the estate of Mary Barnard, and her husband, Bruce Bell, over the past ten years. From the moment I stepped off the plane at Portland International Airport in summer 2003, a complete stranger, they have done nothing but encourage and assist me in my happy Mary Barnard projects. Through email, letter, phone, and cherished visits, Betty has gone above and beyond to read my work, offer clarifications, suggest directions, and fuel my research with such golden materials that I have never once forgotten the great privilege afforded me. Heartfelt thanks are due to Bruce for his wisdom, insight, good humor, and, it must be said, his knack of selecting the very best wine to round off a hard day's scholaring—and for teaching me to drive on the wrong side of the road. Both have become dear friends to me and my family.

Neither this friendship nor my interest in Mary Barnard would have evolved without Ellen K. Stauder at Reed College, who introduced me to Mary Barnard's work in 1995 and then to Betty Bell in 2001. Thank you for quietly watching as I got on with it and for generously giving your time to the Mary Barnard Centenary at Reed in 2011.

Thanks are due to other friends and colleagues in the Pacific Northwest: to James Anderson, Mary Barnard's publisher and long-term champion, for enchanting Barnard conversations and for the gift of letters that I've since donated to the Beinecke; to Thomas Donovan, a close friend of Mary Barnard's, who did me the kindness of alerting me to the KBOO radio recording of Barnard reading; to Anita Helle and Peter Sears, for their profundity of knowledge and their magnificent contributions to the Mary Barnard Centenary; to Mary Barnard's friends, including Anita Bigelow, Dorothy Blair, Harris Dusenberry, Sue Hennum, Cynthia Kimball, Mary

Pat Peterson, and her cousin, Suzanne Ila Gray, all of whom have helped to illuminate my picture of Mary Barnard through the generosity of conversation and, in the case of Sue Hennum, through a wonderful sharing of papers accompanied by the world's most delicious blueberry pie. Thank you to Robin Tovey, James Kahan, and all at Reed College who enabled the Mary Barnard Centenary to take place and to Reed alumnus Constance Puttnam for kindly talking to me about her correspondence with Mary Barnard.

On the other side of the Atlantic, I cannot forget the thanks due to friends and colleagues at Goldsmiths, University of London: to Helen Carr, for supervising my PhD thesis on Barnard (and for all the "after sales service"); to Maura Dooley, for examining it so warmly; to Chris Baldick and Caroline Blinder, for their early encouragements; and to Padraig Kirwan, for keeping my spirits high and my coffee cup filled. Thanks are due to scholars and poets across the two nations: Richard Deming, Nikolai Duffy, Suzanne Heyd, Emma Kimberley, Emily Jeremiah, David Murray, Katrina Naomi, and Eric White. Your interests in my project gave me the confidence to keep doing it.

This may be a slim book, but it is one built out of archives. In addition to those provided by Betty Bell, I have enjoyed substantial assistance from Gay Walker and Mark Kuestner of Special Collections at Reed College Library and from Patricia Willis, Nancy Kuhl, and all the staff at the Beinecke Rare Book and Manuscript Library at Yale University. I was greatly honored to receive the H.D. Fellowship in American Literature at the Beinecke over 2007 and 2008 to complete the research of this book.

An earlier version of the discussion of Mary Barnard's "North Window" in chapters 1 and 2 was originally published in *Western American Literature*; an earlier version of section 2.3 in chapter 2 was originally published in *Paideuma*.

A shortened version of chapter 3 is due to appear in the "Hellenism Unbound" edition of *Synthesis* scheduled for Fall 2013.

Thank you to James Peltz, Jen Stelling, Laurie Searl, Anne Valentine, and Catherine Chilton at SUNY Press.

Thank you, finally, to Louise, for being there from the beginning, and to Zachary, for arriving at the end. This book is my gift to you.

Grateful acknowledgements are due to James Anderson, for permission to print from the unpublished transcript of the address given by him at the Memorial Service for Mary Barnard, Vancouver, Washington, September 4, 2001; Bob Arnold, for permission to reprint from his unpublished correspondence; Elizabeth J. Bell, for permission to reprint from unpublished and published material by Mary Barnard, including cover art and illustrative material under copyright by Barnardworks and now held at the Beinecke Rare Book and Manuscript Library, Yale University; Elizabeth J. Bell, for permission to reprint from her unpublished correspondence; Robert Bertholf, for permission to reprint from his unpublished correspondence; Farrar, Straus and Giroux, for permission to reprint an excerpt from an unpublished letter dated May 6, 1973, written by Elizabeth Bishop to Mary Barnard, copyright © 2012 by The Alice H. Methfessel Trust, printed by permission of Farrar, Straus and Giroux, LLC, on behalf of the Elizabeth Bishop Estate; Reed College, for permission to reprint previously unpublished correspondence by Victor Chittick; Erik Reece, for permission to reprint from previously unpublished correspondence by Guy Davenport; Aletha Decker Carlton, for permission to reprint a publicity photograph of Mary Barnard taken by Hermine Duthie Decker; Germaine Greer, for permission to reprint from her unpublished correspondence; the New Directions Ownership Trust, for permission to reprint previously unpublished letters by James Laughlin, copyright © 2013 by The New Directions Ownership Trust; Paul Mariani, for permission to reprint from his unpublished correspondence; Paula Paige, for permission to reprint previously unpublished correspondence by D.D. Paige; New Directions Publishing Corp., for permission to reprint from previously unpublished correspondence by Ezra Pound, copyright © 2013 by Mary de Rachewiltz and Omar S. Pound; New Directions Publishing Corp. (agents), for permission to reprint from previously unpublished correspondence by William Carlos Williams, copyright © 2013 by the Estates of Paul H. Williams and William Eric Williams.

Every effort has been made to obtain permissions from holders of copyrighted material published herein. The publisher would like to apologize for any omissions and will be pleased to incorporate any missing acknowledgments in any future editions.

Chronology

1905 Samuel Barnard meets Bertha Lee Hoard in Greenfield, Indiana.

1907 Samuel and Bertha marry in Walton, Kentucky. They travel west on a one-way homesteader's ticket, arriving in Portland, Oregon, during the Panic of 1907, in November.

1908 Samuel Barnard finds work with the Pittock and Leadbetter Lumber Company at a mill in Vancouver, across the Columbia River from Portland. The Barnards move into a local rooming house.

1909 Mary Ethel Barnard born in Vancouver, Washington, December 6.

1914 Samuel Barnard forced to leave Vancouver after a fire burns the mill down. He takes a job as manager at a sawmill in Buxton, Oregon. Mary Barnard begins school in nearby Hillsboro. A savage attack on Barnard's maternal grandmother, who lives with the Barnards, by a local youth with an axe greatly shakes up the family.

1918 Samuel Barnard opens the Barnard Lumber Company in Vancouver; the family returns to Washington.

1926 Mary Barnard attempts translations at high school in Vancouver. Studies Greek dramatists.

1928 Enrolls at Reed College, a liberal arts college in Portland, Oregon. Excels at Greek. Studies literature and creative writing under Lloyd Reynolds, who introduces her to the work of the modernist poets and who later assists with the publication of *A Few Poems*. Joins Gawd-Awful poetry group, led by Reed professor Victor Chittick.

1932 Graduates from Reed with a BA degree. Returns to Vancouver and forms a study club, where she teaches a course on Ezra Pound and T. S. Eliot. Reads "A Few Don'ts by an Imagist" and Glenn Hughes's *Imagism and the Imagists*.

1933 Sends six poems and a request for guidance to Ezra Pound in Rapallo, having looked up his address in the *Who's Who* in the Vancouver Public Library. Receives a quick reply; extensive correspondence ensues, lasting until Pound's death in 1972.

1934 Reluctantly starts social work job with the Emergency Relief Administration, for whom she works intermittently for three years. Begins correspondence with Marianne Moore, who encourages her to send poems to *Poetry*, and with William Carlos Williams.

1935 Comes to national attention when "Shoreline" is published in *Poetry* in February by editor Morton Zabel. Zabel prints more poems in the April issue. Barnard is awarded *Poetry*'s distinguished Levinson Prize in November.

1936 Using Levinson prize money, Barnard follows Pound's advice and travels to New York, going first by train to New Orleans, calling on relatives in California on the way, then taking the *SS Dixie* up the East Coast. Arrives in New York on April 9.

Pound's introductions lead to meetings with William Carlos Williams, Marianne Moore, E. E. Cummings, Robert Fitzgerald, T. C. Wilson, Harriet Monroe, and Florence Codman of Arrow Press. Codman introduces Barnard to James Laughlin, who later publishes her early work, and Muriel Rukeyser, who assists with an invitation to Yaddo, the writer's colony in upstate New York.

In the summer, Barnard takes up a fellowship at Yaddo. Meets Malcolm Cowley, Babette Deutsch, David Greenhood, and New York composer Edwin Gerschefski, who sets her poem "Lai" to music.

Returns to Vancouver, funds exhausted, in the autumn.

1938 Takes up a second summer fellowship at Yaddo. Returns to New York in August, where she resolves to settle. In an effort to make ends meet, stays with various friends and holds down a range of temporary jobs, including work as a babysitter, a short stint sending out catalogues for New Directions, and assistance with Hanson Duval's bibliography of Aldous Huxley. Fails to get a sales job at Macy's owing to her modernist tastes. "They could see I wouldn't be the kind to insist on customers' taking *Gone with the Wind*, when they were looking for [Williams's] *White Mule*," she tells her parents in a letter of October 11.

1939 Meets Ford Madox Ford in January and Ezra Pound in New York in May. Spends two months in the summer in the nearby countryside at Lake Schoolhouse with the painter Edna Gluck, a long-term friend. Works on an operetta and a play ("a satiric, feminist, anti-war piece," she tells her parents in a letter of July 20).

After Pound's intervention, takes up position as first ever Curator of the Poetry Collection, Lockwood Memorial Library, University of Buffalo, New York. Establishes the William Carlos Williams archive. Reviews detective stories in spare time and begins experimenting with prose fiction, writing mystery stories.

1940 Debut poetry collection, *Cool Country*, published in *Five Young American Poets, 1940*, by New Directions.

1942 Meets Viola Baxter Jordan. Extensive correspondence begins. At some point in the 1940s, after the war, Viola Baxter Jordan introduces Barnard to Perdita Schnaffer, H.D.'s daughter.

1943 Leaves Buffalo and briefly returns to parents in Vancouver, having fallen ill. Returns to New York, taking up long-term residence at Minetta Street in Greenwich Village. Becomes a researcher, doing indexing and other literary work for the next seven years. Combines research with temporary work for the Educational Division of the War Prisoner's Aid organization, for Simon & Schuster publishers, for Edward James, and indexing for Mark Van Doren.

1944 Begins a novel, *Ashe Knoll*. Around this time begins a novella, *Swamp Lake*, and works on a verse drama with a Greek chorus, *The Trap* (quite possibly the same play she was working on in 1939). None are published, but Williams expresses admiration for *The Trap*.

1945 Mark Van Doren introduces her to his brother, Carl. Assists Carl Van Doren with his Benjamin Franklin biography until he dies suddenly in the summer of 1950.

Pound committed to St. Elizabeths Hospital, a psychiatric facility in Washington, D.C. Barnard, a frequent visitor to Washington on account of her research work for Carl Van Doren, calls in regularly.

1946 Disillusioned with poetry, is taken on by fiction agent Diarmuid Russell. Publishes stories and mysteries in periodicals and anthologies, including *Harper's Bazaar, Yale Review*, and, in 1948, the *Kenyon*

Review. "The Cat," a supernatural mystery, is published in *Today's Woman*, much to the delight of feline lover Pound, then reworked as a radio play broadcast by Nelson Olmsted on his *Stories of Pacific Powerland* program.

Meets Charles Olson, at Pound's suggestion.

1949 Travels to Italy for three months in the spring on an itinerary drawn up by Pound. Meets Olga Rudge and her daughter, Mary. Returns to New York in July.

Samuel Barnard sells business and invests a third in Mary Barnard's name, enabling financial independence.

After visiting Pound in October, agrees to his suggestion that she work on a guidebook to Italian paintings. Produces *A Pagan's Guide to Italian Frescoes* but is unable to find a publisher for it.

1951 Falls ill with two near-fatal viruses and is hospitalized. Spends months recovering, first in New York, then back home in Vancouver. While convalescing, starts reading Greek again. Begins translating Sappho.

1952 *A Few Poems*, a pamphlet of twelve poems, is published and circulated privately by the Reed Graphics Workshop in Portland, Oregon.

Returns to New York in November. Travels to Greece via London, Paris, Brunnenburg, and Venice. Develops cataracts.

1955 Returns to Vancouver for an eye operation. With her parents ageing and increasingly infirm, and finding that the pace of life in New York had become too quick for her, Barnard decides to return to the Northwest for good, although makes many trips to Europe and to New York for research and pleasure over the coming decades.

1958 *Sappho: A New Translation* published by University of California Press. Remains in continuous print, selling more than one hundred thousand copies. In the course of her research into the background of Sappho's poems, Barnard becomes seriously interested in the origins of myths and ethnobotany, as well as archeoastronomy and the calendar, including the Phaistos Disk.

Pound released from St. Elizabeths, returns to Italy.

1959 Barnard visits Pound in Rapallo. Undertakes several visits to Europe in the immediate years that follow, visiting Pound again in 1961 and 1964.

1962–1965 *Sappho: A New Translation* set to music in *Fragments from Sappho*, for soprano, flute, clarinet, and piano, by David Ward-Steinman.

First performance takes place April 29, 1966, in La Jolla, California. Recorded circa 1969 on CRI Records.

1963 Williams dies.

1966 *The Mythmakers*, a study of mythology, printed by Ohio University Press. Two essays first published in *American Scholar*. In its anti-Jungian stance, *The Mythmakers* anticipates Lévi-Strauss's seminal work on myth and coincides with correspondent Gordon Wasson's work on the hallucinogenic mushroom.

1969 Samuel Barnard dies.

1972 Moore dies in February; Pound dies in November.

1973 Barnard meets Elizabeth Bishop, who, while teaching at the University of Washington, visits Barnard at her home in Vancouver.

1975 "The Pleiades" is set to music in *The Pleiades*, a cantata for mezzo-soprano, choir, and orchestra, by Tibor Serly, a friend of Pound's from Rapallo then living in Longview, Washington.

1977 Bertha Hoard Barnard dies.

1978 Mary Barnard awarded Doctor of Humane Letters by Reed College (honorary degree).

1979 *Collected Poems* published by Breitenbush Books and wins the Elliston Award that same year.

1982 Barnard receives the Washington State Governor's Award for achievement in the literary arts.

Although she had always turned down reviewing work, Barnard becomes advisory editor for *Tulsa Studies in Women's Literature* after much persistence from Germaine Greer.

1983 *Three Fables* published by Breitenbush Books. First published by the *Kenyon Review* in 1948.

Barnard stays with Mary de Rachewiltz, Pound's daughter with Olga Rudge, in Brunnenburg, to write her memoir.

1984 *Assault on Mount Helicon*, a literary memoir, published by University of California Press. Previous to publication, excerpts appeared in *Iowa Review*, *Malahat Review*, and *William Carlos Williams: Man and Poet* (Orono, Maine: National Poetry Foundation, 1983).

Despite a reluctance to teach, Barnard accepts invitation to be a guest lecturer at the Rochester Writers' Workshop.

1985 Becomes contributing editor to *Northwest Review*.

1986 *Time and the White Tigress*, an essay-in-verse published by Breitenbush Books. Wins the Western States Book Award for Poetry the same year. Although she had originally planned it as a prose sequel to *The Mythmakers*, Barnard found that the work flowed more easily as poetry.

1987 Awarded the May Sarton Award by the New England Poetry Club.

Poem "Journey" is set to music in *Journey: Cantata for Mezzosoprano, Baritone, Choir and Orchestra*, Op. 127, by Tomas Svoboda. Text taken from *Collected Poems*.

1988 *Nantucket Genesis: The Tale of My Tribe*, a genealogical essay-in-verse exploring the Barnard family history, published by Breitenbush Books.

1994 Portland Poetry Festival dedicated in Barnard's honor.
Paideuma prints Mary Barnard special issue.

2001 Dies, aged 91, from complications of cancer, at home on August 25.

Chapter One

"Spare but Musical"

The Poetry of Mary Barnard

In the year before Mary Barnard wrote the letter to Ezra Pound that was to change her life, she picked out a new bright red student's notebook by the Chief Company, its cover emblazoned with a Native American in full headdress, and set a goal. "These four years," she wrote on the first page, referring to the intellectual and creative awakening she had experienced at college, "must be crystallized into one clear stone." Among scatterings of wistful observations about art, love, melancholy, and memory, interspersed with ideas and lines for poems that might somehow crystallize it all, is an important entry dated October 31, 1932—"one clear stone" of thought regarding what this passionate young woman of twenty-three wanted for her poetry:

> Things have a certain starkness about them in an autumn rain. I should like my writing to be like that—hard substantial colors, *on* something, not transparent. The cherry tree limbs are black, round, shiny, the leaves yellow crescents scattered among curled brown ones on the greening [grass?]. Newly turned earth is a heavy red color. Shapes of things are emerging from their summer mistiness, their disguise. The dancer has cast off her floating satin, and her movements are the pure, true lines of beauty.[1]

It's easy, from this, to see why Barnard was so determined to make contact with Ezra Pound the following October when she looked him up in *Who's Who* in the public library in Vancouver, Washington, the frontier town in the Pacific Northwest in which she had grown up, where "the Roaring Twenties . . . hardly roared at all"[2] and sent him some poems with a plea to "consider the geographical state of Washington, and how unlikely I am ever to meet anyone who could help me."[3] Barnard's desire for a poetry of "things" with a "certain starkness," of "hard substantial colors" devoid of "mistiness" and superfluous wrappings of "floating satin," recalls what Pound had wanted when he was of a similar age; indeed, in Barnard's prose here, one can almost catch a glimpse of the one poem that came to typify his Imagist movement, the "wet, black bough" of Pound's "In a Station of the Metro"[4] flickering in Barnard's image of the "black, round, shiny" limbs of the cherry tree in autumn rain.

As this book will explore, the "Pound connection,"[5] as Barnard termed it, took her to New York, where she was to spend the best part of the next twenty years mixing in modernist circles, and brought her to the attention of the influential literary journals of the day—*American Prefaces*, *New Democracy*, *New English Weekly*, *Partisan Review*, *Poetry*, and *Townsman*—as well as to the notice of Pound's publisher in America, James Laughlin, whose newly established New Directions printed Barnard's first collection, *Cool Country*, in 1940. The "Pound connection" also landed Barnard a job as the first Poetry Curator at the Lockwood Memorial Library at the University of Buffalo, where she worked collecting manuscripts of the modern poets between 1939 and 1943, as well as introductions to "someone NOT so much in sympathy with the contents"[6]—Marianne Moore—and someone who was: "Better send a carbon of yr / stuff to ole Bill / might cheer him. Billyum Bullyums, 9 Ridge Rd / Rutherford," Pound encouraged Barnard in 1934.[7] As they did Pound, Barnard's poems certainly cheered William Carlos Williams, as well as Moore, and both, too, became lifelong friends and mentors. It was Moore who first recommended Barnard to Morton Zabel at *Poetry* in 1934, which awarded her the distinguished Levinson Award in 1935 (two years after Moore herself had won the prize), as well as to the Library of Congress for the position of chair of poetry (which unfortunately came to nothing). In 1949, Barnard visited Italy, at Pound's encouragement, touring places that featured in *The Cantos*, as she improved her grasp of Italian and returned to New York, fired up with thoughts of Europe and eager to begin new writing projects.

But then events appeared to take a bad turn. Early in 1951, Barnard fell seriously ill with not one but two successive, near-fatal viruses. In February, she came down with "the Bug-of-the-Year" and entered Lennox Hill Hospital on Manhattan's Upper East Side for a long stay.[8] Upon discharge, considerably weakened, exhausted, and with no partner to look after her, Barnard travelled home to her parents in Vancouver, where, as their much-adored only child, she was sure to make a good recovery. She was wrong. Almost as soon as she arrived she developed serum hepatitis and was swiftly admitted once again to hospital. The heady days as "a provincial in New York," as Barnard put it, tearing around the metropolis in her distinctive green beret, were over.[9] Permitted to sit up for fifteen minutes a day for one month, half an hour a day for the next month, Barnard soon realized "that it would be not just one month, but many months, before I would be able to live a normal life again."[10]

Such confinement, however, was to prove pivotal to Barnard's career. Rattled by the advice of her doctors, Barnard felt

> that I must do something to make this catastrophe *pay*, to move it somehow from the loss column to the profit column, to make it turn out to be, like all the disasters in English history since 1066 and all that, "A Good Thing." I wanted to feel, when at last I was able to be active again, that I had accomplished something.[11]

There were two rules for the "good thing"—it would have to be something that she would not have done had she been on her feet, and it would have to be something she could do manageably while propped up by pillows. Having allowed her Greek to lapse after working at Sapphics in the early days of her correspondence with Pound, Barnard set to re-reading the classical Greek poets when she received an unexpected gift from a well-wisher. Hearing about her illness while in Rapallo editing his book of Pound's letters, the poet and translator D. D. Paige mailed Barnard a copy of Quasimodo's slim volume *Lirici Greci.* Buoyed by her improved command of Italian following her recent tour of the country, Barnard not only devoured the book but found that it enabled her to return to the puzzle of translating another poet renowned for writing with a "certain starkness": Sappho. The task had perplexed her for years; Barnard had tried to read Sappho in the original, but she felt that she needed a crib, or notes, or a lexicon. What she found in English "only left me wondering what all the fuss was about."[12] But the Italian translations changed all that. Being shown the text through the medium of a language that was not English had a distinct advantage; it left Barnard with a mind free "to balance between the Greek phrase and the Italian phrase, while I searched for the truly equivalent phrase in living, not lexicon English."[13] Within a year, she had a draft of the manuscript that was eventually to become her most commercially successful book, *Sappho: A New Translation*, a continuous best seller since its publication in 1958. The "good thing," as Barnard had hoped, had come.

But if it led to the one "good thing" of *Sappho*, then Quasimodo's Italian volume surprisingly led to another, for Barnard's critical audience at least. In her recollection of the power of the *Lirici Greci* can be found a neat articulation of the aesthetic that has eluded many of Barnard's critics, compelling as her verse may be, an aesthetic Barnard herself was deeply reluctant to specify outside of the poetry itself. Of the *Lirici Greci*, Barnard recalled:

> I found here, in Sappho's Greek, as revealed to me now through the medium of the Italian, the style I had been groping toward, or perhaps merely hungering for, when I ceased to write poetry [for a

> time in the mid-1940s]. It was spare but musical, and had, besides, the sound of the speaking voice making a simple but emotionally loaded statement. It is never "tinkling" as Bill Williams . . . characterized it. Neither is it "strident" as Rexroth described it. It is resonant although unmistakably in the female register.[14]

"Spare but musical" is exactly how one might define the poetry of Mary Barnard. The phrase itself is a delightful compression of the very Imagist principles that Barnard took to heart upon reading F. S. Flint's "Imagisme" and Pound's supplementary essay "A Few Don'ts by an Imagiste" for the first time in 1933, where she encountered the now legendary three rules of Imagism that had appeared in the pages of *Poetry* twenty years earlier:

> Direct treatment of the "thing" whether subjective or objective.
>
> To use absolutely no word that does not contribute to the presentation.
>
> As regarding rhythm: to compose in the sequence of the musical phrase, not in sequence of a metronome.[15]

Born on December 6 in the same year as Pound's involvement with the "forgotten school of 1909," as he was to refer to T. E. Hulme's club of nascent Imagists, Barnard might be best considered as a something of a late Imagist, her "spare but musical" minimalist idiom an emblem of the kind of rhythmical terseness that typifies much of her poetry, most notably that of her formative years, the 1930s through the early 1950s, mostly spent in New York, that are the focus of this book. Take, for example, a stanza from Barnard's poem "Shoreline" that Zabel printed in *Poetry* in 1935:

> Litter of bare logs in the drift—
> The sea has had its sharp word with them. The smudged odor
> Of wild roses, wild strawberries on the dune shoulder
> Stains as with color the salt stench of the sea.
> It is a naked restless garden that descends
> From the crouched pine
> To shellfish caught in flat reflecting sands.[16]

There is an alluring tension throughout, the varying line lengths endowing the stanza with a lushness appropriate to the image of the "naked, restless garden" of wild flowers and fruits, yet kept in check by the clipped grammar of the first and third lines; the paring away of the excessive padding of articles and conjunctions effects a prickly rhythm commensurate with the starkness of "bare logs" and the physical restraint of "the crouched pine" and "shellfish caught in flat reflecting sands." But it is the "musical phrase" that wins through here; the spare, staccato rhythm recedes as the stanza develops and is all but dissolved by the single sentence at the stanza's close, which flows effortlessly over three enjambed lines without the jarring interruptions of punctuation. Intriguingly, Barnard specifies that the "naked restless garden" lies *between* the crouched pine at the head of the beach and the shellfish entrapped in the sands at the shoreline, and in this she might be said to be making a gesture toward her Imagist sympathies—bracketing an image of sumptuous plenty with images of restraint is suggestive of the way in which the Imagist poet's restrained language enables the "naked restless" growth of the "emotional and intellectual complex in an instant of time."[17]

The verbal restraint of Barnard's "spare but musical" poetry parallels other kinds of restraint that have textured the poet's reception so far. She published two collections of short poems, *Cool Country* (1940) and *A Few Poems* (1952), during her years as a "provincial in New York," but the recent recovery of manuscripts from Barnard's literary estate since her death in 2001 indicates that Barnard's output was prolific in this period, with enough material for at least two more books, if not more. True, some of this material includes the kind of typical high school "doggerel" that is the poet's rite of passage, as Barnard was the first to admit, but much of it is not, and perhaps nowhere is Barnard's late Imagism more accomplished than in one poem she had tucked away for more than sixty years, "North Window," written shortly before she first departed for New York:

North Window

A book with a green binding
And snow dropping out of a shallow sky:
The falling away of light and blood,
Of all yellow and rose
Leaves only

Forced passage to another country,
To a beach without wharf, quiet
Like a lake beach.
    Green cloth and polished horn,
    Stairways of unstained wood.
We sit among grasses,
Among bloodless stones
Or lie at night upon white fur
Watching mist gather under the rafters,
Speaking of the queen's emeralds.[18]

There is again that tantalizing balance between tautness and expansion; the verbal restraint of the first two clauses, terse in their itemizing tone, is gently replaced by a sentence that falls over several lines with all the combined delicateness yet consequent thickness of the snowfall alluded to in the poem. This sentence, beginning "The falling away," is at first entrancingly pared back into the margins over the course of three lines, only to rapidly grow into lines that are suddenly longer and denser with assonance and consonance, reminiscent of the way spare flurries of snowflakes can form thick carpets of snow surprisingly quickly, a swiftness not lost on Barnard, who locates sheets of "white fur" in close proximity to "mist" toward the end of the poem. In the imagery, too, there is a paring back, a sense of the life of things draining out of them. The sky is shallow; light and blood slip away; the result is "forced passage to another country," but even there lie further extinctions—excommunication from the world in the form of a "beach without wharf," "bloodless stones." And yet among all this scarcity, there is wealth and lavishness. Like the "naked restless garden" that blooms amid the restraint of the beach, the scene is suddenly graced by images of "white fur" and "the queen's emeralds."

The influence of the Imagists is acute in both "Shoreline" and "North Window," particularly that of H.D., of whom Pound was reminded when he first read Barnard's work. In part this was due to geographical circumstance; the coastline of the Long Beach Peninsula, Washington, that inspired many of Barnard's poems such as "Shoreline," had about it the same kind of plain, hard grittiness found in the windswept seashore of H.D.'s *Sea Garden* poems. Just as H.D. registered emotional intensity in the "hard sand,"[19] the discarded "amber husk" of dried-out fruit,[20] the "meagre flower, thin / sparse of leaf" of a sea rose,[21] so, too, did Barnard find elevation in the spare and the abandoned elements of the beach with its "litter of bare logs in the drift" and "flat, reflecting sands," freighted with emotional significance. Something of the sharp but mysterious, otherworldly qualities of *Sea Garden* is present in the "queen's emeralds" of "North Window" that seem, at first, quite out of place in this specific, rural scene—perhaps this is a metaphor for the rich, jewel-like shine of snow melting on the evergreens outside the "North Window" of Barnard's Washington home? Read beside the "green" of the "book" and the "cloth," the "emeralds" evoke northwestern color. Yet combined with the "white fur" on which the speakers lie, they suggest an entrancing, if slightly puzzling, opulence; we may not be able to make a confident grasp of their meanings, but these images give the poem a marvelous glaze, as if adding varnish to "unstained wood." They endow the poem with the same kind of "accurate mystery" that was attributed to H.D.,[22] whom Barnard admired, and whose work, F. S. Flint said in "The Poetry of H.D," had "the precision of goldsmith's work, in ultimate effect it is mysterious and only to be comprehended by the imagination."[23] Indeed, it is interesting to speculate that Barnard's work, with its American brand of Hellenic hardness and use of Greek themes, is suggestive of what H.D.'s work might had been like had she not gone to Europe[24]—and might, in part, explain H.D.'s reluctance to correspond with Barnard. As that formidable correspondent of the American modernists, Viola Baxter Jordan, saw it, H.D. was a "jealous thing—she never mentions you and I always say something about you or your work in my letters," she explained to Barnard.[25]

Yet perhaps Barnard's late Imagism resonates most strongly with the kind of work put out by the American modernist poet who vehemently defended his choice *not* to uproot to Europe, "Ole Bill" Williams. Barnard's attentiveness, in her red "Chief" notebook, to the "shapes of things emerging from their summer mistiness" in the autumn reminds one of the praise afforded by Williams to the "twiggy / stuff of bushes and small trees," the "stuff" of "patches of standing water," of "reddish / purplish" bushes that come into stark clarity as objects are defined "one by one" in the first poem of *Spring and All* (1923).[26] Her choice of autumn, rather than spring, as the time of creative stimulation is perhaps a reflection of Barnard's more measured and composed relationship with the outside world, as befitting a generation which, Edmund Wilson felt, had arrived after "the last hysteria of the boom and the stock market crash" and whose "sobering effect" had yielded a "literary revival" in American writing.[27] Of Williams's importance to the questions she was asking of poetry, Barnard was in no doubt, as the October 2, 1932 entry into her Chief red notebook—before she had begun writing to him—testifies:

> A day like today makes a physical demand which I cannot meet. The tautness of the spiderweb in the holly tree, the evenness of the lawn, the long tendrils of red Virginia creeper demand song and I am silent. The slight wind, the curved wings of the woodpeckers in flight demand high deeds and I am inactive. The sunlight, too brilliant to last . . . demands sudden, intense lovemaking—most absurd of all. I am passive, unexpectant. The significance of these things—who can say what it is? W.C.W.? the red wheelbarrow[28]

The direct "statement" feel of "Shoreline" (where the sea's rhythms are likened to speech) and "North Window" (which uses variations in sentence rhythm to emphasize changes in scene) comes from the keen ear that Barnard had, like Williams, for the easy musicality of common speech. "I believe in the sound of words. By that I mean words that sound as if they grew together, although they may be common and not particularly beautiful in themselves," wrote Barnard in a preface to the poems she submitted as part of her senior thesis at college.[29] Like Williams, Barnard takes American vernacular speech and, directed by its rhythms, makes poetry out of it; she does not "poeticize" live speech. To aid her, Barnard formulated her own special measure, the "balanced line," which, like Williams's "variable foot" or the "open formation" he noted of Whitman's example,[30] allowed for the endless variability of spontaneous, common speech to be set in verse that used the principle of elapsed time, as in music, rather than the accent as a means of "measuring the measure," as we shall see later. "This . . . approach to free verse, which I could accept, simply meant that, instead of using the interminable iambic pentameter, you wrote for all variations," Barnard recounted to Jane Van Cleve amid the publicity for *Collected Poems*; "that is what I worked on—trying to work out other arrangements of stresses and syllable lengths that would work in English [language] verse and would make a thing hold together."[31]

Added to this, there's the intense focus on the local; not the adopted local of New York that furnished a good number of Barnard's poems (although the city inevitably featured in some of her work), but the local of her beloved Northwest, with which she felt a primal, deep-rooted connection. Like Williams, Barnard was eager to write the American local in modern idiom. And, in some ways, Barnard's personal experience of her region, I will argue, furnished Barnard with the coordinates for producing her "spare but musical" style. Although it is easy to detect the recognizable lush and fecund "wet, heavily wooded wild country"[32] of the Northwest in Barnard's poetry—there is plenty of what she called the "cool country" of rain, fog, mist, mountains, evergreens, salmon, and huckleberries in her writing—there were two spaces that formed her "local" and inspired much of what she wrote that contrast with this lushness: the isolated sawmill settlements she experienced as the daughter of a lumber merchant, spare and minimal in their construction, that inspired poems such as "North Window" and, of course, the desolate Long Beach peninsula of "Shoreline," which, although densely blanketed with evergreens, is characterized by its bare, plain coastline and deserted beaches. This localized version of the Northwest comprised of quiet, spare, lonely places not only played a significant role in her formation as a poet, it made her particularly sensitive to a poetics, like Imagism, so thoroughly focused on the minimal.

These are important contours to identify, for some have missed them. Despite being admired and championed by important figures in literary modernism, wide publication in the leading poetry journals of the 1930s and 1940s, and numerous accolades (as well as the *Poetry* Levinson Award, she won the Elliston Award for her *Collected Poems* in 1979 and the Western States Book Award for her long poem *Time and the White Tigress* in 1986), Barnard has, curiously, drawn limited critical attention. For all her association with Pound, both as an apprentice ("one of Ezra's string of ponies,"[33] said Williams) and, in time, as a close family friend (Laughlin saw her as "Ezra's daughter"[34]), until very recently Barnard has been considered as an occasional footnote in accounts of the more familiar names in American modernism and not as a subject worthy of study in her own right.[35] This marginal attention is strange, given the richness of scholarship that has emerged in recent years on members of the so-called "ezrauniversity" and those heirs of Williams's legacy, and it is stranger still if we consider that such recoveries have coincided with efforts calling attention to women in Anglo-American modernism. The most substantial examination of Barnard to date is in the form of a special issue of *Paideuma*; yet even here critics fall short of adequately defining Barnard's oeuvre, some saying it is "uncategorizable."[36] This lack is what this book aims to fill: to fully investigate the character of Barnard's poetry and lift the footnote to the center of the page in the story of American modernism in its later period.

Of course Barnard's neglect is not simply the fault of the academy. Partly there are pragmatic issues—Barnard lived a very long life (1909–2001), with her archive finally being acquired by the Yale Beinecke Library in 2005[37]—and it is a challenge to situate a life being led, especially that of a writer like Barnard, who fiercely eschewed personal examination. There is also the chaos and mess of human relationships that affect reception; the new Barnard archives show that, for example, much of Barnard's correspondence with Pound was omitted from D. D. Paige's *Selected Letters* on the say-so of Olga Rudge. "As he made you his ambassador [in the United States], you entered, perforce. And perforce she is jealous," Paige told Barnard privately in 1950 as he tried to deal with Rudge's demand that he "cut *all* letters to women."[38]

But there are also issues of changing literary trends. Perhaps the poetry world of the 1930s and 1940s was not quite ready for Barnard's poetry of "a certain starkness" after Pound, Williams, and H.D., who were seen to have moved far beyond their Imagist phases. For some, Imagism expired with the First World War, and a specifically "new" poetry was incapable of emerging until after World War II; the interwar years were "about" something seemingly more profound than questions of form. According to John Crowe Ransom at *The Kenyon Review*, Barnard's work did not appeal to his "metaphysical" tastes:

> I think your poems are singularly consistent, and in a certain mode which continues to strike me as a little limited. Probably I am opinionated about this. I like them but not enough. It may be that 17th Century poetry, to which I am addicted, and "metaphysical" poetry such as is written by your contemporaries, have spoiled my tastes.[39]

Macmillan editor Theodore Purdy thought her manuscript, given to him damp and curling after being caught in a heavy downpour as she resolutely made her way down Fifth Avenue to deliver it by hand one wet September afternoon in 1938, showed "exceptional promise . . . you have the equipment and material for writing verse of real importance."[40] Like Ransom, though, Purdy thought Barnard's work had its limitations; as with the best of Moore's poetry, Purdy observed that "these poems exert primarily an intellectual appeal . . . and [so] have a limited readership."[41] So it seemed that editors, although they liked Barnard's "singularly consistent" work, simply did not think there was a contemporary audience for it—among their readers, at least. For Williams, there was some virtue in Barnard's poetry of "a certain starkness": "I like the steadiness of the feeling back of the poems," he wrote to Barnard in early 1935 after receiving the letter of introduction that Barnard had been encouraged to send by Pound; "you have succeeded in matching this with a line which while full of restraint is never forced."[42] Florence Codman, editor of Arrow Editions, which published E. E. Cummings and Robert Fitzgerald, also perceived something of Barnard's exacting subtlety. Encouraged by Williams to "go to see Miss Codman *at once*" upon her first arrival in New York in the spring of 1936,[43] Barnard wasted no time at all and Codman, who had been reading Barnard's poems in the magazines with increasing interest, quickly requested a manuscript. "You do have the most delicate, almost hurting fineness of perception locked in one of the most certain techniques that I have met in a long time," Codman later told Barnard in 1937; "it's so very quiet and so very sure."[44] However, the Arrow reader report was mixed. The reader admired the measured restraint of Barnard's idiom and its "stretched out clarity":

> The statements themselves are pleasantly perceptive and often freshly perceptive; usually the poem is made out of three or four or five statements of this kind arranged in a particularly open, detached sequence: the effect of particles reflectively dropped to make a pattern.[45]

Yet this very "open, detached" quality, in which language emulates the spare grace of "particles reflectively dropped to make a pattern," was also a cause for concern for Arrow's reader, who complained elsewhere that Barnard's poems were "too slight to sustain themselves." H.D.'s early Imagist poetry had caused similar alarm: she was praised on the one hand for writing a poetry of "accurate mystery" yet derided on the other for writing a "petty poetry that can be said in the one minute before lunch."[46] F. S. Flint had written:

> You take a poem like ["Sitalkas"] for instance. . . . And you cannot argue it out by syllogisms. It might have come out of the Greek anthology; but that does not bring you any nearer to it. In fact, the more you attempt to reason about it the less will you get out of it. It must work on you like an evocation.[47]

Flint's notion, here, that "you cannot argue it out by syllogisms" might explain the problem that John Crowe Ransom had with Barnard's poetry, for the metaphysical poets he aligned himself with produced a poetry rich in syllogistic rhetoric that was anathema to the "direct presentation" of the Imagists Barnard was influenced by. And so, despite her initial enthusiasm, Codman felt obliged by the reader's report to decline Barnard's manuscript, but she maintained her support, suggesting employment leads and making Barnard a gift of fifty dollars to keep her in New York to improve her writing. "I feel like a racehorse—having somebody gambling good money on what a month in bluegrass would do for me,"[48] Barnard told her parents.

The gamble paid off, or so it seemed. Following success with his *New Directions* magazine, by the late 1930s James Laughlin was looking to extend into book publishing and had in mind a selection of work by young American poets who had appeared in his magazine. With four men signed up (John Berryman, Randall Jarrell, George Marion O'Donnell, and W. R. Moses), Laughlin was determined that a fifth poet be found and that that poet should be a woman; the choice was either Bishop or Barnard. Holding out for publication of a book of her own, Bishop declined the invitation, but, a little beleaguered by rejections, Barnard accepted at once. The result was *Five Young American Poets*, a New Directions showcase anthology of debut collections by emerging midcentury poets. But where Laughlin saw some depths to the poems collected as *Cool Country* ("they require several readings. Your gift is not ostentatious,"

FIGURE 1. Publicity photo of Mary Barnard (1940) for *Five Young American Poets*. Photo by Hermine Duthie Decker. Mary Barnard Papers. Courtesy of Aletha Decker Carlton.

he told Barnard[49]), there were others who did not warm to her spare, subtle lyrics with their focus on lonely, natural spaces. Allen Tate's review of *Five Young American Poets* passed over Barnard's *Cool Country* in two cruelly dismissive sentences, devoting several paragraphs instead to Randall Jarrell's *The Rage for the Lost Penny* and John Berryman's *Twenty Poems*, doing much to establish their reputations. Tate's verdict had some impact; the anthologist Oscar Williams left Barnard out of his *New Poems: 1940*, telling Barnard at a New York party that he "expected that I would agree with [Tate's assessment]. He did."[50] She was further shunned by another prominent anthologist; *Cool Country* was " 'nothing but Imagism,' " Louis Untermeyer sniffed on a visit to Buffalo,[51] but perhaps this was no bad thing, for Untermeyer's judgments did not endear him to many. "Louis Unt. has done more than any man living to discredit poetry," Pound was fond of quoting Eliot as saying, as Paige reassured Barnard[52]; another of Barnard's voluminous correspondents, the poet and critic Babette Deutsch, put it rather more bluntly—Untermeyer was "worse than exhausting."[53] Having taken Barnard under her wing in her early years in New York, Deutsch told her to pay no attention to Tate, either. "I saw Mr. Tate's strictures on you," Deutsch wrote on May 30, 1941; "I've been thru that mill too."[54]

Maybe there has always been something a little difficult to define about Barnard, making her perplexing to some, entrancing to others. "You are a strange creature," Williams told her in a letter of March 26, 1937, but this was not a put-down. "Every once in a while I think of you as a romantic, then you stick something in my eye to wake me up. I wish you could circulate more in every way," Williams continued, finding a vital currency in her work.[55] But to most of her New York contemporaries on the Eastern seaboard, it was Barnard's regional background that was unusual and incomprehensible, and in their presence, she said, she felt like "an awkward young woman with sawdust in her hair."[56] Her Northwest of the Cascade mountains and Coast Range forest logging camps was, she would say, "a little-known landscape"[57] that continually found its way into Barnard's poetry and that, she felt, marked her as an "awkward" kind of writer. In 1936 and 1938 she secured invitations to the artist's summer colony at Yaddo, in Saratoga Springs, Upstate New York. It quickly became clear to her that a poetic language gap existed on account of where she had come from:

> It was at Yaddo that I first realized how little chance my poems had with born-and-bred New Yorkers who thought they heard hawks cawing in the woods, and supposed that all railroad trestles were of iron construction. I hadn't known of the existence of iron trestles until that summer. What I meant by "mountain" was something quite different from what they meant by the same word.[58]

Deutsch "enjoyed what [Barnard] said about saw-mills" and thought that "they should make good poetry," as she told Barnard in a letter while she was at Yaddo in the summer of 1938—but they were "all so foreign to a native New Yorker."[59] A few months earlier, Deutsch had felt that "it was odd to have you speak of the Massachusetts coast as 'domesticated,'—it is so much wilder than the meek suburban or semi-suburban or pseudo-rural landscape that I am accustomed to."[60] As a result, Deutsch was not surprised that Barnard was not quite clicking with some of her contemporaries whom she met at Yaddo: "Muriel [Rukeyser] I do know, and like. But I can imagine her coolness to your verbal landscaping."[61] Not that it was easy to relate the subject of this "verbal landscaping" to the native New Yorkers, for the "little-known," "remote" landscape of Barnard's Northwest was still finding its feet as a region even when Barnard was growing up. By the 1920s, Vancouver, Washington, was a busy port town shipping out lumber and grain from the region's growing lumber trade, having for a long time been the only settlement in the Pacific Northwest to be continuously occupied—and not to be confused with Vancouver, Canada. And yet almost as soon as the town founded on the banks of the Columbia River by Captain Vancouver had reached its commercial peak, another, bigger city, Portland, had sprung up on the Oregon side of the Columbia River, becoming the region's economic and cultural epicenter. If Downtown Vancouver had any identity at all for Barnard while she was growing up, it was that of "Portland's convenient 'little Las Vegas' "[62] because of all its card rooms, pawn shops and quick loan establishments, which proliferated well into the 1980s. This all added up to what Barnard called "an amorphous blob. . . . Vancouver, poor girl, like many of our young people, has had a hard time trying to find out who she is."[63]

If it was difficult to communicate this "new" land, it was also difficult to communicate the "new" model of liberal arts education that Barnard had enjoyed at Reed College in Portland, Oregon, which positively nurtured an independence among its students that would have been alien to some she met East during the "era of the Vassar girl: Rukeyser, Eleanor Clark and Mary McCarthy,"[64] as Barnard put it. There were no fraternities, sororities, or intercollegiate sports typical to American college culture at Reed. Contrary to Eastern conservatisms, women students enjoyed unprecedented freedoms, being allowed to smoke anywhere on campus and living in dormitories left unsupervised. "Education at Reed undoubtedly had a lot to do with the independent life so many of us chose to lead or fell into—marriage a possibility but definitely not a necessity," Barnard later explained to a cousin. "But then Reed attracted women who were, even in high school, more interested in their own intellectual development than in marriage and maternity. Co-eds who were primarily husband-hunting didn't go to Reed or if they did, they didn't last long."[65] To those on the outside, Reed was a breeding ground for immorality.

The fact that the college was nondenominational inflamed its infamy, as did its employment of supposedly radical professors. "Rumor persisted that the principal subjects taught at Reed were 'atheism, communism, and free love,'" Barnard recalled.[66] Added to this, during Barnard's time there, Reed insisted upon a genuine diet of the liberal arts. There were no English courses or English majors. All students read classical and European literatures and were encouraged to read them in the original, an education of which Pound would have approved. As part of the comprehensive sweep of literature, Reed professors were teaching the work of modern poets long before colleges in the East; "when I was in the east I was shocked to learn of the benighted condition of most of the colleges, at least [as] regards the modern poets," Barnard informed Pound in 1937.[67]

Thus Barnard found herself in the unusual position of being thoroughly grounded in what is now regarded as the modernist tradition while it was still contemporary, and she was developing her own voice as a poet as she was taking classes on Eliot, Joyce, Hart Crane, Edith Sitwell, H.D., and, of course, Ezra Pound, at a time when his work was deeply unpopular with Americans ("at Reed College you are practically venerated," she told him in 1934).[68] If American colleges were taking notice of Laura Riding and Robert Graves's damning assessment in *A Survey of Modernist Poetry* in 1928 that Imagism carried little literary weight for the twentieth-century poet, Reed was not one of them. By 1937, William Carlos Williams was a staple feature of the Reed creative writing curriculum, long before he made the reading lists of the now ubiquitous master of fine arts (MFA) course. It is small wonder, then, that Barnard saw no gaping schism between herself and the work of the modernists; *these* were her "contemporaries," she felt, rather than those "metaphysical" contemporaries of what she would later call the "Lowell, Berryman, Jarrell wave."[69] Jarrell, we might remember, regarded modernism as a complete and finished event by 1942 in his essay "The End of the Line," something for poets to respond to and to distance themselves from, certainly not something that had scope for development.[70] For him, although modernism had provided "the most successful and influential body of poetry of this century,"[71] it had also run its course, producing a terminus at the end of a track out of Romanticism. So while the likes of her contemporaries Jarrell, John Berryman, and Howard Nemerov were turning away from the kind of spare, direct presentation of the Imagists at "the end of the line" in favor of a difficult, technically complex, deeply ironic poetry, Barnard was enthusiastically pursuing modernist lines after Pound, H.D., Moore, and Williams, refining Imagist aesthetics grounded in the local, cultivating free verse lines governed by musical principles and American speech patterns, and courting an exactness and coolness of lyric with the "sound of the speaking voice making a simple but emotionally loaded statement." Modernism, for Barnard, was not an expired aesthetic standing in the way of a new poetry; it was an ongoing project of which she was a part.

Works like *The Cantos* did not leave her feeling that a finite point had been reached from which she had to depart; instead, Barnard treated modernist work as working material to be used toward the achievement of as yet unfulfilled goals. Her American measure, for example, refined over two decades, developed in part from her assessments of Pound's use of classical meters from *Personae* to *The Cantos*. Just as she had always had older friends at college—she was more at ease with students in the year above her than with her immediate peers—so too did Barnard feel more comfortable with the earlier modernists than she did with other midcentury poets in her peer group, with the exception of Elizabeth Bishop, perhaps, the only contemporary with whom she felt she had anything in common; Bishop, too, had her own version of the "Pound connection" in Marianne Moore.

If Barnard's affiliation with modernism made her stand at a tangent to her peers, then matters were not helped by the fact that she was resolutely apolitical at a time when the New York poetry scene was dominated by Leftist poetics. Although she published many poems without "political implications," as she told her parents in 1938,[72] in the *Partisan Review* and *New Democracy*, she did so not out of political conviction but because she thought political journals looked more favorably upon modernist work like hers; she hoped, as Deutsch did, that she might be "set up by being accepted by the experimental magazines."[73] Williams was perplexed by the fact that she had "the will and courage to . . . face the modern world without bitterness," he told her in 1937,[74] and Marianne Moore's first impressions of Barnard were similarly clouded by puzzlement at her surprising disconnection from the political world, although unlike Williams, Moore saw no "courage" or virtue in this. Barnard, Moore reported privately to Pound, "ought to 'read the papers' and be not wholly in the dark about politics and interests of others."[75] Barnard's apoliticism only intensified as major conflicts such as the Spanish Civil War and the Second World War stirred up political fervor among her contemporaries. Although Pound tried—and quickly gave up—to interest Barnard in his politics, he was still scolding her during her visits to him in St. Elizabeth's for "sitting up on the fifth floor at Minetta St. taking no interest in the world about [her] and never going to see anybody."[76]

But Barnard was not as naïve, or as insensitive, as her contemporaries thought. When Wall Street crashed in 1929, during Barnard's college years, many fledgling northwestern businesses, including her father's lumber business, took a sharp knock, and Barnard felt it keenly. With the Barnard house mortgaged to the hilt and the family surviving on borrowings from her father's life insurance, Barnard financially scraped through college by "hashing" for meals (waiting on tables in the student cafeteria in exchange for meals). When she graduated in 1932, it was to increasingly bleak job prospects, and she took what employment she could get. Ironically, this turned out to be working for the Emergency Relief Administration, doling out unemployment benefits that she herself came close to drawing. As a case worker on and off for several years before she arrived in New York, Barnard worked directly with the poor, interviewing the long-term unemployed in "the constant noise and confusion and smell" of the Vancouver relief office or making visits to homes with "a filthy interior where children peed on the floor as a matter of course, and the front yard was heaped with empty but unwashed food cans."[77] Such firsthand experiences did not make Barnard a socialist, for she found that the members of the American proletariat that she met were "unrepentant capitalists" who sought dollars, not social justice.[78] So when Barnard found herself surrounded by poets and artists spitting revolutionary invective at New York gatherings, she found *them* to be naïve, not herself: "The revolutionary aspirations of a Vassar beauty in pink culottes from Bonwit Teller seemed to be totally unreal and probably born of guilt combined with a desire to be in the swim. I could not take her seriously."[79]

If Barnard stood out among her peers for poetics that embraced Poundian modernism and eschewed politics, the difficulty of placing her was compounded by the fact that, as modernists go, she was simply *not* experimental, at least not overtly. Throughout her career, Barnard remained sceptical of "modernist pyrotechnics."[80] Louis Zukofsky, for example, left her "speechless," she told Pound; "Nothing in the western wildernesses aides me to a comprehension of his poems."[81] As for Gertrude Stein, there was only one thing to do with her work, as she explained to her parents while she was looking for work in the Manhattan temping agencies in 1939:

> I've discovered the real . . . use for Gertrude Stein—typing practice. She's much better than the exercises in the manual, which are not quite as repetitious as she is in her most repetitious moments, and she doesn't have the moral flavor the manual has. . . . Another advantage is that you have to keep your eye right on the book or you get lost.[82]

Nor did she have much interest, at the time, in writing the kind of modernist long poem that seemed to Pound, Eliot, H.D., Williams, and others almost unavoidable in the interwar years, amid increasing cultural fragmentations that demanded some cohesion, and although Barnard lived her emergent years in bohemian New York, she steadfastly refused to poeticize the new forms of the city in favor of a poetry on the themes of nature and mythology, which, she lamented, were "utterly out of fashion from 1930 onwards for almost forty years."[83] But she took some comfort from Marianne Moore: "it is NOT necessary to be Bohemian" like "Dr. Williams and his friends," Moore counseled when Barnard first arrived in New York,[84] encouraging her to keep up what Williams described as "the more or less conventional surface" of her work if it sufficed.[85] None of this eventually mattered, for, like Williams, Barnard had some influence on those open form poets that Donald Allen called "the new

American poetry" in his groundbreaking anthology of 1960. Gary Snyder was one admirer, who had attended Barnard's Reed College with Philip Whalen and Lew Welch; Ed Dorn was another, who considered her work to be "of the highest quality," recalled Robert Bertholf, one of Barnard's successors as Curator of the Poetry Collection at Buffalo.[86] But Barnard was happy to keep a measured distance from the pyrotechnicists, to play the part of "a feminine and extremely muted obligato to the male impetus of Ferlinghetti" as she described a rare public appearance with these other poets to Williams[87]—happy, in fact, to sound a quiet, but confident, defiance against the expectation that to be avant-garde one had to be *evidently* formally difficult.

But being "extremely muted" had its drawbacks, of course, in terms of reception. For one, Barnard held many more poems back than she published, regardless of the judgment of others. The decision not to publish, by Arrow Editions, was a major knock-back, however kind and generous Florence Codman had been to Barnard in those early New York years; very few of Barnard's early poems, including the remarkable "North Window," were ever presented to publishers again. The fact that such poems were neatly preserved at the time of Barnard's death suggests that she had felt them to be of some worth, for Barnard's friends and peers knew that she made very selective decisions about what of her work was worth keeping and what was not. Anything she felt superfluous or dispensable, she discarded.[88] Such self-imposed restraint in publication was also practiced by Barnard's contemporary Elizabeth Bishop, who chose, like Barnard, to publish around ninety poems in her lifetime but whose posthumously published *Complete Poems* contains at least double that number. Despite their common friendships with Marianne Moore and the critic Victor Chittick, who had taught Barnard at Reed before moving to the University of Washington, Barnard and Bishop did not meet until 1973, when both poets found themselves both to be in the Northwest at the same time, Barnard having returned home to Vancouver to look after her parents, Bishop having reluctantly accepted a teaching position at the University of Washington. "It was a great pleasure to meet you Friday and the strangest thing about it is that we never met before" wrote Bishop after dropping in on the Barnards in Vancouver.[89] Part of the delay was due to a natural reserve, like Barnard's. "For most of her writing life," Ian Hamilton observed, "Elizabeth Bishop was known for not wanting to be known."[90] The same might be said of Barnard. "I dislike personal questions, whether they are coming or going" she declared in her literary memoir *Assault on Mount Helicon*.[91] Bishop despaired of the so-called confessional poets ("You just wish they'd keep some of these things to themselves"),[92] and Barnard was equally aggrieved by public outpourings of the soul; a poetry reading by James Agee, for example, gave her "the uncomfortable feeling that I was eavesdropping on a man who was saying his prayers."[93]

Just as Barnard shied away from writing reviews, even if she knew her name emblazoned in bylines might have brought her more notice, so too was she reluctant to comment on her own poetry. She felt, like Bishop, that her poetry said all that she wanted to say, declaring in the preface to *Assault on Mount Helicon*, that she carried a "conviction that lyric poems should be able to float free of biographical anecdote or footnotes, so that the reader may appropriate them as an expression of his own experience, observation, or emotion, or at least as an extension of his own experience, not the writer's."[94] When in 1939 she was asked to supply formal commentary on her poetry to the public, Barnard's self-effacement was to mark her out as very different from her peers. Barnard's contribution to *Five Young American Poets* stood out not only because she was the lone female voice ("the sexapple," as Laughlin teased her[95]) but because she said so little about herself in the preface that Laughlin had made mandatory for publication. Against Jarrell's six-page preface, Berryman's three-and-a-half-page preface, three pages of introduction from Moses, and two and a half from O'Donnell, Barnard's preface weighed in at a mere three paragraphs, not even filling the page. "Your note on poetry is terribly short," Laughlin had chided her in the run-up to publication; "are you sure you don't want to say more? You say almost nothing about your forms and nothing about your attitude to contemporary methods."[96] Barnard was sure she didn't want to add anything further, for Laughlin had missed the point. For all of Jarrell's faux modesty—he began his lengthy preface with the words "I may as well say what the reader will soon enough see, that I don't want to write a preface"[97]—Barnard's trim offering was cool and measured in tone, as befitted her aesthetic:

> Any artist is to me a person who takes nothing for granted; one who, while perceiving the thing's traditional wrappings, sees the thing itself with freshness, as though never encountered before; sees the article as itself, the package as something else, and neither as a reproduction of the picture in the ubiquitous advertisement.
>
> If I have made myself clear, it must also be clear that I could ask nothing more important of poetry just now. Poets, in their particular field, work with words—not only the meanings of words, but the sounds of words, and this to me is extremely important. Beyond these two things, poetry may do different things and be good in different ways; but without freshness of vision, and craftsmanship in the building of metrical and melodic patterns, the poetry might as well be journalism.
>
> What I am trying to do in my own work must be apparent in whatever I have accomplished. My approach to almost any experience is, by an accident of life, through a little-known landscape which proves a barrier to some readers. I think of

> that accident as the luckiest chance of my life, and cannot be sorry for it. Very few of the poems collected here have been written during the past two years, when I have had little opportunity for writing; but I feel that my aims have been sharpened rather than changed, as the world changed.[98]

For those curious about her aims, Barnard directs them to the work itself—"what I am trying to do in my own work must be apparent in whatever I have accomplished," a mantra somewhat reminiscent of what Williams had said to John Riordan in 1926, that "it is the making that is the articulation."[99] But she gives away her Imagist influences in the first paragraph, "the thing itself" resonating with "the thing" of which Pound called for "direct presentation . . . whether subjective or objective," the "freshness, as though never encountered before" reminiscent of the immediacy of the intellectual and emotional complex that the image presents, the insistence on "melodic patterns" recalling Pound's insistence on the musical phrase. While acknowledging the commercial realities that surround the circulation of her work, Barnard insists upon the primacy of "the thing itself" over the need to satisfy the desires of consumers with "a reproduction of the picture [of poetry presented] in the ubiquitous advertisement," a sentiment she expressed to Williams when she had begun working on the "good thing" of her Sappho. "If I have my way, we'll circulate things privately—no reviews, no bookstore sales, no advertising"[100]—all that mattered to her was "your good opinion [more] than a dozen ecstatic reviews."[101]

When it came to writing *Assault on Mount Helicon*, Barnard was at pains to make it "more about other people than about me," as she told James Laughlin; "I'm just not that interesting." With her curatorial and researcher's background (she assisted Carl Van Doren in the 1940s with the editing of Benjamin Franklin's papers), *Assault* was a work of socioliterary documentation, an "intellectual autobiography," thought her editor August Fruge, which reflected her researcher's sense of the need for accurate description rather than a story of the self, or a "tell-all" of those famous writers she knew. Barnard could perhaps have carved out more of a name for herself with *Assault on Mount Helicon* if she had divulged more about the private lives of Pound, Williams, and Moore, but she didn't, and she cared little for those reviews that criticized her for leaving out sex and politics. Appalled by the recommendation of one of the manuscript's readers that she supply full excerpts from her correspondence with Pound, Barnard reiterated in her preface that she possessed "a reluctance to set forth the dramatic details of other, more interesting lives in order to satisfy a public (and editorial) craving for gossip,"[102] a longstanding reluctance that she had been perfecting since the 1930s, when others began to notice the shine Pound had taken to Barnard ("Won't you write me a good long letter telling me all about E.P.?" Deutsch begged Barnard in the early days of their friendship).[103] On Pound and the midcentury New York literary milieu, Barnard wanted to set some critics straight as the first major accounts of him and Williams began to emerge. Although she did not tolerate Pound's notorious politics, she did feel that his nurturing of young talent and his continuing influence on American poetry of the 1930s and 1940s had been somehow forgotten in the scurry to canonize his celebrity. And so *Assault* became "essential reading" about Pound, as Peter Levi is said to have declared in a damning assessment of Humphrey Carpenter's 1988 biography of Pound in the British national newspaper *The Independent*[104]; Carpenter, Levi thought, played down the cultural value of the "Pound connection" to America's midcentury poets. "Your book," May Sarton told Barnard in 1984, "does [Pound] a service in that he comes through as such a life-giver—all that getting poets to meet each other and the cogent severe eye."[105]

But it would be a mistake to conclude that Barnard was not interested in making a name for herself—a name as a poet, that is. She was shy, yet not unwilling to write, out of the blue, to Ezra Pound; she was modest about her ability, yet resolute about breaking into respectable national print; and for all her apparent timidity, Barnard stood up to Pound's critical (and, in the early years, personal) punches. "I was on the receiving end of Ezra's blasts for twenty-odd years," she told the editor of her *Collected Poems*; "I well remember one that began 'You damn fool!'"[106] Although she abhorred the idea of doing poetry readings ("I am not a performer," she told the prize givers of the May Sarton Award she won in 1987),[107] she tenaciously attended the many literary parties she was invited to, followed up contacts, and frequently fired off letters to anyone she thought might help her get published (anyone who she thought it worth being helped by, that is). She was not put off by drawing blanks, as when she went to tea with Ford Madox Ford. "Ole fatty (M. Ford) is at Ten, Fifth Ave / encourager of young talents. . . . I don't know if he has a phone but you don't need a letter of introd / if you say I sent you" wrote Pound in 1939.[108] Immediately Barnard wrote to Ford and was very quickly invited round. But the whole affair was "a very strange experience. Nothing like I expected"[109]; Ford had misread Barnard's intentions, and instead invited her to one Mrs. Ford's open afternoon teas, which was even more insufferable for one guest's gossip. "When I left I still don't know whether they knew how I happened to be there,"[110] Barnard concluded, but she was not discouraged, and soon made acquaintance with other New York writers at Pound's suggestion, including T. C. Wilson and E. E. Cummings, as well as, of course, Williams and Moore, both of whom she had begun correspondences with while she was still living in Vancouver.

Added to this, Barnard left behind a very complete and well-organized archive. Every travel journal earnestly typed up, every letter to her parents retained and in order after they passed to Barnard after their deaths, notebooks clearly marked, sketchbooks and photographs bound together, Barnard curated her own life as much as she curated those of modern poets at Buffalo; one cannot help but feel that Barnard's meticulous protection of her own work was in part a quiet act of anticipation of some future recognition. One of the most intriguing self-referential poems to appear in *Collected Poems* is "Late Roman," a tiny poem which looks, and sounds, like one of Barnard's fragments from Sappho:

Late Roman

I shall be
an historic
figure also,
Mr. Achilles.

One digit in
one of Gibbon's
many footnotes
will denote ME![111]

Nothing less than being "an historic / figure," Barnard demands, if we identify Barnard with the "I" speaking. After all, "ME" is comprised of Barnard's first initials, "Mary Ethel," the name she was commonly known by when she was younger; being of a different case and appearing at the end, this "ME" literally "footnotes" the poem. There is the familiar swift movement from restraint to expansion seen in "Shoreline" and "North Window," this time in the tone rather than in the imagery; the poem moves from humility, as the first stanza depicts a patient figure making a deferent address to "Mr. Achilles," toward bombast in the second stanza, as the speaker demands recognition. Any charge of arrogance is immediately countered by the implicit humor of discussing footnotes with Achilles, the mythical Trojan hero with the vulnerable heel that hastened his death. Despite the tone of muted but high ambition, it turns out that the speaker's desired fame is to be suitably recognized, her contribution properly noted, the "digit" in "many footnotes" given its *full* due—hence the unconventional capitalization of the footnote "ME," a sardonic gesture against those critics who had barely credited Barnard's presence on the American poetry scene. The "Late Roman" that Barnard seeks justice for in accepted accounts of the Roman Empire such as Edward Gibbon's can thus be interpreted as a defense of her own role as a "Late Imagist" within standard accounts of American modernism; here, then, is Barnard's message to literary historians to appropriately reference her achievement; one honored, I hope, in this book.

Chapter Two

Late Imagism

2.1 "The Only Really Worthwhile Piece of Poetry Criticism I Had Ever Read": Pound's Imagism

Pound changed everything. Although Barnard was drawn to the same Greek forms that appealed to the early Imagists, there was little to suggest, at first, that she would become part of his modern movement, even if she had clung to traditional form, as Pound once had, during her early days at Reed College. As a member of the Gawd-Awful Society, named, tongue-in-cheek, after the "gawd-awful silence" that greeted the end of their poetry readings, Barnard realized that she was "the only rhyming poet on campus. Everyone else wrote free verse. . . . I was still using conventional meters and end-rhymes in my poetry,"[1] as is evident in the opening stanzas of her appearances in the Gawd-Awful Society's anthologies of 1928–1929 and 1929–1930:

The Carver

O the night's a carver, carving worlds of ivory,
Carving towns and villages with a silver spoon,
Carving gleaming landscapes of the world of Faery
With the hard, bright chisel of the thin-edged moon.[2]

Disillusionment

I shall go a princess
  But clad like a young knight,
And striding through my chambers
  Shall put my maids to flight.[3]

Over the Hill with the Moon

I sat in a glen in the hour after dark
    When the fern-fronds were dripping with dew,
And I played all my tunes on my old fairy fiddle,
    The strangest and sweetest I knew.[4]

Against such traditional form, however, can be detected the strains of Barnard's emergent modernist disposition, as well as her propensity to articulate, or "carve" out, the landscape. "The Carver" (here given in its entirety), for example, is reminiscent of the measured intensity of an early Imagist poem about the moon that featured in an appendix to Pound's *Ripostes* in 1912, T. E. Hulme's "Above the Dock." Although "The Carver" is largely in iambic pentameter, it is difficult for any listener to force the iambic beat of the first three lines onto the unusual rhythm of the final line, heavy with concrete images of the "hard, bright chisel" of the "thin-edged moon," each phrase comprising three consecutive stresses.[5] The weighted voice of the poem thus becomes commensurate with the solidity of the "ivory" that substantiates the worlds "carved" by the night. As Hulme had explored in "A Lecture on Modern Poetry," the new technique of the "vers libre" that inspired Poundian Imagism demanded that the prosodic form be governed more by the images used by the poet rather than by syllable counts or line endings; Barnard's poem is a step toward this program.

Just as Hulme galvanized Pound's Imagist aesthetic, so did Pound galvanize Barnard's. The arrival of a new literature professor at Reed, Lloyd Reynolds, provided the impetus. Taking Reynolds's creative writing course in her junior year, Barnard began, sometime between 1930 and 1931, to read "the poets I think of as the real moderns: not Masters, Sandburg, the Benets, but Eliot, Pound, H.D., Edith Sitwell, Hart Crane, and . . . Cummings," although "I am sure we did not get as far as W.C. Williams,"[6] who at this point was not much known in the United States beyond the little magazines.[7] She found herself drifting toward Pound because he was not as remote to her as Eliot, whose earlier work and religious poetry "was foreign to me."[8] The choice of wording was not accidental; for Barnard, poetry was to become deeply connected to ideas of "the native," so it is unsurprising that Eliot, an American living in Europe with tenuous poetic ties to his homeland, held limited appeal. Pound, on the other hand, always energetically maintained his links with America and cared for its poetry, even if he chose not to live there. In Pound's *Personae*, Barnard reflected in her memoir, "I was beginning to know at last the country I wanted to explore,"[9] particularly the "country" of free verse metric, as will be seen later.

Exploration of "Pound's country" took up almost all of Barnard's remaining time at college, resulting in a collection of poems that made up her senior thesis, "The Horae of Mary Ethel Barnard" ("The Hours of Mary Ethel Barnard"), which she had pleaded with the humanities faculty to allow her to submit in place of a critical thesis. To reassure those sceptical of her critical competence, Barnard prefaced the thesis with a "Creed":

> I BELIEVE in the simplicity and sincerity of word and movement and idea.
>
> I BELIEVE that compression and image are essential to good poetry, but are not an end in themselves.
>
> I BELIEVE in experimentation and not in cults.
>
> I BELIEVE in the sound of the words. By that I mean words that sound as if they grew together, although they may be common and not particularly beautiful in themselves.
>
> I BELIEVE and regret that everyone is caught in the flow of some poetic movement and is greatly influenced by it.
>
> I BELIEVE that the excellence of a poem is to a great extent measured by whether its meaning increases or decreases with repeated readings.
>
> I BELIEVE that everything good has its place in poetry, but I have a greater weakness for some things than others.
>
> I BELIEVE that perspective is far more important than criteria in judging the worth of poems.
>
> I BELIEVE in Shakespeare and Shelley and Keats and Ezra Pound and Eleanor Wylie and Edith Sitwell (although I often have my doubts there) and I should probably mention Homer. I had a passion for Alfred Noyes when I was in the eighth grade and may have one for Hart Crane by next year. One can never be sure about things like that.[10]

Advocating "simplicity," "sincerity," "compression," "image," "words that sound as if they grew together," Barnard's creed eloquently strikes a chord with Flint's "Imagisme" and Pound's "A Few Don'ts by an Imagiste," and yet, staggeringly, she had not yet read the Imagist manifestoes when she wrote it, at least not directly. It was when she returned home from college to Vancouver, jobless, the Depression severely limiting her options and her father's lumber business having collapsed, that Barnard's eye alighted on Pound's famous lines. To carry them through the "bleak winter" of 1932,[11] Barnard and several other graduates formed a study club, meeting regularly to exchange papers on the literature of the day. Barnard, for one of her turns, chose to discuss the moderns. In preparation, Barnard read some of Pound's criticism, as well as local academic Glenn Hughes's *Imagism and the Imagists*, which had just been published to coincide with Ford Madox Ford's nostalgic volume of Imagist poetry that had come out in 1930. More important, Barnard read "A Few Don'ts by an Imagiste," commenting that

> It seemed to me the only really worthwhile piece of poetry criticism I had ever read—worthwhile for the maker, that is, as opposed to the consumer. I also realized for the first time how much he [Pound] had done for other poets. I decided that Pound was the poet that I wanted to write to. . . . I thought he knew more about the technique of writing poetry than any other living poet.[12]

She also knew that Pound had a passion, like her, for Greek, and that he had probably tasted something of the loneliness that she was experiencing earlier in his career at Wabash College. Plus, she later said, "I always knew, if the work wasn't any good, he'd be honest enough to say 'You'd better take up crocheting.'"[13] Thus in October 1933, precisely a year after she had expressed her desire for a poetry of "a certain starkness" in her Chief Company notebook, Barnard sent off six poems with a letter asking for advice or assistance. Sympathetic to "the shattering wail of the segregated and lone poet on the far, far coast,"[14] in return Pound sent advice evocative of "A Few Don'ts by an Imagiste": "thing is to cut a shape in time" says Pound in one communication;[15] "several adjectives don't seem to do too much," "rewrite this, with greater economy;" and "NO, not TOO much condensation" he says in another.[16] One can almost hear the slashing of pencil that H.D. famously recalled from 1912 when Pound said "'But Dryad,' (in the Museum tea room), 'this is poetry.' He slashed with a pencil. 'Cut this out, shorten this line.'"[17] The allusion to H.D. is no coincidence, since in these early letters Pound almost seemed to be treating Barnard as he did H.D. in 1912. Whereas H.D., for Pound, had the grace of a "dryad," Barnard had the grace of a "gazelle"—and this was to distinguish her from that other female Imagist, Amy Lowell. In response to one of Barnard's letters apologising for her poems' "lightness"—she was concerned that she did not have a subject—Pound wrote: "Don't worry about LIGHTNESS / you aint an Amy Lowell / shall the gazelle mimic the hippo / 'be yerrsellf!!.'"[18] Barnard was all too ready to take Pound up on his call to "be yerrself"—although influenced by Imagism, she was not too ready to commit herself to any preformed molds. Like Imagism's detractors, Barnard was aware that good poetry could be written outside of the ready formulations of literary movements, as articulated by two "beliefs" that she eventually omitted from the final version of her "Creed":

> I BELIEVE that most poets and students of poetry have essentially the same ideas about what is good poetry; but they become stubborn about the words they use to describe it.
>
> I BELIEVE that good poets who have theories forget about them when they write.[19]

Thus, although Barnard's aesthetic may be regarded as a result of the "pounding" and "flinting" of the literary heritage bequeathed to her by the moderns, bearing the force of Pound's outpourings and the scratches of his pencil, there is, at the same time, a resolve toward an authentic, individual poetry, born of the moment and circumstances in which it is written. It was these circumstances—Barnard's immediate local—that became integral to Barnard's late Imagism. "Compression and image are essential to good poetry," Barnard had written in her creed, "but are not an end in themselves." Pound's Imagism certainly crystallized some of the thoughts that Barnard had been having regarding style in her poetry, but her purpose, her "end," lay in the American landscape, in a project not too dissimilar to that of Williams. In some ways it appeared that the nature of the "little-known" landscape of her Pacific Northwest local had predisposed Barnard to thinking along Imagist lines before she had even heard of Pound, as we shall now see.

2.2 Barnard's Imagist Local

Part of the mystery of Barnard's poem "North Window" comes not only from the beguiling image of "the queen's emeralds" at the close but from the very ordinary image at the beginning: what, exactly, does "a book with a green binding" have to do with what lies outside a northwestern window? The answer lies in the poem's subtle play on the association between the literary and the local, where ideas of writing and space overlap and become entwined. "North Window" announces its regional affiliation blatantly in its semantic content, dominated by "green" and "emerald" colors and the paling sky spreading "mist . . . under the rafters," but there is also the sense that regional space is inextricably caught up in the verbal. This is immediately detectable in the title: in the self-conscious use of the letters "N" and "W" that begin each word of the poem's title, suggesting that the poem is about the "NW" of the American literary compass. The "book" of the poem is stitched together by the "green binding" of its regional focus. This association made between the literary and the physical, geographical world, shows the same kind of desire Williams had to make the local *literary*, the literary *local.* Furthermore, the "book with a green binding" can be read as a visual metaphor for the timbered building that the poem presents metonymically, bringing the literary and the physical into a sharp double focus. Elements of the "green" book, for example, appear in the "Green cloth" of the unspecified space beside a beach—is this "Green cloth" some kind of protective rooftop covering, as well as the jacket of the book? "Stairways of unstained wood" might be interpreted as the book's nonglossy, scratchy pages staggering, stair-like, into a heap. Perhaps more convincingly, the book's "binding" is recollected in the "rafters" that bind the roof to the body of this unnamed building in the penultimate line.

Barnard's recollection of her childhood experience of the Northwest local yields further clues for interpreting such images arranged, as the Arrow reader had observed, in "a particularly open, detached sequence." As soon as she was old enough, Barnard accompanied her father on his mill trips through the Coast Range forest, rattling around the bumpy northwestern roads in the family car to tiny clearings deep among the evergreens. While her father negotiated with the mill owners, Barnard read or made sketches of the mills, whose spare structures fascinated her.[20] Moreover, the trips gave purpose to her life's writing:

> I was constantly looking, feeling, registering and trying—*always* trying to find words that would capture something of the experience so that I could put it down and keep it. . . . whatever else was happening [in my life,] these mill trips were constantly recurring, a part of my Vancouver experience, yet outside Vancouver.[21]

Thus, the unspecified building in "North Window" is most probably a sawmill; the "Stairways of unstained wood" suggest newly cut wood and the laying of plank upon plank of wood beside a sawmill, in a stepped "stairway" fashion, ready for transport. Imagery and language are arranged in such a way that they evoke the startling austerity of the sawmill settlements, the shock of the blank space created by them amid the deep green of the Coast Range forest, perhaps most tellingly in the indented couplet, "Green cloth and polished horn, / Stairways of unstained wood." In the "Green cloth" there is a suggestion of the rich green of a region densely blanketed by the Douglas fir trees that have earned the state of Washington the nickname "The Evergreen State"; the pointy height of these firs is articulated in the "polished horn," and something of their spikiness is sounded in the staccato rhythms of that first, itemizing stanza, in the monosyllabic jab of "like a lake beach," and in the initial iambic pulse of "We *sit* a*mong* grasses" (italics mine). But in this couplet, there is also a suggestion of a clearing and perhaps a building within it. Indeed, the indentation is itself a clearing in the "forest" of the poem. From this point onward in the poem, the perspective becomes rooted in the flat, blank space outside: it moves across low-ground "grasses" and "bloodless stones," and finally the speaker claims to "lie upon *white fur*" (italics mine)—we might read this as an image for snow, or even for a blanket, but it is also possible to interpret the image of "white fur" as a metaphor for the unmarked, smooth "white" space of a clearing, its suggestion of a shorn coat evocative of the logging industry cutting down the forest.

Something of this spare, empty space can be seen in one of Barnard's watercolor sawmill sketches, which depicts an anonymous, green-roofed building (like "a book with a green binding") very similar in description to the one in "North Window," where the thick blotch of evergreens to the rear is tempered by the pale colors of the clearing in the foreground, fading from grey to white:

FIGURE 2. Untitled watercolor by Mary Barnard (12" × 9"). Mary Barnard Papers. Courtesy of Elizabeth J. Bell.

"It is impossible to exaggerate the sketchiness of some of these sawmills. One, I remember, was powered by a Ford truck engine. Some of them would get out perhaps one car of lumber in six months," Barnard later recalled.[22] This structural sparsity was matched by the austere lives the sawmill residents led, surviving on the local venison and wild blackberries and huckleberries that grew nearby, as well as the minimal provisions that they grew on garden patches. "They survived," Barnard observed, "and most of them preferred their independence to a steady job for wages even if they could have found one."[23] It was an austerity that Samuel Barnard admired and respected, so much so that when the Portland/Vancouver area was rapidly expanding, he refused to cut off his business with even the tiniest, most isolated of sawmills. Despite having a higher standard of living than the sawmill owners, the Barnards kept their family residence simple and spare in decoration and appearance, predisposed as the family was to the same kind of austerity seen in the families who lived in the settlements. It was a quality that Mary Barnard quietly cultivated over her long life and that her publisher so eloquently drew upon in a speech at her memorial service. "Mary Barnard's work was never about quantity or extravagance and she lived her life as she wrote. She left this world like a clean tungsten flame, perfect until the end, nothing wasted," reflected James Anderson.[24] When I came in the summer of 2003 to visit Mary Barnard's apartment, left much as it was at the time that she died, I made a journal entry that similarly connected the spareness and apparent simplicity of her poetry to the way in which she arranged her home:

> Mary Barnard's apartment, like her poetry, is lacking in ornament. What is displayed has been carefully selected for its significance. There are several art works—many by the painter and Mary's acquaintance Edna Gluck, with whom Mary lived one summer in the 1930s (after Yaddo), and some paintings by Mary herself. Overall the apartment is functional in presentation, perhaps reflecting the modesty and resistance of augmentation that her Presbyterian upbringing had produced within her. The sitting room, for example, contains purposeful objects, rather than ornaments: two chairs sit around a tall table which contains a knife for opening letters and a magnifying glass for reading. The apartment is itself in some kind of time warp, as exemplified by the absence of technology—there is one small television in the study and very little evidence of popular culture, except for a copy of *Anodyne*, the Portland-based free pop culture monthly. . . . And that was all.

FIGURE 3. Sketch by Mary Barnard: Washington sawmill (external view), ca. 1920s. Mary Barnard Papers. Courtesy of Elizabeth J. Bell.

FIGURE 4. Sketch by Mary Barnard: Washington sawmill (internal view), ca. 1920s. Mary Barnard Papers. Courtesy of Elizabeth J. Bell.

It was not only the "sketchiness" of sawmills that shaded Barnard's regional memories and shaped her poetics but also the "sketchiness" of the roads that the Barnards took there to make their lumber deals:

> We drove corduroy roads, sawdust roads, plank roads, almost perpendicular roads; we forded little brooks, rattled across bridges thrown together apparently without spikes, and could at any blind curve expect to meet a logging truck. The car got stuck in red clay and had to be pulled out by a team of horses, or we cut two tires at once on crushed rock, or we lost our way. A new one had to be tracked down by sound, smell, and the tracks of log or lumber trucks in the mud.[25]

Although her poems are rich in images of "roads spongy with sawdust" and "wood-road / . . . tracks bright with chips,"[26] it was not so much the bumpy roughness of these roads that Barnard was drawn to as much as the peace of their quiet stillness that she apprehended as almost constant. In "Highway Bridge," it is through the passage of occasional traffic (like Barnard's own passage through the landscape) that this peace intensifies:

> When a hill stream enters a river at flood
> It is abashed into stillness, welling
> Between grass blades and small clover.
> Its surface becomes the green of leaves obstructing light,
> Tranquil between piers.
>
> Although the bridge has a purpose other
> Than the quiet under it, a peace
> Exploded by the rapid wheels overhead,
> After their passage this that we thought shattered
> Absorbs the falling fragments of sound.
> There is a deeper silence than before
> Where two ruts dip under the river's border
> And do not reappear.[27]

With its easy enjambment simulating the turn of car wheels, this sustained meditation on the landscape enables the speaker to find an unexpected cohesion between the "rapid wheels overhead" and the "quiet under" the bridge. The resulting "deeper silence than before" allows the speaker to see a road that takes them into the tranquillity of the river, in the image of the "two ruts" that "dip under the river's border / and do not reappear." The ruts may be the remnants of a barely passable track, not unlike those on which Barnard traveled with her father, but they may also be a transcendental passage seen in the imagination, enabling the viewer to be just like the hill stream that "enters a river at flood"—in her awareness of the "deeper silence" that proves the speaker wrong (having "thought [the peace] shattered"), the speaker is as "abashed into stillness" as the hill stream.

The sawmills, however, not only provided Barnard with a geography to articulate in writing but also a model for handling poetic language. Many of Barnard's poems are full of images in which rough meets smooth, loud meets quiet, a reflection of the process of writing in which the poet puts the raw stuff of life through an imaginative mill of alterations, erasures, and reformulations to produce something more honed and resonant. So in "North Window," raw, unprocessed natural materials (the "grasses," "stones," "snow," "unstained wood") are placed alongside images of smooth, refined products (the "book with a green binding," "green cloth," "polished horn," a blanket of "white fur," the "queen's emeralds"), products that seem to have been formulated from the land's colors and textures. There is a paring down, a cutting down of language like the effect of a saw on wood, as lines are trimmed, then expanded. It is as if a crafted product—a plank, a timbered frame, a poem—is emerging from the serrated teeth of the line, with its heavy load, in the first half of the poem, of sharp, guttural consonance ("book," "green," "binding," "sky," "blood," "like a lake," "green cloth.")

Indeed, as Barnard's late Imagist aesthetic developed, so too did the influence of the sawmills and their processes of refinement, with her poems becoming increasingly pared down as she cultivated tight verbal economy. Her first poems in *Poetry* in 1935 sprawled at variable lengths across the pages, with "Shoreline" running to sixty-eight lines (and cut even further for *Collected Poems*), "Faun in Exile" running to forty-five lines (also cut—and renamed "Wine Ship"—in subsequent printings), and "Ondine" coming in at forty-two lines long. By the time Barnard printed *A Few Poems* in 1952, almost every poem was noticeably short and confined to one page and often in three stanzas, as if to represent the minimum number of moves a poem needs to make (introduction, expansion, and conclusion) in order to assume coherence. As she told August Fruge, "generally the best clue to the chronology [of her poems] lies in the number of words in the poem. The fewer, the later."[28] Of course, Pound and Williams played their parts. In his first few letters to her regarding poetic technique, Pound issued orders to pare down and prune her verse, complaining that a poem like "Fable from the Cayoosh Country" was "mattressed and quilted down under the verbiage."[29] Williams continued in the same vein: "cut out the first and third stanzas," he wrote in 1938 in response to her poem "The Rapids." "There is usually one intense note in a short poem," Williams observed, "the objective of the writer can't be much else than to make that as penetrating as possible."[30]

But it was not only Barnard's experience of sawmills deep inland that sponsored such a sensibility; the Washington coast mattered, too. Indeed, in her poetry, the two spaces seem intricately entwined as vital components of her regional memory. Of her sawmill trips, she had said that "we went in all seasons, in all kinds of weather except snow, when the mills would be shut down for lack of logs."[31] One would assume that in real life, the snow kept the Barnards inside and at home; but in "North Window," Barnard replays this situation and is "forced" somewhere else. In an alternative reading of the poem, the building is not that of a sawmill but of a family home, keeping in a child wistful for the "queen's emeralds" of the forest because the snowed-in mills are shut down. So when snow is seen "dropping out of a shallow sky," preventing a sawmill trip, there is only one other place this mind can go: "To a beach without wharf, quiet / Like a lake beach." The alliteration and consonance of "like" and "lake" create a strange aural texture of soft and harsh sounds, the "l" lapping the line like "quiet" waters, the consonantal "k" whipping the line like a ferocious Pacific wind on the beaches that Barnard knew intimately. One area of the coast was particularly significant. Ocean Park, a small resort along what is now known as the Long Beach Peninsula, was a place where the Barnards often holidayed, and it triggered a good number of the poems that marked Barnard's arrival in national print ("Lai," "Ondine," "The Silk Leaf," "Faun in Exile" and, of course, "Shoreline"). Located at the point where the Columbia River meets the Pacific Ocean, the Long Beach Peninsula is itself a stunning, bewildering, finger-shaped strip of land of extraordinary dimensions. Twenty-eight miles long yet barely one mile wide, it soars resplendently out to sea as it is gnawed by the eroding waters of Willapa Bay on the east side and the Pacific on the west side. When the tide is out at Ocean Park, the beach presents a stretch of glistening wet sand that peels away for at least a quarter of a mile. No fence, stream, or headland breaks up the beach for more than twenty of the twenty-eight miles. It is a coastline that is, like the purest of Imagist poems, stripped down and devoid of ornament, all the more intense for the lack of human presences. When Barnard was a child, "only one cottage peered over a dune-top, and it was always empty. Often there was not another soul on the beach, or only a few tiny figures doubled in a mirage effect far in the distance."[32] Upon a visit to Ocean Park in June 2005, it seemed to me that little had changed. Despite having a Main Street, a supermarket, and a handful of diners and souvenir shops, Ocean Park is almost as much a ghost town as the settlement that lies completely deserted on the opposite side of the peninsula, Oysterville, which still has decrepit wooden signs advertising the sale of oysters even though its tiny fleet of oyster boats has been crumbling into the waters of Willapa Bay for years.

Yet for Barnard, this space was "Utopia," as she called it in the long letters she would send home to her parents when she was old enough to spend long summers there by herself, taking a similar delight in the spare desolation as that taken by the speakers of "North Window," whose sitting amid the flat, blank space of "bloodless stones" and "white fur" leads them to fantasize about emeralds. Although in Ocean Park poems such as "Shoreline" there is some suggestion of the sumptuous northwest as "a place where almost anything would grow, where growing things had a kind of furious life about them, a kind of lavishness," as fellow northwestern poet David Wagoner has recalled,[33] it is again the pared-down spaces that captivate and drive the emotional tone. "Faun in Exile," for example, imagines what the Long Beach coast could offer a shipwrecked "sharp-eared foreigner":

> Here were no myrtle groves,
> No familiar shrines,
> Only the splintered casks and the sweet wines
> Spilt in the sea.
>
> Here were no grapes,
> But bitter berries grew in the marsh.
>
> Here was no moss,
> But sea worn logs and the harsh
> Grass on the dune top.[34]

FIGURE 5. Ocean Park, Long Beach Peninsula, Washington, ca. 1920s. Photo attributed to Mary Barnard. Mary Barnard Papers. Courtesy of Elizabeth J. Bell.

There is a subtle shift from loss to gain in this excerpt. Although there is little to replace the "familiar shrines," the cold northwestern beach of "here" offers gritty equivalents to the soft, tender growth of warmer shores—there may be "no grapes," *but* there are "bitter berries;" there may be "no moss," *but* there are the "sea worn logs" and the "harsh grass." In this scheme of parallelisms, "only" is replaced by "but," a word that subtly suggests that there are some compensations in what the poem goes on to call "this forlorn meeting of sea and land." They are compensations that were keenly felt by Barnard herself in this desolate coastal space. "Nowhere else have I ever been so alone and so little lonely," she said of Ocean Park.[35]

2.3 "Sand Is the Beginning and the End / of Our Dominion": Barnard, H.D., and the Gender of Imagism

She had wanted to explore "Pound's country" as well as "the forlorn meeting of sea and land" of the coast of her "cool country," but Barnard found herself encroaching upon the imaginative territory of another poet who was also drawn to Greek forms and the symbolic capacities of the beach: H.D. Despite repeated suggestions from Pound, Barnard did not cultivate a correspondence with H.D. "Through [Pound and Williams], I feel somewhat acquainted with you," Barnard wrote from Buffalo in 1943, requesting a donation of manuscripts to the library, but that was the only letter she sent.[36] Why Barnard shied away from H.D. (or, if we are to believe Viola Baxter Jordan, why H.D. shied away from Barnard) is unclear from the spare references to her in *Assault on Mount Helicon*. Barnard's poetry, though, may hold the key: the remarkable similarity of style and content suggests to me that maybe Barnard felt that she had *too much* in common with H.D.; that she would not find the kind of distant, yet sympathetic, critic that she needed and had found, like so many other new writers, in Pound. Or perhaps Barnard felt that she might be accused of imitation, a fear aroused by a biting comment from Pound in 1936 that her manuscript was a premature "repetition (pretty much) of what H.D. had already said in 1913."[37] Possibly that is why H.D., although she sent the University of Buffalo some poems, decided to have nothing to do with Barnard socially.

Pound's charge was a heavy one and intended to humble Barnard into working harder at her technique, yet the parallels between Barnard's work in the 1930s and "what H.D. . . . said in 1913" are intriguing. There is scope to compare these two poets along many different lines—for example, their considerable appropriation of Sappho's poetry, as I discuss in the next chapter—and yet one single refrain from Barnard's "Shoreline" seems binding. "Sand is the beginning and the end / of our dominion," wrote Barnard in 1935; she may well have been talking about the poetic dominion she shared with H.D., for in both poets' early work, sand is a recurrent image, widely distributed like the very grains being presented. Sand features in eleven poems in H.D.'s *Sea Garden*; in Barnard's first collection *Cool Country* (1940) and in unpublished poems from the 1930s only recently made available by her literary estate, sand is referenced in no fewer than sixteen poems.[38] Although neither poet set out to explain the nature of their poetic practice as readily as Pound—who himself used a series of metaphors to explain his notion of Imagism (the psychoanalytical complex, the vortex, and the ideogram)—there is enough evidence in their early poems to suggest that both Barnard and H.D. highly favored the qualities of crystalline particles as a poetic model. After all, H.D. apprehended that her poetry contained "the center they call 'Air and Crystal,'"[39] although critical attention has not focused specifically on *sand* crystals.[40] As a self-styled "sand flea," as she was affectionately known to her parents for her love of the dunes at Ocean Park,[41] Barnard's refrain "Sand is the beginning and the end / of our dominion" is so markedly audacious in temper in contrast to a poetry characterized by restraint and subtlety that it demands to be read as a significant metaphor.

Sand as a substance lends itself well to poetic appropriation. A translucent material, it has the ability to transmit light, thus making it a powerful image through which a poet might radiate messages—for H.D., sand is as "clear as wine."[42] For Barnard, the shoreline is a site of "reflecting sands," as she writes in "Shoreline"—not only a creative site of light-play but also a psychological site for thought and contemplation, an appropriate backdrop to highly self-reflexive poems such as those found in Barnard's early lyrics and H.D.'s *Sea Garden*. Composed of grains of variable colors, textures, shapes, and crystalline composition, the image of sand has the power to evoke a range of feelings. Sand is sensuous—a single grain feels rough and jagged, yet a handful feels smooth. Sand is alluring but elusive. It glistens and sparkles, yet it escapes upon approach, slipping away at the shoreline under waves, to be coughed up further up shore, dispersing at the breeze of coast winds or the pound of footsteps, disappearing through the cracks between fingers of scooping hands. Sand is a real-world equivalent of the kind of "accurate mystery" that F. S. Flint observed of H.D.'s poetry, which is "in ultimate effect . . . mysterious" despite having "the precision of goldsmith's work," possessive of those qualities that Arrow's reader saw in Barnard's poetry, with its propensity for statements arranged in "a particularly open, detached sequence: the effect of [sand-like] particles reflectively dropped to make a pattern."

Sand provides a model for arranging syntax and stanzas. "The hard sand breaks," H.D. announces in the first line of "Hermes of the Ways,"[43] setting a pattern of breaks for the rest of the poem, which undergoes continual reformations of line lengths so that lines resemble the "piles" of "little ridges" of sand arranged by the wind. Barnard follows suit in "Shoreline." The first instance of Barnard's refrain is sandwiched between two geographical images: stanza one, a depiction of the sea; and stanza two, a windswept shore:

The sea has made a wall for its defence
of falling water. Those whose impertinence
leads them to its moving ledges
it rejects. Those who surrender
it will with the next wave drag under.

Sand is the beginning and the end
of our dominion.

The way to the dunes is easy.
The shelving sand is stiffened in the rain
And loosened again in the sun's fingers.
Children, lustful of the glistening hours,
Drink and are insatiate. Wind under the eyelids,
Confusion wailing the ears, their bodies glow
In the cold wash of the beach.

Visually, the refrain stands out like a grain of sand caught between the two forces that shape it, the sea waves and the transient climate of the beach—after all, Barnard concludes, sand is "submissive to the sea and wind." Such friction between images suggests that the poem itself is a rock at which the poet has to chip away, a task familiar to the speaker of H.D.'s "Garden" who, upon perceiving the Image as a hardened thing ("You are clear / O rose, cut in rock / hard as the descent of hail"), presents the handling of the Image in terms of cutting rock: "I could scrape the colour / from the petals / like spilt dye from a rock."[44]

Sand is a metaphor for the type of perspective favored by both poets. Theirs is a roaming, flitting perspective that seems to get everywhere and jumpily switch its focus, moving much in the same way that sand does at the mercy of changeable shore winds. In "Hermes of the Ways," the perspective is partly attuned to the miniature, focusing on the grains of hard sand, clinging here and there on wisps of sea grass and the twists of apple trees. But the perspective is also attuned to the panoramic, stretching out across "leagues" of sand, to dunes, to a hillside, to the "great sea." In "Shoreline," it is difficult to get a feel of the space—the poem flits from sea and shoreline (stanza one) to dunes, beach, and town (stanza three) to a menacing, foggy space of "darkening kitchens" shrouded by "coastal fog" (stanza four) back to dunes (stanza six) to sea-drift (stanza seven) and then to an unspecified shore. In the last stanza, there are traces of these spaces in a collage of "transitory ponds," "clear lagoons," "dune rim," and "sea." Spaces are established, eroded, and reformed, each image itself vulnerable to the rhythmic editing of the poet.

Sand is also a metaphor for Barnard and H.D.'s articulation of time as a series of compressed, ground-up moments carrying marks of other moments like the way sand carries traces of all contact with rocks and waves. Gathered together, these ground-up moments form a stretch of time rather like a stretch of beach, by turns rugged and smooth, evocative of the experience of time passing in varying degrees of intensity. Pound's Imagism might have campaigned for an "intellectual and emotional complex in an instant of time"[45]; between them, H.D. and Barnard produce the complex in a *series of moments in time*, all different in duration, like Barnard's "thin movements" of sea grass dancing on the dune rim in "Shoreline." Stanza three of "Shoreline," for example, sees time made strange, speeded up to consist of "glistening hours" and rapidly changing weather patterns ("wind," "glow," "sundown," "cold," "rain," "fog," "shadow"). This is followed by a long section in which weather—and by implication, time—goes unmentioned, as if the prior moment had been stilled and expanded.

Both poets are sensitive to sand's versatility and ability to evoke a range of physical states to which they can attach selected meanings, dramatizing specific experiences. As a hardened mineral, sand is a solid composed of many types of sediment. It is the physical equivalent of the kind of "verbal grit" that the Imagists were after for their poetry. A porous material, sand can secrete gases and liquid—much of the world's drinking water comes from water-filled sandstones, as do the world's fuel reserves of oil and gas. Barnard and H.D. manipulate this affinity of sand with the three prime physical states of being in order to create multiple layers within their poems, layers as inflated with intense symbols as grains filled with minute deposits of rich sediment. So in "Hermes of the Ways," H.D.'s sand is solid and liquid at the same time: "the *hard* sand breaks, / and the grains of it / are clear as *wine*" (italics mine), an analogy for the torpor of emotion secreted beneath an outer shield.

It is the porous quality of sand that H.D. manipulates the most in *Sea Garden*, producing images that often link sand with fruit, as in "Sea Poppies." A piece of fruit is not simply "on the sand" but is itself composed of sandy colors and textures:

> Amber husk
> fluted with gold,
> fruit on the sand,
> marked with a rich grain,
> treasure
> spilled near the shrub-pines
> to bleach on the boulders:[46]

H.D's fruity-sandy treasure is "spilled," like sand grains gathered and spilled by blustering waves or coastal winds. Fruit, like a grain of sand, has a firm, protective exterior but secretes a softer, juicy interior. Such associative binaries of hard/soft, moist/dry, opacity/transparency offer H.D. scope to dramatize the various sexual conflicts in other *Sea Garden* poems. There is no sand in "Orchard," but one can link the fruit (and nuts) offered to the love object in the last stanza to the sand of "Hermes of the Ways" and "Sea Poppies":

> these fallen hazel-nuts,
> stripped late of their green sheaths,
> grapes, red-purple,
> their berries
> dripping with wine
> pomegranates already broken,
> and shrunken figs
> and quinces untouched,
> I bring you as offering.[47]

The offered hazelnuts are "stripped late of their green sheaths" (like sand grains washed of color by the sea; like the "treasure" left to "bleach on the boulders") in a revenge move by the speaker to return the orchard god's earlier flaying of the speaker "with . . . blossoms." From the hardness of the nuts the focus moves swiftly to liquid imagery, of "berries / dripping with wine" and "pomegranates already broken," recalling the hard sand of "Hermes of the Ways" breaking and becoming "clear as wine." The mix of fruit in different "states" of hardness and liquidity is far from appetizing, for although the berries drip with wine, the focus soon moves onto what is dried up, the "shrunken figs." This is an offering that has been carefully selected, designed to tantalize but quickly disappoint (and perhaps disgust) the intended recipient. The "quinces untouched" may have a double meaning; they might refer to quinces "untouched" because they are fresh but also to quinces "untouched" because they are not wanted or desired. In a flash of an image, the speaker conveys her own sexual anxiety (it is what she is "offering"), simultaneously forcing the love object to experience a declining (sexual) appetite.

In "Shoreline," Barnard's sand imagery is hard too—sand is "stiffened" and forms a shelf, but it is also "loosened" like water or air particles. In another poem from 1935, "Ondine," there is "firm sand" and "dry sand," but in "Note to a Neapolitan," sand is located within a liquid metaphor: "And Miranda emptied her shoes / of little *pools* of sand" (italics mine). Similarly, "Faun in Exile" presents an intermediate state of "half-liquid sand." In addition to the different physical states that sand evokes, Barnard's sand imagery registers a range of contrasting temperatures that can shift quite rapidly, moving from "the beginning" to "the end" of the scale almost instantaneously. In "Shoreline," there is an image of sand cooled by the rain followed swiftly by sand warmed by the sun. In "Faun in Exile," the half-liquid sand undergoes a quick change: "the sand / lies *suddenly* cold under the hand" (italics mine). The speaker in Barnard's unpublished poem "For Jane" complains that "the sand [is] too cold" to walk upon and chooses instead to "walk in perilous ways between the grasses / where the sun warms."[48]

For Barnard, these varying states and temperatures of sand often carry regional meanings. When Barnard wrote "Sand is the beginning and the end / of our dominion," she was writing partly of her experience as an American at the end of a long line of Barnards who had come ashore at Nantucket in the seventeenth century and moved steadily westwards toward Washington, where Barnard was born in 1909. Through nine generations, the Barnard clan had crossed the American "dominion," beginning on sands stretching out of the Atlantic and ending on sands washing away into the Pacific, their westward migration a mirror of the migration of sand grains across land. But Barnard was also writing of her experience as a northwesterner. The product of the collision of natural forces, ground from rocks chipped and cracked from the action of glaciers, volcanoes, and rivers and refined by the pulverizing beat of the wind, sand is certainly suggestive. Barnard's "little-known landscape" was an area of dramatic geological activity, surrounded by mountains pushed up as a result of gaseous volcanic action millions of years ago and by the Columbia River Gorge, a mighty river canyon carved from fast-flowing lava. Indeed, one of Barnard's enduring memories from childhood included a tour that she and her family took through the lava and ice caves near Mount Adams, led by one of her father's sawmill clients.[49] The three states and varying temperatures associated with sand, then, and the forces they relate to offered Barnard a way of articulating the cycle of violent transformations that had shaped the geological "dominion" of the northwest.

For both poets, sand is an empowering substance that accompanies scenes of transformation and recovery. For H.D., sand occasions the renovation of the battered and their renewal into wholes. It reinvigorates flowers like a magical powder. In "Sea Rose," a single brittle rose, "harsh" and "meagre," finds a partner in the equally spare "crisp sand," the mirror of the sand's texture offering some comfort to the weathered, discarded rose "flung on the sand."[50] Indeed, it is at the point of contact with sand that the rose's fortunes are reversed: far from disintegrating into sandy dust (as the poem's earlier images of "stint of petals," "meagre flower," "sparse of leaf" and "stunted, with small leaf" prime us to believe), the flower is resurrected by the sand. The rejuvenated rose is "lifted / in the crisp sand / that drives in the wind," as if pushing up through a flowerbed anew; sand is as nutritious as a rich soil. The restoration of a flower through the action of sand is also a theme in "Sea Lily." As with "Sea Rose," the reader is again primed by imagery to expect disintegration but ends up with an image of an armored flower fit to defend itself against further attack:

Myrtle-bark
is flecked from you,
scales are dashed from your stem,
sand cuts your petal,
furrows it with a hard edge,
like flint
on a bright stone.[51]

Sand emboldens the flower, sculpting it into a sharp weapon whose furrowed, hard-edged petals would repel the approach of forces that seek to destroy it. Sand refines the flower, just as wind refines rock into sand, and grants it the ability to promote life and death, the beginning of a dominion for itself and its allies, the end of a dominion for those who strike it.

In Barnard's "Shoreline," sand occasions the imaginative renovation of the "shattered hulk" of a shipwreck: "The cracked ribs of a wreck / *project* from the washed beach" (italics mine). Like the sudden uplift of H.D.'s emaciated rose in "Sea Rose" or the emergence of the armored flower in "Sea Lily," Barnard's shipwreck is shown in a moment of renewed energy, projecting from sand as if straining to launch into the sea, lubricated by the "dripping brine" that "plucks at the silence of slant chambers" that are caught "opening / seaward." There is a vibrancy about the wreck like the glowing bodies of the children who, earlier in the poem, roll in the surf in metaphoric anticipation of this transformational moment. The connection between shipwreck and the regenerative powers of sand is one that pervades other Barnard poems from the 1930s, such as "An Evening by the Sea," in which the shimmer of sand foretells the enchanting movement of a wrecked mast. The poem ends with an image of *The Alice*, the wreck of a wine ship (and inspiration for "Faun in Exile") washed up close to Ocean Park and a local Washington landmark for years until it was eventually dragged further back into the sea:

A wee bird follows the ripples
And pecks at shining sands.

Silhouettes on the bright horizon
The ships go by afar,
And the mast of the Alice leans seaward
Though sunk in the prisoning bar.

As with the "cracked ribs of a wreck" that "project" in "Shoreline," Barnard endows the action of the shipwreck with an active verb, where the "mast of the Alice *leans* seaward" (italics mine) in marked contrast to the passive verb that follows to remind the reader of the ship's demise—the ship leans and twitches with a hint of life, in spite of its apparent doom.

Such shipwrecks, which pervade Barnard's 1930s poetry and H.D.'s *Sea Garden*, might be considered metaphors for the way both Barnard and H.D. felt about their status as women poets, whose individual experiences in relation to the literary canon meant they might well have felt that they were marooned upon their own islands watching "the ships go by afar," as Barnard put it in "An Evening by the Sea," or observing "men in ships," as H.D. wrote in "Sea Gods."[52] For Barnard, ships passing in the distance might have symbolized the literary worlds that lay beyond the Northwest—the Eastern Seaboard, Harriet Monroe's Chicago, avant-garde New York, Europe—worlds that she craved as a college student. Her early letters to Pound sting of isolation: "I wasn't cut out for a recluse, and that's the only possibility in Vancouver. The people who are all the time arguing about why E. Dickinson was a recluse ought to put themselves in her shoes and ask themselves what they would go out for. They would take off their shoes and go home," wrote Barnard to Pound in 1938.[53] Having copied a good number of Dickinson's poems into her notebooks, perhaps the young Barnard felt at times like a northwestern Emily Dickinson, marooned in Vancouver and yearning for travel and finding some liberation in poetry. Just as one of Dickinson's speakers finds release at the point of wreck ("I saw no Way—The Heavens were stitched—/ I felt the Columns close—/ The Earth reversed her Hemispheres—/ I touched the Universe—"),[54] we might make similar connections between Barnard and the mast of *The Alice* that "leans seaward / Though sunk in the prisoning bar [of sand]"—although trapped in the "prisoning bar" of Vancouver, there is also forward movement, leaning "seaward" as if to "touch the Universe" of Pound's Europe and Moore and Williams's New York, places Barnard would later come to inhabit and travel extensively.

Indeed, looking at an early draft of "Shoreline," it is clear that Barnard visualized the poem as an expression of female experience. Originally entitled "For Those Who Dwell on the Marches," the poem was initially presented through the eyes of a solitary young girl, "bare-legged" and wearing a "middy blouse"; it chronicled her experiences "along a sand beach."[55] Given Barnard's continual references in interviews, essays, and her memoir to the significance of her childhood experiences playing alone at Ocean Park, it is easy to suppose that this young girl was an incarnation of herself, who would go on to write, like H.D., many poems situated along the same "sand beach." However, the draft is not merely indicative of forthcoming content; its very title hints at the kind of gender concerns that both Barnard and H.D. deployed in their early poetry as they forged their poetic identities. Barnard's girl in the "middy blouse" is not simply a nostalgic self-presentation; she might be considered as a sketch of an archetype of the modernist woman. As one of "those who dwell on the marches," she resides in an area marked by political nuance. One meaning of "march" is "boundary" or "frontier," a term not too unusual to Barnard the northwesterner, having grown up at the outer edges of the American frontier. But "march" also reflects the metaphoric "frontier" of modernist women's poetry, where one might locate Barnard and H.D. at different ends of a poetic frontier, sweeping across time between the wars: H.D. one of the first poets to push forth the female modernist frontier in Europe as one of Pound's "Imagistes" in the years immediately prior to the First World War, Barnard one of the later poets to pursue the modernist frontier in America as an apprentice to Pound in the years leading up to the Second World War.

The nature of this ground between H.D. and Barnard—and the ground depicted in their sandy-shored poems—is divulged in a second meaning of "marches": a disputed tract of land between two boundaries. This is a strange kind of no-land, a land in suspension prior to some kind of resolution, where H.D.'s battered speakers await transformation into empowered wholes or Barnard's shipwrecks languish in anticipation of restoration. These "marches" characterize the dominion of a modernist female aesthetic that both H.D. and Barnard strove to possess and animate despite the interference or "dispute" from masculine forces—in both cases, principally from Pound—regarding the shape and direction of the "tract" of their work, however much they appreciated external support. At Barnard's suggestion, it is sand that can resolve the dispute, for it is my contention that the sandy shoreline as constructed by both Barnard and H.D. is an *affirmative, gendered* space, where "marches" are transformed, like Barnard's own edit, into a "dominion" where modernist woman is sovereign. It is a vital move: for "shore" means "shorn off," analogous to the way in which women's poetry has been cut off from the canon—to possess the shoreline for its own sake is an act of empowerment. For H.D., this dominion demands a vibrant, new language. She coins fresh compounds for a coastal topography wrought from sand where the geography of the beach and the geography of a land mass merge: there's a "sand-hill" in "Sea Violet," multiplying into "sand-hills" in "Sea Gods"; the "sand on the stream-bank" in "Pursuit" offers an inland image of a stream, yet the elements of this image are reassembled in "Sea Violet" in a related image of "torn shells / on the sand-bank."[56]

In H.D.'s case, sand imagery can be placed within various combative narratives, including a narrative of gender conflict between her and Pound. Interestingly, H.D. uses hard, dry, coarse sand imagery to describe plants and fruits, whereas Pound's Imagist poems from the same period as *Sea Garden* often depict soft, moist plants immersed in or laced with water. Against H.D.'s sand texts comprising hollowed flowers like "amber husk / fluted" with the "gold" of sand grains ("Sea Poppies"); flowers where "sand cuts your petal, / furrows it with a hard edge" ("Sea Violet"); and where sand is a growing place for "weed, moss-reed / root tangled in sand" where "roots drag up color / from the sand" ("Sea Iris"), one can find contemporaneous oppositions from Pound: "A wet leaf that clings to the threshold" ("Liu Ch'E"); "The petals fall in the fountain" ("Ts'au Chi'h"); "Petals on a wet, black bough" ("In a Station of the Metro"); "As cool as the pale wet leaves" ("Alba"); "the dew is upon the leaf" ("Coitus"); or even the more acerbic "frost on the grass-blade" ("Fan-Piece for Her Imperial Lord").[57] H.D.'s "sand text" fashions a feminine sphere through imagery of hard, dry textures that find no correlation in the damp, soft textures styling Pound's Imagist sphere at this time, as elegant and arresting as these poems are. Speculating further on the contrast, one might say that the feminine and the masculine become inverted: the female poet sculpts formidable flowers that withstand the blast and bluster of fierce coastal winds; the male poet scatters wet leaves that cling, curl, or fade in dews and rains.

One could argue that H.D.'s sandy sphere—as Barnard's—is an emboldening space because sand is a protective *layer* against deluges of water that seek to erode the core of a landmass, as much as it is eroded matter itself. Porous, sand can absorb water and thus insulate and protect what is beneath it, so that it lives on long after the retreat of a wave. In this way, H.D.'s sand imagery can be seen, on the one hand, as a response to the forceful sea of Pound's editing during their days spent in the British Museum tea room, providing a protective layer against his claims on her creativity, and on the other hand storing up useful advice in pockets of consciousness like the crystalline pockets of sand grains absorbing valuable energy resources of oil and gas that can be converted later, upon refinement, into power. Certainly, the idea of being able to crack open hard objects and release rich inner deposits is one that courses through *Sea Garden*, no doubt referring, in part, to H.D.'s ambivalent feelings toward Pound as both guide and guard. Perhaps it was a mutual ambivalence. Pound's wet flowers, in contrast with H.D.'s dry, hardened flowers, might also be considered as personal symbols that disguise his own sense of inadequacy as an Imagist in contrast to the perfection he—and others—saw in H.D.'s early work. Against H.D.'s poetry of firmness and clarity, Pound might have felt that his poems literally wilted in comparison like the sodden leaves he eulogizes.

In Barnard's case, the intense use of sand and relational "earthy particle" imagery might be read as backlash against the "gale" of Pound's continual insistence that she should focus on translation. As much as she held Pound in high regard, Barnard nevertheless wanted to find her *own* subject, not that of another poet's. Sand imagery supplied the "contents" that she thought were lacking in her poetry when she first began corresponding with Pound. Although Pound had curtly enquired "Contents??" in his initial communication, he soon lost interest in helping Barnard locate her subject matter when he realized she had an appetite and talent for Greek.[58] As Pound pushed Barnard to experiment with Sapphics ("If you really learn to write quantitative sapphics in the amurikan langwidge I shall love and adore you all the days of your life"), Barnard continued to worry about the "lightness" of her verse, despite the technical advancement she was making in her prosody under Pound's tutelage.[59] Sand imagery gave Barnard's verse a subtle weight, commensurate with the "spare but musical" style she sought for her work.[60]

In many of the poems that closely followed "Shoreline," sand foregrounds the use of other earthy particles: "stones," "pebbles" and "gravel," "muddy playgrounds," "boulders," "silt," and "sand" all appear in poems published after "Shoreline" that were collected into *Cool Country* in 1940.[61] These poems seem to creak under the sheer weight of the northwestern rock that bore down upon Barnard, demanding refinement into a higher purpose. Furthermore, in the breadth of adjectives that precede Barnard's use of the word "sand," there is a sensuousness commensurate with the variable, rugged yet lush landscape of the states of Washington and Oregon. In poems such as "Roots" and the titular poem "Cool Country," Barnard depicts a landscape that, though craggy and jagged, is moist, tender, and squashy, where roads are "spongy with sawdust" ("Roots")[62] and the wet grass is "deep and sweet in all seasons" ("Cool Country").[63] Contrasting states, where the land like "hard sand breaks" to reveal a soft, watery interior, are central to "Cool Country":

Cool Country

This green is the pod,
The enveloping color of our triangular valleys
Where rivers still young spring
From the coast range into salt estuaries.

Mist blown between promontories
Saturates the earth's every crevice,
Making the grass deep and sweet in all seasons
And the forest heavy.

From these come the red cheeses,
The apricot-colored lumber, deckloads
Moving into the green like lanterns.
The pod is broken for vermilion steaks of the salmon,
The chill wave itself opened
For the red-ripeness of harvest.[64]

The central images flit between those of an exterior ("This green is the pod, / The enveloping color of our triangular valleys," later abbreviated to "the green" and "the pod") and those of internal textures and secretions ("the earth's every crevice," "the red cheeses" and "vermilion steaks of the salmon," which together bloom as "the red-ripeness of harvest.") As if cracking a grain of sand for its secretions of water and oil, Barnard cracks the pod of the valley to get at its valuable, luminous reserves of freshly cut lumber, where the green skin of the valley is peeled back to reveal at first air and water ("mist," "rivers") and then the prized goods, the "deckloads" of "apricot-colored lumber" that have matured like a good red cheese. There is a real tenderness that lies within the land, despite the jaggedness of "triangular valleys," the "coast range" of mountains, or the "promontories" that poke out toward the sea, as Barnard suggests in the closing image, where she associates the red lumber that lies beneath the green pod with the raw flesh of salmon, a fish native to the Columbia River (implied by the "chill wave"). In a grain of sand, Barnard was able to encode the spareness of the logging camps that she grew up among, as well as to make palpable Washington's lush forests as she observed them being cut down and down like sand from rock. Sand was "the beginning and the end" of her Washington experience; if Barnard was translating anything, it was the translation of this landscape's contours to the page, rather than a "greek, latin or chinese" author that Pound had so adamantly told her to "get."[65]

Barnard's recurring image of choice, then, offers an appropriate metaphor for the kind of poetry sought by Pound, particularly at the time of the Imagist revolution, and to which she aspired as early as 1932, looking for a "hard" writing of "a certain starkness"—after all, both sand and Imagism are forged from a moment of crystallization, one of rock mineral and one of literary ideas. Sand is a metaphor that perhaps Pound did not stumble upon—the closest he comes to it is when he expresses hope that the new poetry of the twentieth century will be "as much like granite as it can be."[66] It is interesting to speculate whether, if he had happened upon sand as an appropriate metaphor, his Imagist discourse would have been far more intense and rigorous in its logic. Sand is the polar opposite of the kind of "doughy," late–nineteenth-century poetry despised by Pound that his Imagist movement aimed to eradicate. "The common verse . . . from 1890," Pound scoffed, was "a horrible agglomerate compost, not minted, most of it not even baked, all legato, a doughy mess of third-hand Keats, Wordsworth, heaven knows what, fourth-hand Elizabethan sonority blunted, half-melted, lumpy."[67] Sand is not an "agglomerate compost" but its opposite, defined by sedimentologists as "loose, noncohesive, granular material" only ever loosely connected with other material.[68] Sand does not dissolve into a "doughy mess"; it holds up to water well; nor does it melt under pressure of heat; it is firm and reflective of the sun's rays. H.D.'s poetry of sharp sand presents an image of a substance that is anything but "blunted"; Barnard's images of sand as soft and cushioning (the "sand pillow" of "Shoreline" and the "pools of sand" that bathe Miranda's feet in "Note to a Neapolitan") present an image of sand that is not "blunted" and robbed of any malevolent power but smoothed and refined into a sensuous substance nourishing to those who walk upon it or the wrecked ships that come to rest there.

Although I have argued that it was through sand that H.D. and Barnard were able to construct a space for a specifically female modernist aesthetic, the contrary may also be true: their use of sand imagery bound their poetry to the aesthetics of Poundian Imagism. If Pound's Imagist poetry was concerned with bringing poetry back to the fine particulars, a move away from expansive verbal gestures, abstractions, and ethereal ramblings, then sand makes the ideal model for this kind of poetry, for sand *is* a fine particular. Sand is the refinement of rock mineral, just as the Imagist poem sought to be the refinement of linguistic material, and it offers a real-world model of the kind of "maximum abruptness" that Pound advocated (the term is one he used in a letter to Mary Barnard in regard to a draft of her Sappho translation[69]), its physical terseness an embodiment of "the laconic speech of the Imagistes."[70] Sand embodies everything that Pound and Flint's essay in the 1913 edition of *Poetry* set down as the ideal for Imagist poetry. Validation of such processes of refinement, of grinding and milling ideas, language, and meter to produce a new material sparkling with infinite possibilities, litter the aesthetics of the American modernist poets, even if, like Pound, they were not to formally liken the process of poetry-making to that of sand formation. Williams advised Denise Levertov to "Cut and cut again whatever you write—while you leave by your art no trace of your cutting—and the final utterance will remain packed with what you have say."[71] Or, as Moore advised Barnard in her first letter to her in 1934, "to be emotionally compressed—even over-compressed—aids one later, by permeation," advocating a similar strategy of packing meaning into the tiniest of spaces.[72] When Barnard came to translate Sappho, she took many of the fragments through almost forty versions, her mind working like the sea, shaping and refining each grain of verse into a smooth, clear crystal.

Sand is the result of "direct treatment of the 'thing' whether subjective or objective," evidence of the direct approach of external forces of sea, wind, and other natural assailants, suggesting that the poet should approach the poem with all the force, focus, and passion that natural forces visit upon rock. "As regarding rhythm," Pound and Flint's 1913 essay continued, the Imagist poet should "compose in the sequence of the musical phrase, not in sequence of the metronome." Elsewhere, Pound's discussion of rhythm can be likened to the rhythm of sand activity along the shoreline, where sand is lifted and moved with each wave, caught in the sea's rhythms like words caught in the "rhythm wave" that Pound finds in poetry:

> Don't chop your stuff into separate *iambs*. Don't make each line stop dead at the end, and then begin every next line with a heave. Let the beginning of the next line catch the rise of the rhythm wave, unless you want a definite longish pause. In short, behave as a musician, a good musician, when dealing with the phase of your art which has exact parallels in music. The same laws govern, and you are bound by no others.[73]

Sand also presents us with a more efficient, sparer model of the "emotional and intellectual complex in an instant of time," as it possesses a capacity to instantly evoke a dual experience of the miniature and the microcosm similar to the way Imagist poetry aims to shift from the precision of the minute to the universal in a minimum number of moves. Pound wrote:

> It is the presentation of such a "complex" instantaneously which gives that sense of sudden liberation; that sense of freedom from time limits and space limits; that sense of sudden growth which we experience in the presence of the greatest works of art.[74]

Sand yokes notions of past and present and of nearness and farness into tight relation. In apprehending the image of sand, one can experience the same kind of "sudden growth" as we connect grains to the rivers, mountains, volcanoes, and glaciers that have molded them time and time again throughout eons of geological time across a range of geographical terrains. It was a feature not lost on H.D., who compresses the enormous temporal and spatial dimensions of sand into the opening stanzas of "Hermes of the Ways," moving from the immediacy of a miniature to the remoteness of something larger only to pull the reader back again to the smallness of things (italics mine):

> The hard sand breaks
> and the *grains* of it
> are clear as wine.
>
> *Far off* over the *leagues* of it,
> the wind,
> playing on the *wide* shore,
> piles *little* ridges
> and the *great* waves
> break over it.

The compactness of sand makes it a worthy real-world model for both H.D.'s figure for the Image as one comprising images "superimposed upon one another like a stack of photographic negatives"[75] as well as for Pound's notion of the Image as an ideogram. From the wealth of geological data shrunk into a single grain, the geologist is able to make rapid associations between stages in that grain's biography, much in the same way that the reader of Chinese is able to decode a whole chain of meanings from a single ideogram stylized by a series of overlaid pictorial symbols, or in the way H.D. is able to see one overall picture by shining a light through a string of superimposed photographic negatives skewered together.

And yet sand also offers the reader a way of thinking about Imagism as nothing particularly new but as a renewal and reformulation of long-standing (but not always abided by) standards for "good" poetry, for like sand, Imagism is a reformulation of old materials into new. One of the questions often asked of Imagism is this: "Is an Imagist poem the product of special avant-garde techniques or the product of techniques that are generally considered to be essential to good poetry?" At the time of the Imagist anthologies, some detractors dismissed Imagism for its arrogance in presenting an exclusive "school" whose proposed, special methodology constituted little more than had been practiced in the past by poets deemed to be "great." In 1915, Harold Monro linked Imagist principles to those exhibited by "important English theorists of the past," finding some past poets much in sympathy with the Imagist principles of precision. "Wordsworth . . . might be called an Imagist in theory," he scowled.[76] Yet this was the point of Imagism: it was a loud, flagrant appeal for a return to the core principles common to all good poetry. After all, Pound's Imagist criticism is full of references to poetry from across the centuries, drawn from all corners of the globe—"if you want the gist of the matter," counsels Pound, "go to Sappho, Catallus, Villon, Heine when he is in the vein, Gautier when he is not too frigid."[77] Wordsworth would have been most welcome in Pound's club, but not "the doughy mess of third-hand Keats, Wordsworth, heaven knows what" of the 1890s of which Pound despaired.

In America, Amy Lowell's preface to the 1915 Imagist anthology said that the Imagist principles "are not new; they have fallen into desuetude. They are the essentials of all good poetry,"[78] a view from which American modernists in particular never looked back, for in the United States Imagism was always much more favorably received than in Britain. Barnard's sand is a visual equivalent for "good poetry"—it is hard to define beyond general principles, yet we all recognize a sand grain when we see it and can distinguish sand from rocks. An "open, three-dimensional network" of "grains . . . in tangential contact" as defined by sedimentologists,[79] a stretch of sand offers an earthy countermodel to Pound's idea of "the vortex" as a metaphor for poetry that draws upon the actions of whirlwinds and whirlpools to convey Pound's ambitions for modern poetry—another example of Pound's discourse rooted in wet, fluid things as opposed to the "sand" or "earth" text of women's poetry as one finds in the Imagist work of Barnard and H.D. Yet both discourses value a poetry based upon luminosity, even if they take separate routes toward it—for Pound, the vortex offers "a radiant node or cluster through which ideas are constantly rushing"[80]; for Barnard and H.D., sand possesses a translucence replete with possibilities, from the "reflecting sands" of "Shoreline," to "grains . . . clear as wine" in "Hermes of the Ways." Theirs is an elegant yet raw poetic program, producing a spare poetry that is both coarse and irregular in places, like a handful of sand grains, yet concealing a portal to the sublime when perceived as a whole, like the awe-inspiring visual spectacle of the beach that has enthralled poets particularly since the Romantic period.

"It is better to present one Image in a lifetime than to produce voluminous works," Pound had directed "those beginning to write verses."[81] Perhaps the young Mary Barnard had borne this in mind when, shortly after reading Pound's list of don'ts, she began to redraft "For Those Who Dwell on the Marches" into "Shoreline," adding the refrain "Sand is the beginning and the end / of our dominion" to position sand as the dominant "Image." But the "dominion" of Barnard's America was ever important, and inseparable from her late Imagism, and in this she found an ally in another of Pound's friends when she went to New York—William Carlos Williams.

2.4 "We Can't Get to the World Hard Enough or Fast Enough. . . . We Just Must Write": Barnard, Williams, and American Imagism

If the northwestern landscape had guided Barnard further toward Imagism, where specific regional encounters with the "sketchiness of sawmills" and unadorned stretches of "flat reflecting sands" cultivated a sympathy with the spare and the austere and helped to fashion her Imagist techniques, then there was a payoff: just as the local went some way to yielding the "spare but musical" style she was after, in time, perfection of technique yielded more of the local, enhancing the realism of the "things"—or, to quote "Shoreline," "things" under "direct presentation." "We can't get to the world hard enough or fast enough. . . . we just must write," Williams wrote to Barnard on April 12, 1935, encouraging her to make her poems as clear and direct as she could make them, but he was also implying that the closest way one could "get to" the world was through the imagination, through writing.

Indeed, it was not until Barnard discovered the modernists and, particularly, Pound, H.D., Moore, and Williams, that she became able to write explicitly and more acutely about her regional experience. Among the early manuscripts that Barnard collated in her college years between 1928 and 1932, there are few poems about the mill trips of her "Vancouver experience" despite the "constantly recurring" memories; most of the poems of this period, including those she submitted as part of a creative thesis, were heavily derivative of European models and subjects, informed, in part, by Barnard's reading of the troubadour poets. Her experience of Ocean Park, though, is recorded in early poems like "The Invitation" and "Lai," but for all their evocation of "stripped . . . trees" of the "yellow tideland" where "shallow waters lap unheard,"[82] there are fantastical qualities that disturb the realism, such as the mermaids who make nightly bonfires on the "dark expanse of beach" in "The Invitation,"[83] or the ghoulish "queens" in "Lai" who, "bearing death upon their lips," escort drowned sailors from the shoreline to their tombs. Prior to her contact with Pound and Williams, Barnard's articulation of the Northwest was, to some extent, hindered by the same kind of indeterminate romanticism associated with the region and bemoaned by Nicholas O'Connell in his preface to his anthology of interviews with northwestern writers, *At the Field's End:*

> The Pacific Northwest . . . has been a region without a distinct literary identity. It is still a late American frontier, a new West, and its literature, until well into this [twentieth] century, has been dominated by the chronicles of early explorers and settlers, romances that could have been set in any fantastical land.[84]

But Barnard wasn't hindered for long, and, like the American expatriates in Europe, she was able to dispense with the compulsion to romanticize the landscape only through taking departure of the "new West." On the back of the *Poetry* prize money, coupled with earnings she had made as a caseworker for the Emergency Relief Administration, Barnard relocated to New York to "dislodge some of the barnacles,"[85] she told Pound, and get into a group as he had advised. In the spring of 1936, she took a cross-country train to New Orleans, then a steamboat bound north, the *SS Dixie,* where she was a guest of the captain's table, arriving in New York on April 9. There, the harder Barnard worked at exploring the "country" of Poundian modernism and called upon Pound's friends, the more she was able to recover, in poetry, the "country" of her native Northwest. Ideas of "country" and place resound in the poems Barnard produced in those first years in the metropolis—after the "dominion" and "country of our choice" of "Shoreline" (1935), there is the "country . . . so gracious to us" in "The Rapids" (1940), for example, and the "green" places of "Cool Country" and "Note to a Neapolitan," both published in *Cool Country.*[86] "I feel myself going regional," Barnard confided in a letter to Pound on February 10, 1937,[87] as she attempted to weed out all "verbiage" in her work. By the time she had relocated further upstate to take up her curatorial post at Buffalo, it seemed that she no longer needed to make the effort to "go regional"; her specific regional experience was almost constantly to the fore and seemed, like the passing freight train in "Encounter in Buffalo," to seek her out in the most unlikely of places:

> The country lies flat, expressionless as the face of a stranger.
> Not one hillock shelters a buried bone. The city:
> A scene as thin as a theater backdrop, where no doors open,
> No streets extend beyond the view from the corner.
>
> Only the railroad embankment is high, shaggy with grass.
> Only the freight, knuckling a red sun under its wheels,
> Drags familiar box-car shapes down long perspectives
> Of childhood meals and all crossings at sunset.
>
> With a look as deep as the continent, with the casual greeting
> Of those who will meet again, it bestrides the viaduct.
> Its span is the span of trestles above mountain gorges,
> Its roar the echo of streams still wearing away stone.[88]

In the "flat, expressionless" space of the deserted eastern city and the "box-car shapes" of railroad freight, the speaker is still able to find the "deep . . . continent" of "trestles above mountain gorges" and the "crossings at sunset" of the ferry that connected the Long Beach Peninsula to the Washington mainland, still able to locate the "familiar" Northwest she feels she "will meet again." In the recovery of space, there is also a recovery of the literary past: in "Encounter in Buffalo," one not only hears the "roar" of northwestern streams in the roar of the freight train, one also hears the roar—the "barbaric yawp"—of the locomotives that join up the continent in Whitman's "Passage to India":

> I see over my own continent the Pacific Railroad, surmounting every barrier,
> I see continual trains of cars winding along the Platte, carrying freight and passengers,
> I hear the locomotives rushing and roaring, and the shrill steam-whistle,
> I hear the echoes reverberate through the grandest scenery in the world,
> I cross the Laramie plains, I note the rocks in grotesque shapes, the buttes,
> I see the plentiful larkspur and wild onions, the barren, colorless, sage-deserts, . . .[89]

Whitman's is a heady, circular lyric, shifting continually between both memory and vision of place with all the energy of "now," like the frenetic revolution of train wheels in motion. Barnard's poem presents a quiet kind of continuity to the theme of "place-as-transport" (or "place-as-transportable"). The restraint suggested by the adverbial phrase "Only . . . only" (as well as by the repeated abbreviation of "freight" to "it"/"its") enacts a kind of reining in of Whitmanesque emotion; the "roar" of the freight leads Barnard to imagine the muted sound of "streams still wearing away stone" rather than a mass reverberation "through the grandest scenery in the world."

If there is memory of the height of logging trestles crossing mountain gorges in "Encounter in Buffalo," there is also memory of the lonely, blank space of the clearings of sawmill settlements of "North Window," devoid of the signs of life, their "bloodless stones" echoed in the Buffalo space where "Not one hillock shelters a buried bone." One might argue that it is precisely the pared-down emptiness of the "scene thin as a theater backdrop, where no doors open" that facilitates this memory and stirs the imagination, rather than the "familiar box-car shapes" of the freight train, just as the speakers of "North Window" are led by the quiet emptiness of the scene to imagine "the queen's emeralds." Similarly, in "The Trestle" (1938; later renamed "Logging Trestle"), a trestle's apparent end is a beginning point for the imagination. Moved by the emotive "chill" of a "trestle fallen into disuse," the poet feels compelled to act and find a use for the trestle in poetry; in doing so, she restores the trestle to life:

The Trestle

Neither cloud nor rain casts
A chill into the valley
Like that of a trestle fallen into disuse.

The rails move out from the hillside
Across the piling lengthening its stroke
Where ground slopes riverward.

Abruptly the rails terminate.
Sky opens between the cross-ties lifted
Each upon five upright timbers. The gray wood

Leads the eye to nothing further.
The broken column stands against cloud
As though an abandoned wharf extended into wind.[90]

Verbs that convey a sense of stopping are outpaced by verbs that convey movement along forward lines, so while "the rails terminate," they also "move out" along a track with "piling lengthening its stroke" down a ground that "slopes riverward." After such imaginative animation, "the gray wood / Leads the eye to nothing further"—what began in the imagination comes to a visual end. Yet in the last two lines there is another beginning, another forward movement of the imagination, as if the trestle animates the imagination just as the imagination animated the trestle. The "broken column" of the trestle is repaired, in the imagination, into the likeness of a sturdy, whole structure that endlessly moves forward, an "abandoned wharf extended into wind." The singular "eye" of the poet and the singular existence of the logging trestle thus seem to power each other in "The Trestle," so that neither is really alone and abandoned but, again, "alone and so little lonely."

Although concerned with the local, Barnard's was no small-scale, self-serving project; underlying the recovery of very specific, known space was an endorsement of the modern nation—that is, Barnard's was an *American* project as much as it was a gendered, modernist, northwestern one. In poems like "Provincial II," for example, Barnard's ragged local is pitted against the grandeur of Europe, the irreducible elements of her reality considered a worthy opponent of Eurocentrism:

Provincial II

The European made his appearance
Wearing velvet and the jewels
Of his inheritance
Gravely, without unbecoming pride.

He courteously made it plain to her
The silk she wore was paper.
Dismayed, caught in the shower
Of his disapproval, she bragged
In buckskin, which (he remarked)
Was outdated fully one hundred years.
At last, cowering in a few rags
Of homespun, she dried her tears with grass
And consoled herself with the large
Plums of the provinces.[91]

The only response available to Barnard's native "in a few rags / Of homespun" to the insults of the European is to make use of the immediate homeland, whose nature provides her with a "grass" handkerchief and "plums" with which to comfort herself. It is no less than what Emerson had instructed the American poet, whose duty was to discover "the value of our incomparable materials" in all their variety and to understand that the homespun—the grass, the plums," the tangible realities of American experience—are as much a profound resource for poetry as anything Homer, Dante, indeed "the European" (subtly mocked here by the assured capital "E" and definite article) had to say. "We do not with sufficient plainness or sufficient profoundness address ourselves to life, nor dare we chaunt [sic] our own times and social circumstances," Emerson wrote in "The Poet," "yet America is a poem in our eyes; its ample geography dazzles the imagination, and it will not wait long for meters."[92] That "plainness" is precisely what Barnard achieves in the frank, straightforward tone that characterizes "Provincial II" and so many of her poems, not unlike the matter-of-fact, dealing-in-details dryness of tone associated with much of Moore's output.

If the native in "Provincial II" finds an alternative to European models in provincial grass and plums perhaps a little too meekly ("at last, cowering in a few rags"), elsewhere there is a much more determined resolve to celebrate the American local and "chaunt our own times and social circumstances," as in this unpublished poem from the 1930s:

Shriek of Defiance (in the manner of Ezra Pound)

Come, my songs,
Let us be unforgivably simple-minded.
Let us gape all afternoon at a Johnny-jump-up
And suck our thumbs in round eyed astonishment at a young
calf.
Let us prefer skunk cabbages in a swamp to Picasso
And not consider it necessary to say so.
Let us sleep, oh! a very great deal,
And drink milk with our dinner.[93]

Picasso is substituted for "the European," a "Johnny-jump-up" flower for "grass," and "skunk cabbages" for "plums of the provinces," but the message is the same—intense concentration on the smallest details of the local (here the "dazzling geography" of Barnard's swampy green Northwest) is the surest way forward for the *American* poet. The wild, primitive "shriek" of the title is by a voice that claims this project as a *right*, demanding throughout "Let us" do this, "Let us" do that. Although Barnard pays tribute to the "one living poet whom I consider a master,"[94] as she told Pound in her first letter to him in 1933, in lines that riff on Pound's poems from the 1914 *Blast*, Barnard's "shriek" is much more "in the manner" of Williams and his call for an American poetics based on all the rough detail of the local. Thus it is easy to see why Williams was so impressed with Barnard when he first read her and why the two poets came to be such good friends when she went out East: they had in common a desire for an American poetry based on the gritty specificity of lived reality, an attempt, as Williams put it, to lift to the imagination "those things which lie under the direct scrutiny of the senses, close to the nose."[95]

What lay under the direct scrutiny of Barnard's senses were the Washington sawmills and the Long Beach coastline; both became essential components of her late Imagism. Such absorption of spare, desolate spaces fuelled a propensity toward simplicity and restraint, a delight in the slightest of things, and an abhorrence of waste and ornament that Barnard carried over, as had her parents, into the domestic realm as much as she carried it into the field of the verbal, making Barnard an ideal candidate for forwarding the Imagist project into the American 1930s, where Depression-wrought austerity dominated the national mood; perhaps this is where Imagism, with its thrifty verbal attitude, really belonged. But there was another element at work in the production of Barnard's late Imagism that drew Pound to her as much as it drove H.D. away, in a pique of jealousy perhaps, an element that powerfully enabled Barnard to "get to the world" of her American local and the "emotional and intellectual complex" of the experiences she had had therein, as well as assisting with the production of the "spare but musical" phrase: peculiarly, a "European"—but of a very different order than that of the dandy bedecked in velvet and jewels.

Chapter Three

"A Would-Be Sappho"

3.1 Sappho and the Imagists

In the sawmills and the seashore Barnard found her style as well as her subject; not only were the grains of sand at Ocean Park and the sawmill clearings beyond a north window hard examples of the kind of localized specifics demanded by American modernism, they were also physical and geographical expressions of the kind of spare plainness to be found in the Japanese haiku form or Sappho's fragments that Pound and other Imagists had sought to find equivalents for in Anglo-American verse as they revolted against the "doughy mess" of "the common verse . . . from 1890." Such links between Barnard's local and Sappho's fragments were not to go unnoticed when she finally published the "good thing" of her Sappho translation in 1958, as the poet David Gordon observed: "The firm, unadorned, and . . . ('polished exact') idiom that Barnard brings to her remarkable translation of Sappho may be related to the 'frontier town' (stoic spareness, high spirits, grit) of her childhood, and tempered by the 'dustbowl' and the Great Depression of 1929."[1] Gordon was perhaps unaware of just how prescient a statement this was; the new Barnard archives pinpoint Barnard's obsession with Sappho at the beginning of the Depression years and her attempt to emulate Pound's example. Following a grilling of her latest manuscript one October day in 1930 by Lloyd Reynolds, the Reed tutor who had introduced her to the "real moderns," Barnard relayed the diagnosis to her mother and signed her letter off with a rather curious moniker. "He said I should study for greater subtlety of rhythm . . . greater 'intensification' . . . and, to some extent, clearer images," she wrote, before scribbling "a Would-Be Sappho."[2]

Time would tell that Barnard would one day write and "be" Sappho in her 1958 translation, but not before her late Imagism had extensively engaged with Sappho's poetry, both as part of her apprenticeship in prosody, as the next chapter explores, and as part of her American modernist project to "make it new" for the nation, as the present chapter does. In a way, Barnard was doing just as her Imagist forebears had done: finding a "spare but musical" voice through the appropriation of an exemplar in the mode. And yet, ironically, Barnard managed to draw out of her "Sappho connection" a thoroughly American "shriek of defiance," as well as a best-selling text that would trigger an outpouring of classical translations by Americans. In order to see precisely how Barnard managed this remarkable feat of spinning distinctively "new" American lyrics from some of the oldest European lyrics in existence without kowtowing to "the European," we need to spend a little time revisiting Sappho's impact on those earlier Imagists to see why this particular Greek poet mattered so much in the first place.

"It all began with Greek fragments,"[3] H.D. had said in *End to Torment*. She could have been speaking for her lovers as much as for herself, for Pound, Richard Aldington, and H.D. discovered Sappho around the same time that they were discovering both themselves and each other, buoyed by the major recovery of Sappho's corpus, which ran, rather tantalizingly, alongside the personal and creative emergences of these three poets caught up together in a triangle by turns erotic and aesthetic. In 1885, the year of Pound's birth and one year before H.D's, Henry Thornton Wharton published *Sappho: Memoir, Text, Selected Renderings and a Literal Translation*, the first comprehensive book of Sappho's lyrics in English, including translations by the Greek scholar John Addington Symonds. In 1901, Pound and H.D. met at a Halloween party. Both would go on to read and draw upon Wharton's text, as would Barnard after them, a text which enjoyed renewed popularity in 1902 when a manuscript of Sappho's work was discovered among the sandy rubbish tips of Oxyrhynchus in Egypt. Taken to Berlin for preservation by scholars from a nation that had churned out more than twenty new editions and translations between the 1770s and the 1850s, the aptly named "Berlin Parchment" was quickly seized by translators.[4] A French edition appeared in 1903, while Pound was still in college.[5] The English edition arrived in England the year after Pound did, having published his first collection, *A Lume Spento*, in 1908. In 1909, J. M. Edmonds began publishing his English versions of the Berlin parchment in the pages of the *Classical Review*,[6] the same year that Pound met the woman who was to appreciate his further experiments in Sapphics, his future wife Dorothy Shakespear, as well as the men who were to inspire his Imagist movement, fellow poets T. E. Hulme, Ford Madox Ford, and Wyndham Lewis. H.D. sailed to Europe in 1911, joining Pound, to whom she had been engaged sometime between 1905 and 1908, in London. There she met the English poet Richard Aldington, who shared her classical interests. As well as the articles from the *Classical Review* that H.D. would copy out in the Reading

Room at the British Museum for Aldington (who, born in 1892, was still too young to gain a reader's ticket), H.D. copied out Edmond's Sappho translations, to which Aldington swiftly responded with a poem based upon Fragment 96: "To Atthis (From the Rather Recently Discovered Papyrus of Sappho Now in the British Museum)."[7] H.D. had her own creative responses to the Oxyrhynchus finds, among them, "Hermes of the Ways," which she showed Pound in the British Museum tea room.[8]

H.D. and Aldington's poems after Sappho crystallized some of the ideas that Pound had been having about the nature of the new poetry. After all, he and Dorothy had been reading Sappho themselves during their courtship when a light had gone on. "Blessed be Sappho who has shown you a path towards Truth," Dorothy wrote to Pound in 1911.[9] Upon reading H.D.'s "Hermes of the Ways" in 1912, Pound famously informed H.D. and Aldington that the three of them were founders of a new poetic school: Imagists. Pound's own work approximating Sapphics appeared soon after in the June 1912 issue of *The English Review*,[10] and in October 1912, Pound forwarded work by H.D. and Aldington to Harriet Monroe at *Poetry*, saying of H.D.'s contribution that "it is in the laconic speech of the Imagistes. . . . It's straight talk, straight as the Greek!"[11] A draft of Aldington's "To Atthis" was published in September 1913 in *The New Freewoman*,[12] above H.D.'s "Sitalkas," another poem in the Greek vein, paired on the same page as the poets themselves were paired in marriage the very next month. In 1914, Edmonds produced more volumes of Greek fragments, and Pound published *Des Imagistes*. By the time Edmonds finally published the comprehensive *Lyra Graeca* in the Loeb classical series in 1922, closely followed by other translations by Edgar Lobel and Edwin Marion Cox, Pound, H.D., and Aldington had each produced work directly after Sappho, as had Amy Lowell, who edited the Imagist anthologies that followed *Des Imagistes*, much to Pound's chagrin; no matter, Sappho bound them all. Pound's *Lustra* (1916) included several poems modeled on Sappho's fragments, as did H.D.'s *Sea Garden* (1916), *Hymen* (1921), and *Heliodora* (1924). H.D. continued her classical scholarship, producing a prose meditation on Sappho probably in the early 1920s ("The Wise Sappho," not published until 1988) and reviewing Cox's new edition of *The Poems of Sappho* in 1925.[13] When he returned from his military duties in the First World War, Aldington resumed editorial responsibilities at *The Egoist*, where he was involved with reprinting the Poet's Translation Series that he had begun before he went off to war. In 1919, Aldington brought together two titles in the series into one volume, *The Poems of Anyte of Tegea and Poems and Fragments of Sappho* (the Anyte translated by Aldington, the Sappho by Edward Storer). He had already printed a small number of copies of erotic lyrics after Sappho in 1917, *The Love of Myrrhine and Konallis*, which was reprinted in 1926.[14]

The recovery of Sappho's work, then, not only formed a backdrop to the early lives of these three poets, it also triggered the experiments with poetic form and content that they found necessary to articulate their respective situations, for classical texts, such as Sappho's fragments, were, as Aldington pointed out in his commentary to each translation that featured in the Poet's Translation Series printed by *The Egoist*, "more alive, more essential, more human than anything we can find."[15] Obsessed with the fragment and the whole, the need to simultaneously foreground the breakup and disintegration of culture as well as speculations of its idealized unities, the eroded form of Sappho's corpus was a tantalizing prospect for European-based modernists. As Margaret Reynolds writes in *The Sappho Companion*, Sappho was seen by modernist writers as "parading modern anxieties," the dispersal of her fragmented texts a metaphor for the modern experience of urban isolation.[16] She was regarded as a model who enabled the moderns, as Erika Rohrbach puts in it in her essay "H.D. and Sappho: A Precious Inch of Palimpsest," "to be what they were."[17]

In Pound's case, Sappho's shredded fragments informed his Imagist theories, giving an example of how a poem may derive its impact from being stripped down to the essentials, a model for intense compressions, where language is seen to convey as much in the spaces *between* words as in the spaces they occupy. So although his "Papyrus" (1916) is an obvious parody of Sappho's recovered texts, it also signals the power of the collage effect Pound was to craft in *The Cantos*:

Spring . . . .
Too long . . . . . .
Gongula . . . . . .[18]

Despite the lack of syntactical coherence, the fragment achieves its effects through the play of verbal echoes, which invest the fragment with a voice of mournful yearning. The cascading consonance of the "ng" cluster combines with the mirrored assonance of "lon" and "gon," so that a fragmented clause appears to come to the fore: "Spring too long gon[e]." As "gon[e]" dissolves into a new word, it becomes apparent *who* is the subject of the yearning—"Gongula" (or "Gongyla"), one of Sappho's names for an absent lover. It is thus the nonsyntactical elements of the fragment that articulate the speaker's predicament (even the punctuation marks suggest that the speaker awaits further news); that is, that Gongula has been gone too long, and now it is spring and time for lovemaking. In the words of Hugh Witemeyer, the poem "enacts a drama of presence and absence"[19] reminiscent of one enacted by Sappho's corpus. And it is unmistakably in Pound's register. The quasicomical chime of the completing sounds of the poem, "Gongula," gives the sense of the utterance collapsing into a gargle, and as well as assuming the appearance of a Greek fragment, it spoofs the telegram. It is humorous yet deadly serious at the same time, as much as in the coarse, elliptical, meandering idiom of Pound's letters and prose as it is in the fragmentary Sapphic mode—indeed, an example of Pound being "what he was" through Sappho, as Rohrbach might phrase it.

Thus, along with other lyrics from *The Greek Anthology*,[20] epigrams of the Roman satirists, and haikus from the classical Japanese tradition, Sappho's fragments were one of the distilled models for Pound's poems in *Lustra*, influencing the production of poems such as "Alba," "Ione, Dead the Long Year," "Ἱμέρρω," "Ladies," "To Καλόν," and "Shop Girl." Sappho's lyrics, however badly eroded, offered an example of the kind of "direct presentation" that Pound was after, an example of work whose direct treatment of the subject was occasioned by as few adjectives as possible, concision of diction, and musical rhythm. "Consider the definiteness of Dante's presentation, as compared with Milton's rhetoric," Pound invited the would-be Imagist, adding "if you want the gist of the matter go to Sappho."[21] Amy Lowell, who used imagery appropriated from Sappho in some of her love poetry, heeded Pound's technical advice, producing some short poems which focused on a specific image derived from the fragments—an apple ripening on a branch, Aphrodite's descent in a winged chariot, and Eros shaking the heart like wind blowing against mountain oaks.[22] Lowell poeticized the "definiteness" of Sappho's technique in her poem "The Sisters," saying of Sappho:

> I know a single slender thing about her:
> That, loving, she was like a burning birch-tree
> All tall and glittering fire, and that she wrote
> Like the same fire caught up to Heaven and held there
> A frozen blaze before it broke and fell.[23]

It was this kind of overpowering concentration of emotive feeling that the Roman rhetorician Longinus had found compelling about Sappho's verse:

> Do you not wonder how she [Sappho] gives chase at once to soul and body, to words and tongue, to sight and colour, all as if scattered abroad, how, at variance within she is frozen and burns, she raves and is wise? For she is either panic-stricken or at point of death; she is haunted not only by one single emotion but their whole company. All things befall a lover, but she took the extremes of love's history and binding them in one achieved a masterpiece.[24]

H.D. was drawn, like Pound, as much to the energy that teeters between the textual substance and the gaps in Sappho's corpus as she was to the "extremes of love's history" that lay compacted in the content. For her, Sappho's work was a site of strange intensity, by turns luminous and shadowy, like an island "with bays and fjords and little straits between which the sun lies clear."[25] In "The Wise Sappho," H.D. likens Sappho's words to "orange blossoms" (bright, yet like delicate blossom flakes, barely tangible), "red hearts," "red lilies," weaving cloth of "purple wool" and "scarlet garments."[26] Added together, Sappho's texts, to H.D., inscribe a brilliant blankness as much as they do a fabric of glorious color, like "all colours in spectrum."[27] The results of H.D.'s fascination with such entwined opposites (the "extremes" of her lyric) are "jagged narratives," as Diana Collecott has called them: texts modeled after Sappho's eroded corpus, which relentlessly present the reader with the same kind of "dilemmas of interpretation" found by the translator of Sappho.[28] The result is an intense yet elusive poetry (or "accurate mystery"), as "clear" and as immediate as the sunlight H.D. imagines over a gauze-like island ruptured by "innumerable, tiny, irregular bays,"[29] yet as riddling as the endlessly fragmentary pools of water that wet the island, like the crack of the wind that disappears almost as quickly as it whips the ankles of the speaker in "Hermes of the Ways." Sappho's verse, for H.D., is a model for imposing an almost impossible-to-bear intensity on a poem, where the reader is brought to the brink of overwhelming sensation only to be spared the full blast of it at the last moment, as if the intensity is reserved for someone other than the reader. By way of example, the final stanza of "Orchard" is not only pertinent for its gesture toward a poetics of sand but also for its much more general structure of oppositions that draws in such poetics that the poem gives "chase at once to soul and body, to words and tongue, to sight and colour, all as if scattered abroad" after Sappho. To revisit, H.D. writes:

> these fallen hazel-nuts,
> stripped late of their green sheaths,
> grapes, red-purple,
> their berries
> dripping with wine,
> pomegranates already broken,
> and shrunken figs
> and quinces untouched,
> I bring you as offering.[30]

The bare hardness of the unsheathed hazelnuts and the bursting color of the grapes instills all the solid, clear brilliance of the kind sunlight that H.D. sees in the verbal geography of Sappho's "island" texts, as much as the glistening grittiness of sand grains. But as with the islands, the perspective is fissured: the wholeness of nuts and fruits, so fresh they could burst, is followed by a bursting that has taken place sometime else, in the "pomegranates already broken." The burning intensity of the freshening of fruits is then cooled in the remaining imagery of fruits past their best, the "shrunken figs" and the "quinces untouched." In the preceding stanzas, the speaker asks the "son of the god" of the orchard to "spare us the beauty of fruit trees" and "spare us from loveliness." In the last stanza, the reader, as well as the speaker, is spared just that, led to a near-climax of hotly compressed imagery of dripping fruits only to be speeded away from the "beauty" and "loveliness" of ripe, desirable fruit. The brilliant sunlight from Sappho's island appears in the earlier part of this stanza in the play of colors, the "green sheaths" of the hazelnuts, the "red-purple" grapes, but then the light is withdrawn as the intensity cracks and cools—no colors are used to describe the pomegranates, the figs, or the quinces. The stanza assaults the senses with the same kind of force that stripped the hazelnuts and broke the pomegranates, only to restrain its effects, an example of the kind of "hurting fineness" that Florence Codman associated with Barnard's poetry some twenty years later.[31]

3.2 Barnard's Sapphic Imagism

Like Pound and H.D., Barnard found herself attracted to the startling directness of Sappho's "polished exact" idiom in her youth, even if, in the end, she was to do something with Sappho that brought her closer to the one poet *less* enamored of European models despite his friendships with the red-haired Romance Languages scholar and the astronomer's daughter that went back to their student days in Philadelphia—Williams, once again. Impressed with Homer and the Greek dramatists at high school, Barnard was among a select group of four students who opted to take Greek as their language choice at Reed. Like the Imagists, Barnard was drawn to the musical rhythm of Sappho's cadences, but she was equally intrigued by the possibilities of the fragment as exemplified by Sappho, by the intense compressions within the fragment as much as by the expressive power of the surrounding gaps, by the use of plain "straight as the Greek" speech in the poem's presentation. Fuelled by a copy of Wharton's *Sappho* that she received for her twenty-first birthday in December 1930 and with Lloyd Reynolds's counsel to write, Imagist-like, with "greater 'intensification' . . . and . . . clearer images," Barnard began to experiment, like Pound and H.D. before her, with classic adaptation.

The early results were far from satisfactory. Barnard scattered allusions to Sappho's fragments in poems themselves unremarkable and derivative of archaic forms, nothing as adventurous as, say, H.D.'s "Fragment

113" or as probing as Pound's "Papyrus." In the heavily end-rhymed "The Invitation" (1927), which Reynolds dismissed as "too much like vacation verse published in the *Oregonian*,"[32] mermaids are washed up from the sea wearing cloaks of foam after a bonfire ritual on the beach, coming forth from foam like incarnations of Aphrodite, the goddess of love and flowers who was birthed, so Greek legend goes, from the sea. In the sonnet "The Fool's Serenade" (1932), "The foam upon the beach, the little flame / Of moonfire creating every wave"[33] causes the subject to sing of her heartache, as if the foam had conjured up Aphrodite herself. Aphrodite's foam froths through the white flower imagery of a troubadour-style poem, "Two Songs for Rosamond" (1932), in which it seals a courtier's appraisal of the beloved ("Whiter than fleur-de-lys / Or foam which now / Blows on the spring sea— / So fair art thou"),[34] and dominates a poem that Barnard dared to send to Moore in the early days of their correspondence, "Blanchefleur" (1933), in which Aphrodite's "white flowers," "wax-white flowers" of "white / Polished flake," blanket water "before the tide."[35] It was, Moore said, too "conscious."[36] Elsewhere are allusions to Sappho's fragments that verge on direct quotation, particularly Sappho's much anthologized Fragment One (or "Ode to Aphrodite") and Fragment Two; some of these are more successful, if only in their attempt to imitate Sappho's plain, direct speech. Barnard's "Love Poem," for instance, is a condensation of Fragment One:

Love Poem

Oh plaguing Aphrodite, hear my prayer!
Give back my sane mind which you stole from me,
Or make me madder, not be aware
How laughable is my insanity.[37]

A fragment of a fragment, reminiscent of, but not as startling as, Pound's example in "Papyrus" from 1916, "Love Poem" was "good enough," Reynolds told Barnard, but, he added, there was very little for the reader to pause over.[38] Reynolds also took issue with "Ode to Adventure" (1928), a meditation on the types of myth available to women poets for poetic treatment based on Sappho's Fragments One and Two, in which Pegasus, the winged horse, is fused with Aphrodite's winged chariot:

Sometimes so very near me thou hast flown
That I have heard the whirring of thy wings
Ring in my ears for days on end, and know
Why, facing death, thy daring rider sings

"Didn't like the second verse," Barnard said of Reynolds's reaction in her letter to her mother,[39] and it is not hard to see why. Not only is the poem hampered by archaisms, it is wholly unsure of its subject matter (is this a lament for the opportunities available to female poets, or a rousing call to arms?) and seems to offer a hotchpotch of elements (the modern ode, fragments of Sappho's ode, iambic pentameter) that do not sit comfortably together. For Reynolds, there was "not much comment."

In other poems that Barnard wrote at Reed College, and perhaps did not show Reynolds, were much more successful adaptations along Imagist lines, as in these two tiny poems from 1932, the second one untitled, which, for all their brevity, certainly gave the reader something to pause over:

Cupbearer

I shall bear
Scarlet and yellow cups on a crystal tray,
With no drop spilled;
Translucent pottery sun-shot
And filled
With wine no cellarer knows,
Clearer than clear air.

Fire, snow, and the night
Create a world
Where two may come together.
But violet, gold, and white
Are one gray
With the rain, the light
And the thawing snow.
In the common day
We walk again remote
With alien gray faces.[40]

"Cupbearer" is a telling expression of Barnard's Imagist intentions; in the "scarlet and yellow cups" made of "translucent pottery," we find a pertinent example of writing made of "hard substantial colors, *on* something, not transparent" that Barnard craved in that revelatory entry in her Chief Company notebook written around the same time. The wine, like Imagist language, is presented upon a hard, clear "crystal" tray like a blank page, devoid of unnecessary ornament. The cupbearer, like the Imagist poet, spills not a drop, in the same way that the poet takes care "to use no superfluous word."[41] The effect is unparalleled clarity, a poem "clearer than clear air," the "greater 'intensification' . . . and . . . clearer images" that Reynolds had instructed Barnard to try for. The poem simultaneously draws on and responds to Sappho's Fragment Four, in which Aphrodite (the "Cyprian") is invited to fill gold cups with nectar, later translated by Barnard as

Queen! Cyprian!
Fill our gold cups with love
stirred into clear nectar[42]

Sappho's "gold cups" are hinted at in Barnard's more ordinary, and less "conscious," "yellow cups" of "translucent pottery"; her "clear nectar" resonates in Barnard's more sober "clear air." Sappho's command to "fill" the gold cups "with love" is heeded by Barnard's cupbearer in her own idiosyncratic way; she bears cups "filled" not with love but "with wine," gesturing toward an autonomy not seen in the direct quotation of "Ode to Adventure" or the derivation in "Love Poem." So despite this somewhat suppressed allusion, the achievement is very different from Barnard's other experiments with Sappho's fragments: "Cupbearer" makes its *own* simple, "emotionally loaded" statement in plain speech *after* Sappho, rather than parading imitative prowess. The fragment does not get in the way of the articulation or become the subject of the poem; instead, it textures the poem, inspiring the tone and register.

The poem beginning "Fire, snow, and the night" contrasts well. Rather than taking a single Sapphic fragment and cutting it across several lines, as in "Cupbearer," in this second poem Barnard does the opposite—she takes images from several Sapphic fragments and shrinks them into one line, into a single phrase. "Violet, gold, and white" alludes to the colors that Sappho associated with Aphrodite, mentioned in many fragments. "Violet" refers to the color of gifts given to Aphrodite in ritual, such as "violet tiaras"[43] or "the folds of a purple / kerchief"[44]; "gold" denotes the color of Aphrodite's winged chariot, which carries her to the aid of Sappho in Fragment One; and "white" is the color of several images related to Aphrodite—the whiteness of the foam, from which she was born of the sea; the whiteness of the flowers of her myrtle groves, where she was said to perform rituals; and the whiteness of the rock of Leucas, from which it was thought she leapt out of mad desire for her lover Phaon.[45] "Violet, gold, and white" is an allusion that Barnard replayed in one of her poems in Sapphics, "Departure" (1935), in which "violet, gold, and white" appear together in an illustration of Aphrodite wading shoreward; rising from foamy waves of golden-hued "amber light," a "white Cytherean maiden" emerges, "crumbling in blossom" with flesh of "flowered terraces," as befitted a goddess deserving of "violet tiaras."[46]

As with "Cupbearer," the Sapphic allusion in "Fire, snow, and the night" works to make the kind of "simple but emotionally loaded statement" that Barnard was after. As well as the covert allusion, the poem is in plain, direct speech. It has about it "the fresh, colloquial directness" that Barnard admired in Sappho,[47] recalling the feeling of "words [that] fit so naturally into the rhythm that they seem like spoken words raised to the highest degree of music and expressiveness," which Sir Maurice Bowra identified as

Sappho's chief virtue.[48] In what is one of Barnard's most overtly erotic poems, however subtle (and, perhaps, euphemistic), "Fire, snow, and the night" suggests the sadness of the separation of two lovers parting in the morning, having "come together" at night and then walking "again remote" in "the common day." The focus is not on how Sappho's experience is *comparable* to that of Barnard's speaker, as in "Ode to Adventure," but on the intensity of the speaker's experience directly. Whether one immediately grasps the Sapphic allusions or not, "violet, gold, and white" presents vibrant visual images that stimulate the senses. They are color metaphors for the "fire, snow, and the night" that is the setting for the lovers' encounter. That the passion suddenly fades—that "violet, gold, and white / are one gray"—is the emotional turmoil of the poem, and Barnard chooses to tell this through adding a color metaphor of her own, "gray," adapting the Sapphic allusion in order to "emotionally load" the statement. Just as the quick presentation of vibrant colors excites the senses, so does the use of "gray," as next in the sequence, have a devastating immediacy. In locating sexual disappointment in the color gray, Barnard follows what Pound had done in his classic adaptations in *Lustra*, in which an abandoned lover is left to mourn "Grey olive leaves beneath a rain-cold sky" ("Gentildonna") or finds despair illustrated in the dull olive branches stripped to the ground like "pale carnage beneath bright mist ("April").[49]

"Violet, gold, and white / are one gray" has some external, geographical reference to Barnard's "North Window," too, in addition to the intertextual link with Sappho; it points to the kind of northwestern light-play noted by Pacific Northwest scholar Laurie Ricou, who cites an illuminating account from Barnard's era by Bertrand Sinclair. "Color is one of the charms of the coast region," Sinclair wrote in 1925; "morning and evening there is every shade from light pearl to deep purple, changing as the sun shifts, like a *delicately tinted mist* that finally clears to a deep, woodsy green, fir-and-cedar green."[50] The mist has not yet lifted in "Fire, snow, and the night"; the speaker experiences the grayness of borders (between night and day, between warm and cold, between intimacy and distance); the only certainty that emerges, or "finally clears," in the mist is the unpleasant sense of being "remote / with alien gray faces." Indeed, the last two lines are rather strange; "remote" and "alien" seem to be rather abstract terms, in contrast to the heavily visual images that precede it. Barnard may well have been referring to images of grey-faced aliens that were increasingly appearing in popular culture, thus highlighting the extremity of the lovers' separation, but there are also some intriguing spatial metaphors here: the former lovers "walk again remote," as if they are distant, remote *places*; and they are "alien" citizens in the space of "the common day," foreign to those they encounter, including each other, unable to "come together" as they did so harmoniously the previous evening. As such, the poem gestures toward its emotional drama through images rooted in the landscape, a landscape that is by turns inviting, warming, intimate, as it is unwelcoming, cold, isolating. Indeed, the "two" that come together in the poem include the two locals, the emotional and physical; this, as we shall now see, became an important part of Barnard's Sappho-inspired late Imagism that spoke to Williams's aesthetic as much as it did to Pound's and H.D.'s.

3.3 Barnard's Sapphic-American Modernism

Despite Barnard's announcement that she was a "Would-Be Sappho," despite all her experiments, under Pound, with Sapphics, despite her early adaptations from Sappho's fragments, what is perplexing about Barnard's late Imagist poetry is that as she refined her technique, Sappho seemed to vanish from her poetry entirely. "Fire, snow, and the night" makes a flicker of a reference to her corpus, and though classical in feel, the connections between "Cupbearer" and Sappho's Fragment Four are, at best, subtle. And yet the 1950s saw Barnard pull off a masterful translation of the recovered Sappho corpus, praised by both Pound and Williams for its fusion of modern American idiom and clean, precise, musical rhythm, as well as by critics for its unprecedented accuracy in capturing Sappho's exacting plainness of speech; "Barnard's Sappho is read as if it *is* the voice of Sappho," declared Yopie Prins emphatically.[51] Sappho made overt appearances in Barnard's free verse poems of the 1950s, too, appearing as the focus of unrequited love in the comic sequence *Three Translations from the Greek* ("But she, being off / prosperous Lesbos, / finds fault with my / gray hairs"), Sappho's laughter sending up the "whiskered mumble-/ment of grammarians" in "Static," and Sappho's fictional suicide leap being the subject of a poem about the northwestern mountains, the self-consciously titled "The Rock of Levkas." But during Barnard's time out East, from 1936 up to the moment she began working on her translation in 1951, Sappho seemed wholly, and strangely, absent from her poetry.

What happened? How did Barnard manage such a skillful transition from hit-and-miss adaptation in the early 1930s to acclaimed translation in the 1950s when she seemed to give up on Sappho during the interim? I would argue that she never did give Sappho up, despite appearances; that the more she explored "Pound's country" of Imagism and free verse, the more she explored the "cool country" of her local and, of course, the more she lived the "extremes of love's history" (in her Chief notebook she had written "If the greatest love is very close to hate, then I love this cursed place with a consuming passion"—the emotional once more conflated with "place").[52] Sappho became a *covert* presence in Barnard's late Imagist poems, rather than an absence, and in this she was following H.D., who, Eileen Gregory writes, "absorbed Sappho at a 'pre-verbal level.'"[53] Gregory implies that Sappho's lyrics existed in H.D.'s consciousness in a flexible form, being "pre-verbal" because they were resources for verbalization into new work: "In some of the early lyrics of H.D . . . traces of [Sappho's] images and tonalities unobtrusively [mark] individual lyrics," Gregory comments. In Barnard's case, Sappho's oppositional poetics, of the kind recreated by H.D. in "Orchard" and then by Barnard in "Cupbearer," were a perfect example for how Barnard might harness into poetry the unusual climatic conditions of the Columbia River Gorge that dominated her local and formed a backdrop to the emotional dramas that demanded to "be crystallized into one clear stone." Snaking along the Washington/Oregon stateline that divided Barnard's Vancouver hometown from Reed in Portland, the gorge is a formidable setting for the creative imagination. On one side of the Columbia, the Oregon side facing north, the gorge is steep; as a result, rain makes it way quickly down to the river via waterfalls, and the land is dark and wet. But on the Washington side facing south, the gorge possesses a gentler slant; there, the land is drier, as rain eases its way down to the river with less ferocity, and sunnier and lighter than the land opposite. Such drastically different climates are normally divided by a mountain range, not a river; the resultant open space between these climates generates amazing light displays such as that of "Fire, snow, and the night," as well as the world's foremost example of a natural hybridization system forged by the cross-fertilizations of the plants and animals that inhabit the opposing climates in unusually

FIGURE 6. Columbia River Gorge, view from Chanticleer Point, Oregon, June 2005. Photograph by Sarah Barnsley.

close proximity.[54] The effect of all this is the blending of peculiarly companionable opposites; the northwestern climate produces physical extremes in a tiny fragment of land, parallel to the "extremes of love's history" that Longinus observed in a fragment of Sappho's poetry.

So in poems like "The River under Different Lights," although there is no overt allusion to Sappho, something of Sappho's oppositional poetics is detectable in the articulation of the conflicting currents of light and water that confuse the speaker's senses. Comprised of three fragmentary sections that Barnard began working on in the 1930s, the first fragment, "The Gorge," begins

> Light has the dull luster of pewter
> and the clouds move sidewise clawing the tops of the crags,
> resting their soft gray bellies
> briefly in the high valleys.
>
> Foam, plowing against the rapids
> gathers all brightness.[55]

Not only are there color oppositions—the "dull luster" against the bright foam—but also oppositions of speed and movement, as the crab-like clouds gently pause for a brief rest while the ship-like foam spiritedly plows against the rapids. The foam's intensity is hastened through the shortness of the sentence that articulates it, in sharp contrast to the dullness of the high-valley light, which languishes like a cloud over four lines. These are oppositions that are continued through the other fragments, from the ship that appears "as though resting from the sea's labor" contrasted against the quick-moving buses that just about allow passengers "snatches of river between madrona and fir" to the "fog with a slow edge" set against the "flux of stream and ocean." The central opposition is between clarity and fogginess, between the light to be had on one side of the Columbia River Gorge and the inclement fog that floats down from the steep, high valleys of the other. The clouds come to ground in the second fragment of the poem, "The Ship," creating "fogging buses"; in opposition, the bright, plowing foam lifts off the surface of the water to reveal a passing ship, "a white vessel / dividing reflected forests." In the third fragment, "The Estuary," the light contrasts are simply compressed into that of "daylight and fog."

These tensions are heightened by the poem's conflicting narrative currents. On the one hand, the poem appears to move from land to sea, progressing from "The Gorge" to the "The Estuary." Yet one element—the ship—is making the opposite journey as it "passes inland," a metaphor, perhaps, for the oppositional movement of the poem. As with "Cupbearer" and "Fire, snow, and the night," Sappho-inspired techniques of compression and fragmentation predominate and intensify the oppositions. Although the poem takes place within a very tight linguistic space, sentences are still maintained; the poem makes sense and also allows itself to be pared down. It appears to simulate the appearance of fragments, with irregular stanzas that grate against the coherence conferred by the numerical and lexical sequencing of the fragments, which sets them into order. The result is that the poem is made to be as confounding as the landscape that accommodates such seemingly incomparable idiosyncrasies. In its oppositional texturing, the poem is evocative of the bewildering oppositions that swiftly move through Sappho's fragments, which Barnard later activated in her translation, from the "tender / feet of Cretan girls" capable of violently "crushing / a circle" in "the soft / smooth flowering grass" (Barnard's fragment number 23) to the "soft hands" that "tear off / dill shoots" to please the Three Graces (Barnard's fragment number 19).

With the lack of prominent narrator—there is no "I" or "we," common to many of Barnard's early lyric poems—there is no obvious human story to "The River under Different Lights"; the only people mentioned are the "riders in the fogging buses" who snatch glimpses of the river, and even then they are strangers, to each other as much as to the eye watching. And yet there is an overwhelming sense of melancholy in this poem; all brightness is gathered by the foam; a greyness descends upon the scene; the bus passengers can see increasingly little of the landscape. Perhaps the poem is an extension of the separation of "Fire, snow, and the night," inflected with the same grayness that arises following a failed love encounter? Certainly there is erotic suggestion in the opening lines, in the clouds resting on crags with their bellies out as if in bed, in the foam brightening with orgasmic intensity, as well as in the movement of the ship "dividing reflected forests" on the river surface. In an early version of the poem, "September" (1932), the erotic is displaced onto the local vegetation, which is tinged with sexual energy that freezes and burns at the same time after Sappho: "By the climbing road vine maple is frosted to fire / And elderberries are ripe with woodsmoke's blue," wrote Barnard.[56] Something of the "alien" relationship that develops between the two former lovers is articulated in "The Estuary," the final fragment of "The River under Different Lights." Here, in the borderline space of the estuary (the river/sea border recalling the night/day border that agonizes in "Fire, snow, and the night"), "fresh water meets salt," two are blended, and then

> Nothing is sure, neither
> tide, season, nor hour
> in this flux of stream and ocean,
> daylight and fog,
> where only the fish,
> a secret presence, move
> surely on spring's errand.[57]

That is, there is no "spring's errand" for the unspecified lovers, "only the fish" have this surety; in this poem, as in "Fire, snow, and the night," the unspecified lovers (themselves a "secret presence") become "remote" from one another.

An intriguing pattern thus emerged in the major period of Barnard's poetry as she produced poems for *Cool Country* and *A Few Poems*; human subjects seemed to desert Barnard's imagination or else become minimal presences. At the same time, her poems became more and more riveted by human emotions: despair, isolation, melancholy, and, to a lesser extent, ecstasy; only such emotions were not attached to people but to places. So just as Barnard takes out the overt allusions to Sappho, she also takes out the lyric "I" and in its place inserts the northwestern landscape. The landscape is the adequate subject, marked not only by its own special geographical character but by the psychic dramas of its inhabitants that unfold there, inhabitants who have, at best, "a secret presence." People are implied in the overpronounced physical space, rather like the way in which Edward Hopper uses large, clear windows and extended floor spaces to dramatize the emotions of the people who have just left the empty space depicted or those who are on the edge of it. So if for Williams, in poems like "A Sort of Song," the aim was to overtly reconcile the American *people* with "the stones,"[58] Barnard was less interested in the people than the stones themselves—or so it seemed. Consider, for example, her 1944 poem "Crossroads":

Crossroads

Rotting in the wet gray air
the railroad depot stands deserted under
still green trees. In the fields
cold begins an end.

There were other-too-long-postponed-departures.
They left, finally, because of well water
gone rank, the smell of fungus, the chill
of rain in chimneys.

The spot is abandoned even in memory.
They knew, locking doors upon empty houses,
to leave without regret is to lose
title to one home forever.[59]

The first stanza reads almost like a version of Williams' poem "The Red Wheelbarrow," the wheelbarrow "glazed with rain"[60] substituted for the "railroad depot" "rotting in the wet gray air." *Place* and *things* command attention over people; at every step, the human aspect of the poem is minimized, shrunk down, put at a tangent—it is but one thematic "road" crossing the poem, no more significant than the other thematic roads concerning what has happened to the railroad depot, the cold fields, the well water, the houses; indeed, the only elements of the poem infused with any sensual adjectives depicting texture, temperature, taste are *the things*. The human story is in the past tense, whereas *the things* command the present—the depot "stands" "rotting" in the continuous present, the cold freshly "*begins* an end" (italics mine); "the smell of fungus" and "the chill of rain in chimneys" are not even bound to time. And yet the "they" of the poem (the general third person pronoun itself another means of distancing the human story) is associated with the only past-tense verbs in the poem: "They *left* . . . They *knew*" (italics mine). The first hint of this remote "they" of the poem is through the metonym "departures," a word itself inflected with ideas of distancing; even the long line in which this word appears, with its string of hyphens, "postpones" the first mention of the human element to the end of the sentence. As a result, the physical space becomes overpronounced in its relentless foregrounding, but the effect is rather curious: rather than diminish the human story, this attention on external particulars enhances it. "Locking doors upon empty houses" is such an odd line, conceptually—why, if the house is riddled with fungus, would you bother to lock it up?—and yet it evokes a heavy melancholy. For Barnard's affixation of *all* affective imagery onto objects of place has the reverse effect of injecting the poem with the "almost palpable" human realism that she had said she wanted for poems like "Crossroads" that she wrote while at Buffalo. This faint merger of people and place is given away not by any elaborate scheme, as in Williams's double play throughout *Paterson* of a central mythic figure between Dr. Paterson-the-man and Paterson-the-place-by-the-falls, but, as is frequent in Bishop's poetry, by the slightest of linguistic maneuvers. Consider, for example, the grammatical trick played in the last line of "Crossroads"; it is easy to misread the last line as a statement about the people and insert a possessive apostrophe at the most critical point: "They knew, locking doors upon empty houses, / to leave without regret is to lose / title to one<u>'s</u> home forever" (underlining mine)—which is what this last line *should* say, having just gestured toward a narrative of unspecified frontierspeople giving up on a life of cold fields and the "well water gone rank." But the poem does not say this; the eye is forced to go back and see that there is no possessive apostrophe and that this statement is not about people but place; the home is simply "one home"—of many—not a particular person's home, not a particular person's story. In this flicker of grammar, "place" and "people" seem substitutable—

the one throws up the other, they collocate. The countable phrase, indeed, points to that fragile sense of home that is often said to inflect American literature—"one home" is lost, but there will be more. So not only does Barnard make the poem very specific on *the local*, in this slightest of grammatical decisions she also makes the poem about *the nation*.

Williams, it is well-known, was quite outspoken on such matters: as he said to Ford Madox Ford, American art should enable its people to "express themselves fully, in all colors and shapes of their living moods."[61] The poet's business in all of this was "to write particularly, as a physician works, upon a patient, upon the thing before him, in the particular to discover the universal."[62] The purpose was not to achieve an impersonal art that, in its final composition, erased the particular, but quite the opposite: a synthesis between poet, place, and poem, for each was dependent on the other in order to be understood. "The critics would have it that I, the poet, am not profound and go on with their profundities, sometimes affecting to write poems in their very zeal as thinkers," Williams scoffed at the very same New Critics who had dismissed Barnard, but yet, he felt, "the poet thinks with his poem, in that lies his thought, and that in itself is the profundity."[63] In other words, Williams saw no such division between "intrinsic" and "extrinsic" criteria in his understanding of a poem, as did the New Critics; poetry was less a stand-alone "verbal icon" or "net" of a poet's thoughts, at a tangent to the poet and the local contexts that created it, and more an active component in the poet's conception of self and world. "So much depends / upon / a red wheel / barrow,"[64] Williams had written, the gesture to what lies *outside* the poem (the unexplained "what" that "depends" upon the local context) is as important as the movement within it. Thus, where the New Critics saw that the form of a work was its essence and its choice of subject insignificant, Williams saw no such disparity between form and content; indeed, they were reciprocal of one another, as he explained of his purposes in *Paterson*:

> To *make* a poem, fulfilling the requirements of the art, and yet new, in the sense that in the very lay of the syllables Paterson as Paterson would be discovered . . . to flutter into life awhile—it would be as itself, locally, and so like every other place in the world. For it is in that, that it be particular to its own idiom, that it lives.[65]

Although Barnard comparatively said very little about her own method outside of the poems themselves, it was clear from poems like "Remarks on Poetry and the Physical World" that she was in firm agreement:

Remarks on Poetry and the Physical World

After reading *Ash Wednesday*
She looked once at the baked beans
And fled. Luncheonless, poor girl,
She observed a kind of poetic Lent—
And I had thought I liked poetry
Better than she did.

I do. But to me its most endearing
Quality is its unsuitableness;
And conversely, the chief wonder in heaven
(Whither I also am sometimes transported)
Is the kind of baggage I bring with me.

Surely there is no more exquisite jointure
In the anatomy of life, than that at which
Poetry dovetails with the inevitable meal
And Mrs. B. sits murmuring of avocados.[66]

The poem presents two kinds of poetry, and, through some clever conceits, makes no bones about which is the superior. The "impersonal" poetry of *Ash Wednesday*, by T. S. Eliot (that exemplar of New Critical ideology), drains the "physical world" of its relevance, an outcome Barnard ridicules in the image of the "poor girl" reader being put off her food (her fleeing of the scene a barb against Eliot's call for the poet's removal of personality): "poetry" and "the physical world" are cleft apart. A more "exquisite" prospect, on the other hand, is poetry like hers and Williams's, one that is consonant with local realities: "poetry [that] dovetails with the inevitable meal," "dovetails" with the routine and custom of "the physical world." The case for Barnard's brand of modern poetry is cemented in the suggestive final two lines. Whereas the reaction of the "poor girl" to *Ash Wednesday* in stanza one is couched in prosaic, matter-of-fact language ("She looked once at the baked beans / And fled"), the reaction of "Mrs. B" (a hip self-reference) to the poetry *she* encounters is presented in language charged with exciting aural correlations. While "Mrs. B. sits murmuring of avocados" has its literal meaning, the sound play yields another meaning—the onomatopoeic "murmuring," the buzz created by the friction between the soft and harsh sounds that blend in "Mrs. B"; all this constructs an image of another "B," a *bee*, a "physical world" constituent here created by poetry. "When you get a strong fishy smell from an envelope," Barnard once wrote to Williams, "it contains poems from me," referring, in part, to their aspiration toward the "physical world" about them.[67]

To Williams the poem was a "fine" effort,[68] and he was pleased to see Barnard put more of herself into her poem, however remotely, for he was always badgering her to loosen up and inject some personal realism. "You cut your verses down but you cut them too much, too much of the details of you," Williams chided in 1940. "Write you, write it intricately, as intricately and as finely, to the last detail of a thin line."[69] In part, Williams was encouraging more emotion, more passion in her poetry ("your objects don't seem to me to have been looked at in moments of sufficient emotional stress. You can see them and you put them down clearly but you don't seem much hurt or elated," he had told her earlier),[70] but Barnard was never as interested as he was in expressing "personality" in art in a literal sense, with singular reference to herself; it was more a collective, American "personality" that Barnard was so keen to embody.

Thus it comes as no surprise that the yellow and rose sky in "North Window" is also the color of blood or that the stones by the lake beach are "bloodless"; that sand dunes are "naked," coastal pines are "crouched" like shivering children, that shipwrecks have "cracked ribs" in "Shoreline" like a "shattered hulk"; that "place . . . grows into the body," that "blood should be clear amber under tree bark" in "Roots"; or even that land can be as "expressionless as the face of a stranger," as in "Encounter in Buffalo." *American* space is *human* space, marked by the "extremes of love's history" as it is by bluster of wind, rain, and other climactic forces. In this Barnard was following Dickinson, who used extremes of geography and weather to convey the intensity and range of emotive suffering through images of deserts, ice caps, earthquakes, volcanic eruptions, storms, and whirlpools, only in a much more specific, Williamsesque way in her use of particular, intimately known American spaces. Indeed, it was Williams who had said, in 1919, that the only way to know the sensuous, external world under the nose was through the emotions. Writing in *Poetry* in 1919, Williams posited that "the world of the senses lies unintelligible on all sides. It is only interpretable by the emotions. It only exists when its emotion is fastened to it. This is artistic creation."[71]

So the disappointments of love and sex, of "Fire, snow, and the night," return again and again in Barnard's *Cool Country* poems (indeed, poems that probe the "cool country" of relationships), surfacing in the deserted Washington shorelines, the chilled forest valleys, the mists and fog of the Columbia River Gorge, the river itself with its currents as changeable as affairs of the heart. "Some poems may seem like nature poems, but they're not that. They are not just descriptive. I would use an image in nature to evoke an emotional situation," Barnard would later remark.[72] Thus the bitter end of the implied love affair that has run its course, like a river, in "The River under Different Lights" (which did not make it into *Cool Country*) is re-staged in "The Rapids" (which did), a poem based on Celilo Falls, the huge area of dramatic falls and rapids along the Columbia River wiped out with the building of the Dalles dam in the 1950s and with them, one of the oldest, continuously occupied tribal settlements in the United States. In the middle stanza of this three stanza poem, Barnard's speaker laments:

> The water we saw broken upon the rapids
> Has dragged silt through marshland
> And mingled with the embittered streams of the sea.
> One might have kept sweet pailsful and kept nothing.[73]

Just as the implied lovers become once again "alien" and "remote" in "Fire, snow and the night" and "The River under Different Lights," so too is the outcome of "the rapids" of this particular affair less than pleasant. In the detail of the transformation of fresh water into silt-laden "embittered streams" is the detail of the end of the love affair—the bitterness of something that once yielded "sweet pailsful" now amounts to nothing. As in the most memorable of Sappho's lyrics, the experience is bittersweet, and it is the land's experience as much as anyone else's. The "one" who "might have kept sweet pailsful and kept nothing" is, at best, distant, part of an axiomatic phrase, the human element placed just on the edge of the frame, just a little too remote for the reader to see, a "secret presence."

However, in this instance there is hope and resilience as well as sadness, and this too is related in geographical close-up at the poem's end:

> But the ungatherable blossoms floating by the same rock,
> The chisel marks on a surface in full flight
> Have flung light in my face, have made promises
> In unceasing undertone.

The "same rock" of the poem is possibly Beacon Rock, one of the more notable monoliths along the Columbia River, thirty-six miles east of Vancouver, which Barnard passed many times when travelling with her father to the lumber camps along the Columbia River Gorge.[74] Here Beacon Rock stands in for the speaker, left behind and affected by the "full flight" of the water, her lover, whose violent flinging back of the implied relationship nevertheless leaves traces of what might be—the "blossoms" of their affair, although now "ungatherable" and hard like "chisel marks," remind the speaker that, as the seasons leave and return, love may come again; this is the promise of the "unceasing undertone" of the river, continuously subject to the energies of rapids.

If Barnard's American project worked with Sappho's oppositional poetics at the level of the image, it worked at the level of voice, too; many of

Barnard's poems exploit tensions between voicing and silence, enshrouded, as ever, in the cool country landscape. Sappho, of course, had set some precedents; throughout her fragments is a ring of voices, each declaring their capacity to speak ("Tell everyone . . . I shall sing beautifully for / my friend's pleasure," "I asked myself," "I said," "I confess," "I took my lyre and said")[75] or endorsing the voicing of others ("We heard them chanting," "People do gossip," "Some say a cavalry corps," "It was you, Atthis, who said").[76] Indeed, Sappho's poems were designed for group performance, either with Sappho's pupils having a part (or several parts) to play or Sappho herself playing a singular role with the pupils as her audience.[77] And yet, as Yopie Prins argues, Sappho's fragments "simultaneously provoke and resist voicing"[78]; any voice is swiftly rendered vulnerable. So in Barnard's fragment number 31, Sappho famously says "my tongue is broken"[79]; elsewhere, the ability to speak or say something worthwhile is the subject of dreams ("Last night / I dreamed that / you and I had / words: Cyprian")[80] or a power best left to the nonhuman ("The nightingale's / the soft-spoken / announcer of Spring's presence," Barnard's fragment number 62 reports). The vulnerable voice, in Sappho, is undeniably that of the lover, riddled with desire one moment, doubt the next.

But Barnard shifts the focus somewhat, from private to public, so that this tension between speaking and not speaking, between the mass power of voices circulating and interacting with one another and the anxiety about the fragility of the individual voice among an increasing populous environment, could be said to be an *American* tension as much it was a textual tension prevalent in Sappho's verse. She knew that Williams had long been preoccupied with the question of what constituted the American voice, as had Whitman before him; Americans, Williams declared, were "yawping speakers of a new language."[81] Some of these "yawping speakers" inhabit "Shoreline," perhaps one of the clearest examples of Barnard's adoption of Sappho's ring of voices in free verse, a poem already shown to be inflected with regional and national concerns. Here, it is never completely clear who or what is speaking, as the poem undergoes several tonal switches in keeping with the raggedy appearance of its lines, and yet voices come and go with all the discernible rhythm of the waves that wash over the shore; maybe it is the voice of the sea? For one, there is a voice that pronounces judgment—"Those whose impertinence / Leads them to [the sea's] moving ledges." The judging voice slips away awhile, only to return later, or so it seems: "Did you, as I, *condemn* the coastal fog . . . ?" (italics mine) the voice enquires, but there is something different here. Quite apart from the shift to first person, such opinion is aired in a very different syntactical frame, in a question that seeks validation from an other ("Did you, as I . . . ?"), rather than in the frame of the opening parallelisms, whose surety of tone signal the speaker's conviction and autonomy. Then, later, "The way to the dunes is easy" is uttered in similar tone to the opening line, "The sea has made a wall for its defence," which leads to the judging voice. Both lines appear to have the sober, plain quality of a voice making a simple statement of observation, and yet "The way to the dunes is easy" sounds as if it is uttered by a child trying to tempt a friend to come follow. The childlike voice does not castigate, like the voice that judges; it voices optimism, possibilities, the fact that the sand will stiffen in the rain but once again be "loosened . . . in the sun's fingers." But then within the same stanza the voice speaks of "Children, lustful of glistening hours." This cannot be the voice of a child, one might conclude; the voice speaks of children with some measured detachment, using a more sophisticated vocabulary, which stretches to the polysyllabic ("glistening" and "insatiate"). And so the voice switches again, as capricious as beach winds that lash "under the eyelids," appearing to belong to that of an unnamed, but articulate, adult observer until it switches again or, rather, breaks up as if the wind is smothering out some of the syntactical glue in the clipped phrases that follow: "Wind under the eyelids, / confusion walling the ears," the voice hollers against the rushes of sea air.[82]

And yet Barnard's voices are not "yawping speakers" in isolation, or even, as we see in the last stanza of "Shoreline," in perpetual conflict with one another; as in Williams's vision, they speak a "new language," but they seem to be in dialogue with one another, too, so much so that they combine and *unify* to produce that aspect of Barnard's work that is "so very quiet and so very sure," which Florence Codman was so taken by in 1936. If anything, Sappho showed the way to a "democraticized" lyric that evinced American ideals of liberty and equality. The recurrence of the pronouns "we" and "our" suggests a sense of agreed purpose and shared experience, a sense of democratic unity. The varying voices may express their differentiation from other subjects in the poem, condemning "those" who confront the sea's "moving ledges," asserting adult authority over the children at the beach, expressing childish innocence, yet at the same time there appears to be a voice that expresses *togetherness*, from the articulation of the refrain "Sand is the beginning and the end / of *our* dominion" to the pronouncement that the shoreline is "the country of *our* choice" (italics mine). Contrasts of voice in the early stanzas go some way to foregrounding the graceful, effusive rhetoric that characterizes the voice in the last stanza; "Clear lagoons / Behind the shattered hulk, thin / Movements of sea grass" trails smoothly off the tongue, eased by the enjambment, just as "the transitory ponds and smooth bar slide / Easily under the advancing tide"; the way to rhythmic American speech, like the "way to the [Washington] dunes," is found to be "easy" when one looks to the American local, as we shall see in the next chapter. So for all the loss that the "we" of the poem experiences ("We lose the childish avarice of horizons"), by the end of the poem a kind of "super" voice articulates possession of the shoreline in terms of co-ownership—"these things are *ours*" (italics mine). There may be many voices, as in Sappho, scattered at different points, but they seem related to one voice, echoing through the poem almost imperceptibly as the "unceasing undertone" in "The Rapids," as the "thin movements" of sea grass in "Shoreline"; this voice is inextricably caught up with place.

Indeed, just as Barnard's image of sand grains could be said to be representational and affirmative of the American experience, of a people migrating across the North American continent, so, too, is her use of voice: she distributes different voices and competing tones across the verbal contours of her verse much in the same way that Americans have moved around the physical space of the United States. Perhaps Sappho's was a model that Barnard had felt was vital to appropriate in order to assert herself as an American poet, even if she carried anxiety about the character and strength of the American lyric. As Margaret Reynolds has argued in *The Sappho History*:

> [Sappho's] collective notion of poetry—where many sing, and many consciousnesses are realised—means that Sappho can assert her own identity within the poem. She makes a persona other than herself who can then look at her, recognise her, name her. Even in the few fragments that we have, one of the peculiarities of Sappho's poetry is that she often names herself, brings herself into existence by signing her own name in her compositions.[83]

It is impossible not to think of Whitman and his intentions for "Song of Myself" in all of this; ideas of "collective . . . poetry" had appealed to American poets long before Barnard, only Sappho, more than Whitman, was to show Barnard the way. Barnard may not name herself directly in her poems, in line with her suppression of lyrical subjects, but she is not averse to inferring her presence, either—take the "ME" in "Late Roman" or the "Mrs. B. . . . murmuring of avocados" in "Remarks on Poetry and the Physical World," for example—and always in company where "many sing, and many consciousnesses are realised," be it that of the children delighting in dunes in "Shoreline," of the "riders in the fogging buses" in "The River under Different Lights," of the remote lovers of "Fire, snow, and the night" and "The Rapids."

It is not clear, yet, who Barnard had in mind as she was writing these poems and how far such poems were about her own affairs, but recent archival finds suggest perhaps they were, that they were as much Barnard's "song of myself" as they were a "song of ourselves," of the "yawping speakers of a new language." In an unpublished and untitled poem, initialed at the foot "M.B." (as if signed in dedication to someone) and very probably from the 1930s, given the typeface used, the "extremes of love's history" are ascribed to "my life" in an arresting story featuring a "still" fir tree, by turns "arrowy" and protective, and the "wilful water" that flows back and forth around it. Intriguingly, no one speaks; there is only the quiet "murmur" of a river ("murmuring" like "Mrs. B."):

> The slenderly poised clean shaft of your fir,
> Arrowy and yet still, might have stood in the station
> Beside the Great Northern rails and the wilful water
> Of my life, flowing so contrarily eastward.
>
> You remember how the trees at Wind River have that air
> Of protecting the water without leaning above it.
> No branch droops willow-fashion, trailing leaves
> Bubbled with silver, making the water murmur around it.
> Without shading the stream, they let fall reflected color.
>
> All time flows down from the same source in the hills.
> The current following those rails as if in hollowed rock
> Overtakes me, hour by hour. Tomorrow is lying
> Now by your drinking roots, green with your love.[84]

This striking poem perhaps depicts the moment that Barnard left the Northwest, along the Great Northern rails, to go and meet poets in New York, "contrarily eastward," in 1936, and suggests that she was leaving more than just land behind. But this is mere speculation; what this poem shows is just how far Barnard came to associate the "I" (and the "you") with elements of her local—and this had implications for her use of Sappho. For Barnard found that there was no longer any need for the prior text of Sappho to assist with the articulation of "the extremes of love's history" as she had experienced them, or any other subjective cause, when the American local, itself, was entirely suitable material; it contained such a range of oppositions and binaries necessary for the dramatization of emotional conflicts (such as "the greatest love [that] is very close to hate") that there was no reason to dredge up quotations and allusions from foreign texts. "The flow must originate from the local to the general as a river to a sea and then back to the local from the sea in the rain," Williams told Horace Gregory in 1944[85]; he was arguing for the universalities of human experience to be found in specific American space (and hence the geographic analogy), and in this Barnard was a co-conspirator.

Like Williams, Barnard was working to make *new* forms, to build America's cultural capital from its own resources, not from Europe's, for that would only lead to cultural subservience. Of course, to begin with Sappho had been a most productive model worthy of attention. She had had something to teach the Imagist poets, and there were good reasons for them to try to emulate her plainness of speech, her verbal economy, her musicality. Sappho had also had something to teach the American modernists, and there were good reasons, too, for poets like Barnard to emulate her oppositional poetics as a means of harnessing the range of human emotions *and* the extremes and ranges of the American landscape comprised of many different locals, her "collective notion of poetry" as a way in which Americans could incorporate the many accents, dialects, viewpoints and concerns of members of the new nation, the "yawping speakers of a new language," as Williams put it.

Indeed, out of all poets, Sappho was among the few who could be considered as an exemplar for American poets shaping a new lyric, for like Homer, Shakespeare, and Dante, Sappho was a poet who heralded the new times for her nation; she had about her what Emerson described as "the timely." Emerson had called for the American poet to go about the "singing" of America with the same sense of prescient purpose as Homer and Dante, who were European models of "the timely man." Addressing Americans, Emerson complained:

> Time and nature yield us many gifts, but not yet the timely man, the new religion, the reconciler, whom all things await. Dante's praise is, that he dared to write his autobiography in colossal cipher, or into universality. We have yet had no genius in America, with tyrannous eye, who knew the value of our incomparable materials, and saw, in the barbarism and the materialism of the times, another carnival of the same gods whose picture he so much admires in Homer.[86]

If Sappho's wider corpus had been available, perhaps Emerson would have cited her too as an exemplar in his passionate appeal for American poets to dare to come into the moment and "chaunt" their "own times and social circumstances," for as Barnard so eloquently argued in her essay-length footnote to her Sappho translation, Sappho had something of this timeliness. "Sappho was not, as has sometimes been assumed by those unacquainted with the tradition, a lonely poet adrift on a provincial island," Barnard wrote, but lived "among the richest and liveliest Greek settlements of [her] period," where "both art and science were flourishing. This was the age that produced the Hera of Samos and the Pythagorean philosophers."[87] This age had some parallel with Barnard's; both Sappho and Barnard were witness to the early stages of their nations' rise to power, their emergent modernity, their increasing dominance in the arts and sciences, their "incessant commotion,"[88] as

Barnard put it in her summary of the times in "Blood Ritual," first published in the *New Directions* anthology of 1937. "[Sappho] was riding the crest of her own wave; her world seemed modern to her as ours does to us, and just about as troubled," Barnard continued in her footnote, and this kind of cultural apprehension of the new was played out in poems such as "Adversity and the Generations," which is sardonically focused on the gadgetry of a 1930s New York deli. Likening the overzealousness of American invention to Cain's "toiling before Eden's east threshold" among the adversities of weeds and "boulders / embedded in arable soil," Barnard writes wryly of the new age of American achievement in the "east threshold" of New York:

But we were not content.
Full of ambition, with capacity
For increased exasperation,
We devise a pancake machine.
The pancake batter, as always,
Creating a delicate situation,
The electrically animated parts
Miscalculate exactly.

Thistles and thorns were nothing
To this dogged inaccurate motion
Producing lunch-counter chaos.
Cain was bitter, but his seed
Suffer hysteria.[89]

One "seed" suffering such "hysteria" was Barnard's New York friend Babette Deutsch, whose letters are electrified by anxiety induced by a city that "eats your days and gobbles your nights" and growing unease about the prospect of war in Europe. "I enjoyed the dry humor of Adversity and the Generations," she told Barnard in September 1937. "But in view of the chaos brought to one's breakfast table (minus a pancake machine) with the morning paper, lunch-counter chaos seems the merest fly-speck."[90] Barnard's was a new age, however fraught and frenetic, and she, like Deutsch, very much knew this; for in poems like "Provincial," Barnard showed her own "tyrannous eye" that knew the value of America's "incomparable materials":

Provincial

Mossy stones, the quilted legends
Warming the villages like a sprigged comforter,
The dead like a smoke webbing the trees,
And all inviting dreaming:

These must be pleasant, but I never knew them,
Have no acquaintance with bronze monuments,
Have never spoken with a ghost on a bridge.
Our concrete piers are white and new in the water.

The dead are sparsely sown as yet.
The rain clouds rising above stumpland
Form no apparitions. Thin wheat by the fir roots,
Two potted geraniums on a stump
By the plank road receive the shower.

More beautiful than flowering moss
The naked rock rises,
Chipped columnar by the liquid
Blades of bright water.[91]

There is an Emersonian pride in America here, as Barnard's "shriek of defiance" is moderated into a voice of dignified authority; this one-time "province" of European expansion is felt to be "more beautiful" than the "flowering moss" that enshrouds the "pleasant" realm of the English tradition with its "dead" (its poets?) "like a smoke webbing the trees." America's "incomparable materials" are devoid of any ornament, as yet untouched by the moss and webs that quilt Europe; its "concrete piers" are "white and new," "naked" even. And this newness is its great strength, as worked out in the cunning adverbial metaphor at the poem's end—America's "naked rock" is "chipped *columnar*" as it rises (italics mine); although Barnard is disconnecting the American story from that of Europe, there is still some parallel to be had with the rise of the great civilizations of ancient Greece and Rome, which innovated enduring, elaborate architectural structures such as the column as a sign of cultural might. America is just as mighty, Barnard's poem tells us. Eliot's suggestion, in *The Waste Land*, that the modern world is broken and dead was as "foreign" to Barnard as the rest of his verse; the third stanza of "Provincial" is as vehement an opposition to the opening lines of "The Burial of the Dead" as Williams's counterimage of spring teeming with new life in the waste fields of "on the road to the contagious hospital" at the beginning of *Spring and All*. Barnard swaps Williams's waste fields for "stumpland," his "twiggy / stuff of bushes and small trees"[92] for "Thin wheat by the fir roots, / Two potted geraniums on a stump" that "receive the shower"—the effect is the same; through vegetative metaphor, Barnard asserts that America is at a point of unprecedented growth, not unprecedented fragmentation, as in Eliot's Europe. Like Williams, who in *Spring and All* observes that "one by one objects are defined," Barnard sees this version of America with stunning clarity—the "naked rock" comes into sharp, alert focus, with definite shape as it is "Chipped columnar by the liquid / Blades of bright water," set apart from the dreamy, smoky, webby confusion of the fragmenting "villages" of Old Europe.

For all the parallels that Barnard saw between the new "naked rock" of emergent modern America and Sappho's time "among the richest and liveliest Greek settlements of . . . the age that produced the Hera of Samos and the Pythagorean philosophers," it was simply not enough for this new poetry, this new literature, this new nation to depend in any way on another culture to hold it up; simply not enough for Barnard's poetry to assert itself through classical allusion, for Barnard to settle as a "Would-Be Sappho"; American poetry *had* to be American, first and foremost, as culturally autonomous as the English, as the Greeks, as the poets of the Italian Renaissance, and in no way deferring. This was what Williams was getting at shortly before he began corresponding with Barnard, when he warned any would-be American writer of certain aesthetic imperatives. "We must invent, we must create out of the blankness about us, and we must do this by the use of new constructions,"[93] Williams had implored. Like Barnard, Williams saw America as "a new world naked," as Paul Mariani effused in his Williams biography that took the phrase from *Spring and All* for its title.[94] *Classic adaptation*, of the kind that Pound and H.D. had done in their early Imagist phases, as Barnard had in hers, got in the way of *American form-making*, which was the priority task. Whitman had set the pace in *Leaves of Grass* and his free verse innovations, and the following generations of American poets were obliged to be just as bold, to have the same "tyrannous eye" for "incomparable materials," to make forms as new as spatial and material conditions of the times, indeed, to catch "the truth of [American] civilization in its own forms." And such forms were always to be found in live American speech rhythms, as Williams was to observe: "Where else can what we are seeking arise from but speech? From speech, from American speech as distinct from English speech. . . . Not, that is, from a study of the classics, not even the American 'Classics'—the *dead* classics—may I remind you, we have *never* heard as living speech."[95]

So this is why Sappho became a "secret presence" in Barnard's late Imagist poetry; her example had to be, in the end, just that—an example, and not a template from which to take a direct cut, for America had its own templates. Coming under Williams's influence when she moved to New York, and having dug through his attic of manuscripts, reviews, and other writings when she was Poetry Curator at Buffalo as she established Williams's archive, there is little doubt that Barnard was aware of all that Williams had written about the new American art and how the American poet should work. As a young poet, she had wanted to write like Sappho, and in time, she came to understand this urge as a symptom of what she was really after in her poetry—a new poetry befitting the "naked rock" of an America civilization that "rises" out of modernity, not a poetry "mossy" or "quilted" with the idiom of another culture, to quote "Provincial." As her American project gathered pace, Barnard realized that her relationship to Sappho had to change. To echo Williams, in order to be like Sappho, to make a new art as worthy and as prescient as Sappho's, Barnard had to write *unlike* Sappho. "When each poem has achieved its particular form unlike any other, when it shall stand alone—then we have achieved our language. We have said what it is in our minds to say," dictated Williams in 1919.[95]

It was this kind of impulse toward autonomy that Edmund Wilson observed in Barnard's midcentury contemporaries, coming of age in the period when Williams's reputation boomed in the United States. Writing in the *New Republic*, in which Barnard had published an early version of "Roots" ("Northwest Anchorage"), Wilson made the assessment in 1941 that there were "unmistakeable signs of the revival of an interest in literature for its own sake—that is, as a department of activity which has its own aims, techniques, and rights," referring mainly to the New Critical school.[97] Or, as Mariani put it, the early 1940s was a period in which "writers were beginning once again to see the world for themselves rather than through a series of prior texts. That was exactly what Williams himself was feeling, as he groped for a new form," and it was most probably what Barnard was feeling as she dropped the "prior texts" of Sappho and focused on the text of the American landscape, which was prior to all else.[98]

Of course, in the end Barnard *did* become Sappho in her critically acclaimed translation of 1958, but this was no act of deference, for even in this remarkable translation, which recovered Sappho for audiences of the modern, industrial age, there is the pulse of her and Williams's American project. What made Barnard decide to take on Sappho after her frustration with Sapphics under Pound in the 1930s, as the next chapter will explore, seems, on the surface, quite accidental; as she tells us in *Assault on Mount Helicon*, she was recovering from serious illness, limited in her movements and in need of a meaty project for the mind to keep herself sane. And yet it is an act of cultural might to say "I am ill; I shall translate Sappho," to feel secure enough in her ability to write in her own idiom the words of a poet so revered and yet, due to the tattered condition of her corpus, so challenging to translate. In putting Sappho back together in American idiom, Barnard emphasizes the strength and character of that idiom; it is a language "chipped columnar," a durable form able to hold up work of cultural distinction.

Perhaps this act of cultural assertion has had something to do with Barnard's phenomenal success with *Sappho: A New Translation* (its subtitle a nod to her and Williams's project for "the new"). It was certainly not what anyone had expected, not even Barnard. Despite having secured an introduction from the leading classical scholar and translator Dudley Fitts,

Barnard's agent Diarmuid Russell had great difficulty trying to place the manuscript with a publisher. Florence Codman's Anchor Books told her that "Sappho would never sell."[99] When the manuscript was eventually snapped up by the University of California Press, not only did the book sell and sell (by the time Barnard wrote her memoir in the early 1980s, the book was ninth on California's list of best-selling paperbacks), other translations within America swiftly followed it.[100] The feeling by critics was that Barnard had brought Sappho to a modern American audience, expressing the bare, lyrical intensity of her verse without recourse to the excessive linguistic ornament or narrative padding that had smothered so many previous attempts to translate Sappho into English—English English, that is, not American English. Just as Imagism perhaps belonged to the spare, austere American 1930s, as I speculated in the last chapter, perhaps Sappho's idiom coincided more comfortably with what Pound described to Barnard as the "amurikan langwidge," as I shall soon speculate. Yet although Fitts's introduction paid tribute to Barnard's capture of Sappho's "pungent downright plain style," there was also recognition of the kind of "new conscious form" that Williams called for:

> Like the Greek, it is stripped and hard, awkward with the fine awkwardness of truth. Here is no trace of the "sweet sliding, fit for a verse" that one expects to find in renderings of Sappho. It is exact translation; but in its composition, the spacing, the arrangement of stresses, it is also high art. This, one thinks, is what Sappho must have been like; and Longinus . . . was no fool when he pointed to her marshaling of sharp details, rather than to the melody of her verse, as the secret of her eloquence.[101]

"It is also high art," Fitts pronounced, and perhaps this is partly why American audiences have been so enthusiastic, for in Barnard's "exact translation," there is also Barnard's "composition," an inventive act by an American poet, affirmative of a national literary identity. "I've always stood in real awe of your Sappho, surely the best Greek translation in American literature,"[102] the Sappho scholar Guy Davenport told Barnard in 1981; it was not just a translation, but also a work of American literature: to recall Edmund Wilson, "literature for its own sake."

And so in Barnard's *Sappho: A New Translation*, we also find Barnard's late Imagism. In skillfully pared-down lines, there is the same kind of conversational ease and cutting clarity detectable in poems such as "Fire, snow, and the night," managed into ribbon-like visual frames that simultaneously suggest fragments and wholes, as in this example:

Tonight I've watched

The moon and then
the Pleiades
go down

The night is now
half-gone; youth
goes; I am

in bed alone[103]

Like Barnard's "Fire, snow, and the night," Sappho finds the move from night to dawn a fitting metaphor for the awareness of a lover's loneliness; the physical local coincides with the speaker's emotional local. As in "Shoreline," the fragment enacts several tonal shifts while maintaining a central, unifying "I" as the speaker moves from a mood of quiet observation ("Tonight I've watched / The moon and then / the Pleiades / go down") to one of introspective regret ("youth / goes," a reference to the departure of youthfulness, but also a play on the departure of the "youth" who once shared the speaker's nights) to a final mood of muted despair ("I am / in bed alone"). Setting the first line off from the rest of the fragment is a device Barnard sustains throughout her translation; in this way Barnard seems to give the fragment a semblance of completion, as the first line doubles as a title. Like an Imagist poem, the connective tissue of this fragment, as with others in Barnard's translation, comes not so much from the verbal content as from the verbal rhythm, which works toward the totality of the utterance—everything is part of "a simple but emotionally loaded statement," each part flowing rhythmically to the next in a "spare but musical" way, oiled by the easy familiarity of phrases following natural word order and the plain, common word, "stripped and hard," as Fitts observed, "straight as the Greek," as Pound had demanded, over anything ostentatious or florid. The fragment is exactly what Williams was after for the American poem—a machine of visual and auditory movement, each part "moving rapidly from one thing to the next . . . a passage through . . . a swiftness impaling beauty," as he said of Moore's example.[104] In a way, Barnard was simply being faithful to the Greek; "one thing is bound to strike the reader" of Sappho and Homer, Barnard said in 1994, "and that is the way their poems *move*. . . . In both poets there is visual movement and there is auditory movement."[105] But this was also what she had wanted for her own "spare but musical" poetry; she wanted the sound of the voice "*making* a simple but emotionally loaded statement" (italics mine), a line in the act of movement as in speech.

"'Sappho's poems are not the work of a young woman, but of a mature, older woman. I could not have translated her poems 20 years earlier,'" Barnard later told David Gordon.[106] In a way, she was right, for the "Would-Be Sappho" who said in her 1932 creed that she believed "in the simplicity and sincerity of word and movement and idea" still had to find her way to it; Barnard needed to discover her own way of managing "simplicity" after Poundian Imagism, and her own way of making her poetry genuine, sincere to its context, both unquestionably hers and unquestionably American. In her late Imagist poems, focused on her American local—on Ocean Park, on sand grains, on the sawmills, on the Columbia River Gorge—that drew her work close to the early Imagist poetry of H.D. and the wider American poetry of William Carlos Williams, Barnard achieved "simplicity and sincerity of word . . . and idea," but there was also the issue of "movement" to consider. "Without the freshness of vision, and craftsmanship in the building of metrical and melodic patterns, the poetry might as well be journalism," Barnard had written in her preface to *Cool Country*. If Barnard had sharpened and clarified the subject matter of her "freshness of vision" through her experiments after Pound and Sappho, then these two poets were just as indispensable in her "building of metrical and melodic patterns." However, as we shall now see, the results of her efforts brought her closer, once again, to Williams's grand project for American poetry.

Chapter Four

"A New Way of Measuring Verse"

4.1 Barnard and Pound: An ABC of Metrics

Writing to Pound in 1937, Barnard complained of the difficulty that she had "listening with a Pacific Coast ear to lines written in an English accent"; to her, "most of the English poets in that Faber anthology [*The Faber Book of Modern Verse*] seemed as posed as mannikins [sic]."[1] What was called for was an *American* metric, one that was infinitely flexible and able to accommodate the live speech rhythms of a widely distributed, rapidly growing American population, attentive to the local in all its permutations, indeed "the sound . . . that was native to me"[2]—that is, "an alternative to the commonplace iambic pentameter that she felt did not reflect American speech patterns," as Elizabeth J. Bell, Barnard's literary executor, has explained.[3] As with the free verse—or "vers libre"—that had developed in Europe, where no good verse was really ever "free," as Eliot had said in 1917,[4] American free verse needed a means of governance if it was to achieve a truly native character. As Williams was to write a few months later in *The Poetry Journal*:

> American verse of today must have a certain quality of freedom, must be "free verse" in a sense. It must be new verse, in a new conscious form. But even more than that it must be free in that it is free to include all temperaments, all phases of our environment, physical as well as spiritual, mental and moral. It must be truly democratic, truly free for all—and yet it must be governed.[5]

Williams had no idea, then, of course, that it would take him almost the rest of his life to come up with some workable model nor that he would be hailing a "little-known poet" on "the far, far coast" as the discoverer of "a new way of measuring verse according to the expanded requirements of the age," as Williams congratulated Barnard in a New Year's greeting in 1952.[6] But as with most things in Barnard's career, her "new way" of ensuring American verse would "have a certain quality of freedom" *and* "be governed" all began with the "Pound connection."

Like Pound and his Imagists, Barnard found the rhythms of classical Greek cadences compelling as she began her quest for a "spare but musical" style. In addition to her formal studies, as a young woman she recited Homer and Sappho into the noisy breakers off the Washington coast on her trips to Ocean Park; Greek verses had immediacy for Barnard, a wild, freeing vitality alike in feeling to the Pacific waves that swept up the beach. And yet, also like Pound, Barnard was not immediately converted to free verse. "I liked rhyme and a swinging rhythm,"[7] she said of her early work, having had James Whitcomb Riley's *Child-Rhymes* "humming in my head from my earliest years."[8] She wrote her first poem at the age of seven, entranced by the power of rhyme:

> My first piece of sheet music was a very simple tune with words—a four-line verse. . . . On the back were the first few bars of two or three similar compositions with the accompanying words, which broke off where the music broke off. One was about a robin, a line of verse that presented me with an uncompleted rhyme. I felt no urge to complete the tune, but the line of dangling verse that needed another line as well as a rhyme-word stimulated my imagination. . . . I completed the verse, supplying the rhyme, and found that I had—almost—written a poem. This was better fun than anything I had found yet. I was off to the races.[9]

The "urge to complete the tune" was to come and, with it, a desire for rhythmic structure. In eighth grade, she devoured Esenwein and Roberts's *The Art of Versification*, which she stumbled upon in the school library; here she found "the lovely words 'iamb,' 'trochee,' 'dactyl' for the first time" in a school milieu where "metric was hardly mentioned."[10] In junior high school, she read Harriet Monroe and Alice Corbin Henderson's anthology *The New Poetry*, which modernized Barnard's tastes somewhat but only where a poem yielded that same kind of rhythmic intensity that she had found in Greek verse: "I read Amy Lowell, Edna Millay, the Benets and Elinor Wylie, who was my favorite. I rejected Carl Sandburg and Edgar

Lee Masters because I was looking for music and did not find it in their poems. . . . I liked conventional form, yes, but I wanted more variety, longer lines, more *music*."[11]

Barnard found this variety in Pound, via Lloyd Reynolds's creative writing class at Reed. As well as urging "clearer images," Reynolds had been taking Barnard to task over rhythm, encouraging her to vary line lengths, avoid sing-song rhythms, and drop end-rhymes in an effort to loosen up. But if free verse still seemed to Barnard a little like "chopping up the prose paragraph," it was Reynolds's attention to Pound that really enabled her to hear something else[12]:

> I no longer remember which came first, the day I wrote a poem liberated, at least, from a whalebone corset, or the day when Lloyd wrote out several lines of Pound's poetry on the blackboard, waved his arms about, and proclaimed, "The man who could do that could do anything!" . . . I copied the lines into my notebook, feeling skeptical, yet intrigued. The lines were from "Homage to Sextus Propertius." . . . They bit deep. I returned to Gill's bookstore the copy of the Harriet Monroe anthology that my mother gave me for my birthday, and brought home *Personae* instead. I was beginning to know at last the country I wanted to explore.[13]

She began this new course of exploration with a poem on a Greek theme, "Lethe," among the six she sent to Pound in that hopeful first letter of 1933:

> Above the brink
> Of that lamentable river I shall lean,
> Hesitant, unwilling to drink,
> As I remember there for the last time.
>
> Will a few drops on the tongue,
> Like a whirling flood, submerge cities,
> Like a sea, grind pillars to sand?
> Will it wash the color from the lips and the eyes
> Beloved? It were a thousand pities
> Thus to dissolve
> The delicate sculpture of a lifted hand,
> To fade the dye
> Of the world's color, to quench forever
> The fires of the earth in this river.

The living will forget
More quickly than I,
Dead, lingering with lips unwet
Above Lethe.[14]

Perhaps the poem reminded Pound of H.D.'s early writing, or perhaps he simply liked to see an American writing on Greek themes; nevertheless, in his response, Pound singled out "Lethe" as the best "because there is more IN it."[15] The "whirling flood" that threatens to "submerge cities" might be read as an articulation of the struggle between the two lines of influence that Barnard was interrogating at this time: the "whirling flood" of Greek cadences that she associated with sea waves and a sense of the natural and the "cities" of traditional, European meters, with their sense of rigid architecture and solid design, which she associated with the English "mannikins" of *The Faber Book of Modern Verse*. But also, the "whirling flood" might represent free verse as a whole, its "whirling flood" of lines loosened and unleashed upon the "city" of the poem upheld by "pillars" of convention. The implied fear is that the "whirling flood"—a deviation from the "pillars" of iambic pentameter—will "dissolve" what the poet has made for its lack of control: the "delicate sculpture of a lifted hand," which is the "delicate sculpture" of a poem, created by the poet who sculpts it with the "lifted hand" as pen moves across paper, as hands rise rhythmically over typewriter keys. It is perhaps no coincidence that the opening line invokes the rhythm of the iambic pentameter, brutally cut short, like a crashing pillar; it is a vivid enactment of the Poundian "heave" against the iambic pentameter described in Canto 81.

The reluctance of the speaker with "unwet" lips parallels Barnard's initial reluctance to fully taste the "river" of free verse and "forget" the "cities" of the iambic pentameter. It was one thing to write freely, as she had tried to in "Lethe," but quite another for that freeness to be identifiably rhythmic *and* measurable, for the rhythm to be "whirling" but not so out of control that it would "flood" the poem. The poem's Greek subject matter was perhaps no accident; if it was in Greek cadences that Barnard had experienced a kind of freeness, as she shouted them into the Washington surf, maybe it only seemed right to use a Greek theme to sponsor an exploration into American free verse. Did Greek have something to offer American prosody? Pound certainly thought so, although his concern was with what Greek rhythms could offer modern prosody in general. After all, the Greek Melic poets that Pound admired had used conversational cadences written in the vernacular and composed "in the sequence of the musical phrase," as he and F. S. Flint had wanted for Imagist poetry, to be sung to the accompaniment of a lyre or woodwinds.[16] Along with his praise for "Lethe," Pound's first communication with Barnard enquired curtly, "Rudiments music???" Although she had appreciated the music of the moderns she had encountered in *The New Poetry*, Barnard felt that she herself lacked any practical musical ability. Because Barnard had "never got to first base with music" as a child,[17] Pound's enquiry struck a nerve, and she replied in a letter of November 15, 1933:

> I know what you think about music and poetry, but please, Mr. Pound! Rhythms don't exist in music alone. I am not a musician. I can't so much as carry a tune, although I do like to listen to music. I am interested in dance rhythms—rhythms felt and seen rather than those heard. If it is necessary, I am willing to study music—music rhythms at least, but I can't believe that is necessary. Messing up one art with another is often bad business. Wouldn't a study of Greek rhythms be just as valuable?[18]

Pound agreed—at least, partially. Encouraging that she "dig in DEEPER in greek," he recommended the chapter on the subject of Greek metric in the *Encyclopédie de la Musique* edited by Albert Lavignac and Lionel de la Laurencie.[19] But he did not let Barnard off the hook about the relevance of music. Aware of her interest in Greek, Pound told Barnard to study the duration of different syllables available in English, following the way that classical meters had been derived from similar understanding of the duration, or "quantity," of ancient Greek syllables. As he explained to her,

> Music rots when it gets too far from the dance.
> Poetry when too far from music . . .
> you needn't worry about not having an exact pitch sense
> NOW . . . but as you go on, IF you go on, it is bound to grow,
> though you can't actually write it down in words.
> Besides the difficulty in WRITING mu-
> sic is in the RHYTHM NOT in pitch . . . any-
> body can tap a pyanny till they find the pitch
> they want. The question of the DURATION of
> the note, is another job altogether . . .
> [. . .]
> Get a metronome and learn HOW long the different syllables,
> and groups of them take.
> and don't go telling everybody I said so/
> I don't want the NEXT "movement" smeared over by
> Lowells and people who WON'T work.
> at least not until we have been at it ten years.[20]

The "people who WON'T work" was a swipe at the modern western tradition, which, Pound felt, had put up a stubborn but lazy resistance to the idea that quantity had a part to play in the rhythm of English language poetry. As his Imagist movement was gathering pace in 1913, Pound emphatically appealed for a revision in opinion, speculating in his essay "The Tradition" that it was not entirely illogical to apply Greek quantitative rules to poetic language in English vernaculars: "As to quantity, it is foolish to suppose that we [in the modern western tradition] are incapable of distinguishing a long vowel from a short one, or that we are mentally debarred from ascertaining how many consonants intervene between one vowel and the next."[21]

But his appeal fell on deaf ears, and it was Barnard who he entrusted to see the task through, to not "go telling everybody I said so" but to quietly "learn HOW long the different syllables." Like the lines from "Homage to Sextus Propertius," Pound's words bit deep with Barnard, who eagerly replied that she was converted to the idea of studying music and immediately set about reading Pound's *Instigations* (1920) and *Pavannes and Divisions* (1918). She had more difficulty, however, in locating the Laurencie and Lavignac encyclopedia to further her knowledge of Greek metric. Relying instead upon her knowledge of Homer and Sappho, Barnard responded to Pound's advice to "dig in DEEPER in greek" by offering him a poem based upon her own understanding of Sapphics, which she felt, perhaps naïvely, as a "Would-Be Sappho," that she could do with some kind of ease. Enclosed with her letter of January 2, 1934, was "an exercise of the kind that I can do 'now and any time,' and I want to know if you think that kind of exercise is profitable."[22] That exercise was "Lai," reproduced here as it came to be published in *Poetry* a year later:

> Nothing availed then in the starless darkness with the sea
> giving a gray light.
> Nothing availed then either by sea or by land
> For the boats were filled with a shallow and unlit water,
> their sails riven.
> But her hands spread upon the bolt of the door refused to
> believe,
> And the waves spoke for her since she had no voice.
>
> I said, striving with her, "He is long since dead.
> I have seen the queens who ride fast along dark roads
> Bearing death upon their lips and love upon the palms of
> their hands.
> I know they now have left the mired ways and the chan-
> nelled meadows.

Where blue roads echo under the stripped, high-singing
trees, tower-ward they bear him.
In the yellow tideland, shallow water laps unheard."

But she shook her head and the waves spoke for her as
they do still,
Sighing a furtive song in the spread foam
While the troubled stones of the beach turn in my heart.[23]

"Lai" demonstrates both the possibilities and the difficulties of translating Sapphics wholesale into English, as Pound was quick to recognize in his response of January 22, 1934: "LAI starts with something nearly a bad Sapphic line." Trying to scan Barnard as Pound might have done, I scan the first line of "Lai" below, distinguishing between syllables that appear "long" (–) and those that appear "short" (◡), with due respect to vowel length and consonant loads as per the rules formulated by classical metrical theorists[24]:

◡ – ◡ – ◡ ◡ ◡ – ◡ – ◡ ◡ ◡ –
Nothing availed then in the starless darkness with the sea
– – ◡ –
giving a gray light.[25]

If one omits the phrase "with the sea," the line approximates the pattern of longs to shorts conventional in the sixteen-syllable greater Sapphic line, with six out of the remaining sixteen syllables deviating from the norm, mostly at the start of the line[26]:

◡ – ◡ – ◡ ◡ ◡ – ◡ – ◡
Nothing availed then in the starless darkness [with the sea]
– – ◡ – –
giving a gray light.

As Pound had found in his well-known attempt at Sapphics in 1912, "Apparuit," Barnard's extra syllables give relief against the heaviness of the long line, providing a means of offsetting the stiltedness familiar to many translators attempting Sapphics in English. This in itself was not enough. "If you really learn to write proper quantitative sapphics in the amurikan langwidge I shall love and adore you all the days of my life . . . provided you don't fill 'em with trype," Pound chided. It is not difficult to see why he cared little for the "trype" of the poem's contents; woven from different cultural strands, with the Sapphics giving it a Greek quality, the title an Eastern quality, and the narrative evoking a "faerie" landscape, with the "queens who ride fast along dark roads / bearing death on their lips" investing the poem with a mysterious, otherworldly feel, "Lai" is a mixed-up poem, unsure of the tradition it is rising out of and unsure of where it wants to go—and certainly not written in the kind of live, modern American idiom of the "amurikan langwidge" that Barnard was seeking. The repeated phrase "Nothing availed then," for example, is rather awkward and seemingly unnatural sounding, although not ungrammatical, and the speaker's reported speech is altogether estranged in tone and syntax order—these are lines perhaps too uncomfortably close to the "posed" stiffness of the English "mannikin" poets that Barnard was determined to avoid. "Lai" is not distinctively American or sufficiently bold and singular in character in any way, qualities reflected by the poem's vague, flat landscapes deprived of light, where the "starless darkness" and "unlit water" allow for only the most nondescript geographies of lands of "dark" and "blue" roads curbed by "yellow tideland" to emerge.

Pound urged Barnard to keep up the experimentation, however, and she did not let him down; over the course of 1934–1935, she worked on several more Sapphic exercises that worked with sense as well as sound.[27] Of note is how *American* these exercises strove to be, utilizing the local for content; how *modern* they attempted to be; and how, all the while, they derived a *musical rhythm* based upon contemporary speech cadences. One untitled exercise concerns a "creek," one of many surrounding the Columbia River Gorge that dominated Barnard's local, usurping the faery landscape of "Lai," with its unplaceable "mired ways" and "channelled meadows" with an observed "wide, thin road-bed of water."[28] Another exercise, "Departure," retells the mythical story of Aphrodite's emergence from the sea clad in foam; yet unlike, say, the vague depictions of an anonymous beach that pervades early allusive poems such as "The Invitation" and "The Fool's Serenade," the imagery of "Departure" acerbically evokes the treacherous Washington seacoast, drawing on its "ravelled breakers," its "rough" foam and "fog-hooded sound" that combine in the poem to feed the image of a typical Washington coastal "storm of light and motion upon the sea's face." The third exercise, self-consciously entitled "A Defence of the Poet's Method," was inspired by Multnomah Falls, one of the largest natural falls in the Northwest, cut into the steep, Oregon side of the Columbia River Gorge. Here, water pours over rock into two pools of differing heights:

> Where the unfractured water at the cliff's verge
> Bent a lucid shoulder above the canyon,
> Where the mist arose in a plume above the
>   Stream's disappearing—

Even in the act of abandoning its
High ravines it grasped at a lyric instant,
Caught it in the white cannonade, spun it half
  Obliterated

In shattered pools, not yet aware of its form
Nor of its full significance, till in still
Pools below, a smoky image split into
  Mist; a remembrance.[29]

The awkward speech rhythms of "Lai" are replaced in these Sapphic exercises with plausible, live speech rhythms; indeed, perhaps the "method" Barnard is defending in this latter poem is the way in which she allowed the "stream" of the Sapphic lines she studied to somehow wash over the "cliff" / the "canyon" / the "ravine" (indeed, the "naked rock") of her poetry so that a "lyric instant," what Williams had called "new verse, in a new conscious form," could be "spun." Compared to Pound's "Apparuit," Barnard's exercises in Sapphics carry off modern idiom with a little more consistency and vigor than Pound's effort, with its archaic sprinklings of "thou," "thee," "thine," "afar," "hast," and so on.[30] They are marked by a tendency to allow whole sentences to run the full course of a stanza or, in the case of "A Defence of the Poet's Method," over the entire poem, having the same "one-sentenceness" about them as Wallace Stevens's "The Snow Man" or Williams's "The Great Figure."

But there were problems, as Barnard suggests in the final stanza: walking such tightropes between "faithful" renditions of Sapphics, with respect to syllable counts, and American vernacular did not, in itself, promise a substantial new kind of form; there was still a "ravine" of difference between classical Greek and the modern "amurikan langwidge." With her letter of April 20, 1935, Barnard sent Pound "some more imperfect Sapphics" and a complaint:

> This time I have tried writing for sound and letting the sense take care of itself. Dr. Williams said I had a "facility" for the form. I wish I did, since I have to write Sapphics, but anybody who had to work harder than I do wouldn't write them.[31]

Yet Pound continued to crack the whip:

> O/K/ keep at it till you get *your* basic . . . I simply do not KNOW enough about question of quantity, I mean use IN English of greek supposed "rule" . . . keep *trying* TOWARD

> the solution // can we in eng / observe the measurements, short = short vowel and ONLY one consonant before the next vowel. Can it be done without paralyzing the speech altogether.[32]

Pound advised Barnard to write to W. H. D. Rouse, who had edited the *Classical Review*, in which the Imagists had read of the Sappho finds at Oxyrhynchus. Barnard promptly fired off a letter to the Cambridge schoolmaster, enclosing some of her Sapphic exercises. Rouse's reply confirmed her doubts:

> Rouse found some of my lines rather good, but seemed to feel that I was attempting the impossible. He feared it was too late to Anglicize classical rhythms. "Chaucer might have done it, but hardly anyone since." [Longfellow's] *Evangeline*, he said, was "truly awful, not only the gabble, but the monotony."[33]

Just as Pound had complained in "The Tradition," Rouse was all too aware of the crudeness applied to the distinctions made between stress and quantity over the centuries, or so some notes marked "Rouse," typed up in Barnard's typewriter (and, with their frequent address to "you," read as if they are a transcript of a letter to her), indicate:

> The Greeks did hear both quantity and accent, but the accent was not stress like ours; it was a musical tone, like a recitative. As soon as the tone changed to a stress (early in the Christian era) the quantities were compressed as they are today. . . . Dionysius on Literary Composition tells us all about accent. This had no effect on rhythm at all (as stress always has).[34]

Also like Pound, Rouse suggested that if she was interested in the relevance of Greek quantity to modern poetry, then she really had better study music—English madrigals, for instance. All this Barnard communicated back to Pound in the summer of 1935 but with a hunch as to how she might break the deadlock:

> I am always trying toward quantitative Sapphics, but as near as I can make out, there simply aren't enough short syllables in the English language as it is written. If we pronounced the final "ed's" of the past tense, or wrote in your epistolary style (dropping the final "g" of the participle) there would be some hope. I seem to be working with different kinds of

> long syllables instead of long and short ones. Shall we reform the language?[35]

4.2 The Weighted Syllable

This "different [kind] of long syllable" that she had found herself working with was one that took account of both quantity and accent; in time she called it the "weighted syllable." The only public comment that Barnard made regarding the weighted syllable appeared in an essay published in 1994 on her approach to translating Sappho in the early 1950s:

> I had given up trying to do strictly quantitative meters, though I took quantity into account. I thought of a long syllable rather as a weighted syllable, weighted with a long vowel, a cluster of consonants, a stress, or an emphasis dependent on sense, a conversational emphasis. A "long" might be one of these or a combination of two or three.[36]

Yet clearly she was thinking along these lines as early as the 1930s, as she strove to apprehend the "form" emerging in her Sapphic exercises. Where these exercises appeared to deviate from the "greek supposed 'rule,'" this may have been because she was selecting syllables on the basis of their weight, as she sensed it, rather than strictly on the basis of their quantity, as determined by classical rules. Consider a stanza from "Commerce," where I have marked the deviations with brackets:

– [–] – [∪] ∪ ∪ ∪ – ∪ – –
All my wealth comes here to the harbor wharves, and
[∪] ∪ – ∪ [∪] ∪ ∪ – ∪ – [∪]
Rich am I, but ominous days appear when
– [–] – – – ∪ ∪ – ∪ – –
Unseen cargoes darken the streets with anguish;
– [– –] – –
Dearly I bargain.[37]

These deviations may not really be that errant if each syllable is examined for its relative weight. "Rich" is technically a short syllable according to classical rules, consisting of a short vowel followed by a consonant load that can feasibly begin a new word. Yet Barnard uses "rich" where conventional Sapphics demand a long syllable. With its consonant cluster at the end and the "conversational emphasis" that the syllable gains from its place in the stanza, I think Barnard is using "rich" as a "weighted syllable," as a "different [kind] of long [syllable]." There is a similar principle at work in "my," the second "I," and the second syllable of "dearly," each of which occupies the place of a short syllable in conventional Sapphics. Although these may be long syllables according to the classical rules, they are markedly lighter in emphasis in the kind of American vernacular presented here. Thus Barnard uses these lighter syllables where a poem in classic Greek would use shorts; they provide a contrasting quality against the heavy syllables necessary to inject the stanza with musical rhythm.

Rouse had perhaps pointed the way. Barnard's typescript for the notes marked "Rouse" continue thus, in a distinct schoolmasterly tone:

> But there is a variety of stress often within the [hexameter] line. No one has worked this out; all you can say is that the dramatic iambics and trochaics have the natural speech cadence in which stress was important, and had exactly the same effect as in English and every where [sic] of shortening longs before and after. (The common speech was less careful of quantity than the educated speech.) Thus the common phrase "my darling" is spoken with different quantity according to the order of the words,
>
> ◡◡ ◡/–◡
> mea voluptas
> but
> ◡◡ – / ◡◡
> voluptas mea[38]

It was no less than what Pound had set Barnard out to find in the first place: "There aren't any RULES/ thing is to cut a shape in time"[39]; that is, Pound recognized that rule deviation was a necessary sacrifice if the "shape in time" was to be effectively "cut." And so Sapphic cadences woven from weighted syllables, as a means of enabling the "shape" to have musical rhythm, thus began to creep into Barnard's free verse—shaping the line, rather than the stanza, as Victor Chittick came to observe of her later Sappho translation ("Take the matter of Sapphics. . . . My text-book definition makes them appear as a *stanzaic* form, a whole stanza. You speak of putting them into a line, as though they were feet, or some metrical unit"[40]). So "Faun in Exile," from 1935, expresses a distinct musical rhythm that unexpectedly invigorates the parallelisms at its center (syllables are marked in terms of their relative weight, as Barnard may have intended):

> [– ◡ ◡ –]
> Here were no grapes,

[–] – ᴗ – ᴗ [– ᴗ ᴗ –]
But bitter berries grew in the marsh.
[– ᴗ ᴗ –]
Here was no moss,
[–] – – [– ᴗ ᴗ –]
But sea-worn logs and the harsh
[– ᴗ ᴗ – –]
Grass on the dune top.[41]

Like Pound's "The Return," this section is almost entirely constructed out of strings of the Adonic colon (– ᴗ ᴗ – –), a signature of the Sapphic form placed in brackets above; they overlap within the line, as well as across the line, but do not demand that Barnard make a "full stanza" in Sapphics for them to round off, as Adonic colons do in the "textbook" definitions of the form. Interesting, too, that the Greek cadence is inscribed in a poem depicting the Washington seashore where Barnard first uttered Greek poetry into the ocean, as if to solder the connection between Greek cadences and the compelling rhythm of the "river" and the "stream" that is revered in both "Lethe" and "A Defence of the Poet's Method." But it is also an attempt to get at the character of direct speech. As Barnard later set out in *Assault on Mount Helicon*, describing the method she took when preparing her Sappho translation, in such approximations she was looking for "an equivalent" to the speaking voice:

> I made no attempt to translate into the original meter. Greek normally has more syllables than English. I have never been able to see any way of rendering a Greek stanza in the equivalent number of English syllables without padding. . . . Underlying the stanzaic form there is, I swear (in the teeth of those who have said otherwise) a cadence that belongs to the speaking voice. That underlying cadence is what I have tried to find an equivalent for, because, so far as I knew, no English translation had yet conveyed it.[42]

Barnard cut other "shape[s] in time" from related Greek meters, finding further "equivalent" cadences. After considerable difficulty in tracking down the Laurencie and Lavignac encyclopedia, Pound mailed the relevant sections to Barnard in February 1935. "Having learned about dactyls and spondees [in high school] I had supposed this was all. Now I discovered that there were glyconics, epitrites, Aeolian tripodies" (all members of the Aeolic class of meters, which includes Sapphics), Barnard reflected in her memoir, adding "at the same time, it occurred to me that the free verse poets whose rhythms I admired were people who knew Greek: Pound, Eliot, H.D. Could there be a connection?"[43] Her suspicions were confirmed when she scanned selections from *The Cantos*, as these scansions from her notebooks confirm[44]:

> Hear me, Cadmus of Golden Prows!
> – – / – ᴗ ᴗ/ – ᴗ – /[Glyconic line]45
>
> Peerless among the pairs
>
> – ᴗ ᴗ – ᴗ – [Aeolian tripodies]
>
> And the vinestocks lie untended
>
> ᴗ ᴗ – – /– ᴗ– ᴗ [Two epitrites]46

How far Pound was himself aware of what he was doing here is anyone's guess, but as his letters to Barnard show, he was somehow in tune with Melic rhythm and, by turns, in tune with Barnard, whose appropriation of such meters soon became evident in her own poems, enabled by weighted syllables. These Aeolic forms (placed in brackets above) glide so effortlessly over the utterance that they sound like choice scraps from conversation. Consider these two excerpts from "The Rapids" and "Playroom":

> [– – – ᴗ ᴗ – ᴗ –] ᴗ [Glyconic]
> No country is so gracious to us
> [ᴗ ᴗ – – ᴗ – ᴗ –] [Two epitrites, with variation]
> As that which kept its contours while we forgot them,[47]
>
> [– ᴗ ᴗ – ᴗ –] ᴗ [Aeolian tripodies]
> Hearing them, no one could tell
> Why they sing sadly,[48]

But although Barnard made a conscious effort to experiment with a range of Greek meters, it was the Sapphic cadence that appealed the most, particularly the four-beat balance of the Adonic colon. "Keep at it until you get *your* basic," Pound had advised; it appeared in Sapphics that Barnard had found just that, a basic sound that could be relied upon to carry off the line and deliver, as Pound had encouraged would-be Imagists, a certain "residue of sound"[49] that would make distinctive the "shape in time." Pound had helped Barnard get going with free verse as she labored alone in Vancouver between 1933 and 1935, tutoring her in what David Gordon called "An ABC of Metrics,"[50] so when she sailed into New York harbor in the spring of 1936, the time was ripe for her path to converge with that of Williams, who was also hung up on cutting shapes in time for an American audience.

4.3 "A Well-Conceived Form within which Modification May Exist": Barnard, Williams, and the Question of American Measure

If Barnard had found, in Aeolic meters, cadences whose rhythms were in some way commensurate with American idiom, then she was still left with the problem of measure. It was one thing to find cadences that sounded right to Barnard's "Pacific Coast ear" and devise a means of registering the "shape" of these cadences through the "weighted syllable" but another matter entirely to have a reliable means of measuring spoken cadences so that the shapes could be set in time, over and over, as the poet willed. At the time that Barnard was swapping the "whalebone corset" for the "whirling flood" of Poundian free verse, Williams was lamenting to Kay Boyle in 1932 that "there is no workable poetic form extant among us today."[51] He wanted, like Barnard, to capture the sound of the American speaking voice ("Speech is the fountain of the line," he told Boyle), and he too felt that an American measure should relate to music and be sufficiently flexible to accommodate the new variables of speech as spoken by the "yawping [American] speakers of a new language," taking special account of time and "the duration of the note"[52]:

> The line must, as a minimum, have a well-conceived form within which modification may exist. Without this internal play upon the stops, it cannot achieve power. . . . It seems to be that the "foot" being at the bottom of all prosody, the time has come when that must be recognized to have changed in nature. And it must be seen to have changed in its rhythmical powers of inclusion. It cannot be used any longer in its old-time rigidities. Speech for poetry is nothing but time—I mean time in the musical sense.[53]

Barnard was aware of Williams's efforts and concurred with his sentiments, but she felt that she, personally, was in want of a different approach:

> I admired the poetry of William Carlos Williams, and approved his endeavor to find an American metric, but I did not feel that he had found the solution, or at any rate, not the solution that would work for me. I did not really expect to find what I was looking for in Greek metric, but I found in the Lavignac something that struck me as a possible answer to my problem.[54]

Besides its exposition of the wide range of Greek meters, the *Encyclopédie de la Musique* furnished Barnard with a solution to her difficulties by way of the musical principle of balance, which, she realized, governed Greek dimeters, or lines of two measures, as well as musical bars:

> I was interested in certain lines, dimeters in which the longs and shorts constantly varied in position, but *balanced.* The Greek text was not given, only the analysis of the rhythm. One was headed, "*Air de l'anonyme*" and went like this:
>
> ᴗ – – / – ᴗ –
> ᴗ – – / ᴗ ᴗ ᴗ –
> – ᴗ ᴗ – / ᴗ / –[55]

Could this means of counting be done in American verse? Barnard found that it could if she counted *weighted syllables*, finding examples in Pound's work:

> I found that Pound's line, "Eyes, lips, dreams, and the night goes," scanned by T. S. Eliot as a spondee, a dactyl, and another spondee, really made better sense as a balanced line:
>
> Eyes, lips, dreams, and the night goes
> – – – / ᴗ ᴗ – –[56]

And so Barnard began experimenting with the "balanced line" in poems like "The Silk Leaf" (1936), where she attempted to balance the number of weighted syllables from line to line. Consider the opening of the poem, marked with my scansions:

> ᴗ – ᴗ – ᴗ ᴗ / – ᴗ ᴗ – –
> The silly foliage dandled in light winds
>
> ᴗ – ᴗ / – –
> Has made my head light.[57]

In the "dimeter" of line one, eleven syllables of varying weights divide into two measures at an approximate midway point. In the first measure, two weighted syllables and four lighter syllables add up to an overall duration of four weighted or long notes, working on the Greek principle that two shorts equal one long. This is perfectly balanced by the second measure, where three weighted syllables and two lighter syllables also add up to an overall duration of four weighted or long notes. What such practice affords is a flow of rhythms that are simultaneously variable yet regulated, as spontaneous in feel as live speech, yet sufficiently arranged into a rhythmic order like bars in music, enabling the linguistic arrangement to assume a form in time. Indeed, even before Barnard had come across the principle of balance in the *Encyclopédie de la Musique*, she was already moving some way toward it—even the opening lines of "Lethe" approximate dimetrical rhythms:

> ᴗ – / ᴗ –
> Above / the brink
> ᴗ ᴗ – ᴗ – ᴗ / – ᴗ – ᴗ –
> Of that lamentable / river I shall lean,
> – ᴗ – ᴗ / – ᴗ ᴗ –
> Hesitant, un / willing to drink,
> ᴗ – ᴗ – ᴗ / – ᴗ ᴗ – –
> As I remember / there for the last time.[58]

Yet Williams had a vital role to play, following on almost causally from Pound's. Among the first poems Barnard sent him were two versions of "Commerce," one in Sapphics and one not. The Sapphics, Williams thought, were "interesting" and "curious," he told her in a letter of March 19, 1935, but ultimately limited. "Perhaps the form is suited to a woman. There is an order which becomes passion in a woman, something which Sappho has typified. It seems as I write to be the opposite of Walt Whitman's Song of Myself which may be man at his worst—but most typical," Williams speculated, a little dismissively.[59] The other version of "Commerce," however, was more promising:

> The free version of the Commerce thing is not "better" but easier for us to feel today than the more studied version which is just something else. I like them both. I think you have taken advantage to the full of both methods and that the looser variation shows your virtuosity to better advantage than the other.[60]

If Pound had provided the "strict exercise" required before "loopin' the loop," as he told Barnard in a letter of December 18, 1934,[61] then it was Williams who tempted Barnard onto the rollercoaster of freer writing as he pushed her to write more intimately of her local. This, he believed, would enable her to write more genuinely as an American, the "free version of the Commerce thing" being "easier for us to feel today," one supposes, because its "looser variation" reflects the "new language" of the "yawping speakers" he was so concerned to represent in poetry. Signaling her agreement, Barnard wrote a poem so concerned with connection to place that she called it "Roots," published in *Townsman* in October 1938. But, intriguingly, this was no departure from her Greek project, for "Roots" shows Barnard blending her study of Greek rhythms and rules of measurement under Pound with Williams's appeal for American specifics in "looser" form:

Roots

[–   ᴗ   ᴗ / –   –] [Adonic colon]
Rain on the / windshield,
  –   [– ᴗ / ᴗ   –   –]
Roads spongy / with sawdust [Adonic colon]
ᴗ   –   / ᴗ ᴗ –
Have meant / in the end
ᴗ –   ᴗ ᴗ –   ᴗ / –   –ᴗ ᴗ –ᴗ
A love of a place that / grows into the body.
  –   –   ᴗ   –   – / ᴗ – ᴗ   –   –
Blood should be clear am / ber under tree bark.

[– ᴗ   ᴗ   –   / ᴗ] ᴗ   – [Aeolian tripodies]
Lacking that, there / are the roads
ᴗ – ᴗ – / – – ᴗ
Extending like / root tendrils
[– ᴗ ᴗ – / ᴗ] ᴗ – ᴗ [Aeolian tripodies]
Under the ang / les of mountains,
[–   –   –   ᴗ ᴗ / –]   –   ᴗ – – [Glyconic form]
Rain sharpening on the / windshield at evening.[62]

"Roots" can be read as a reflection of the process of cutting a shape in time as the poet assesses rhythm and makes adjustments as the line is set among other lines. The line is a "root" to which, like childhood memories, the poet keeps going back. The line is also a "road," with an observable shape, an idea buttressed by images that point to beginnings ("roads / Extending") and endings (the closure of the day in "evening") and suggest that there are parameters, that growth takes place within a holding framework under "the angles of mountains" that hem the tendril-like roads into the landscape. The "angles"—units of measurement—are direct metaphors for Barnard's measure, keeping check over the terrain of the poem. All the while, the road, like Barnard's balanced line, is variable in surface yet sufficiently regular to allow balanced movement across it—a visual metaphor for the "well-conceived form within which modification may exist," as Williams had told Boyle—as well, of course, as another example of how Barnard's experience of the physical world shaped her poetics, the spongy northwestern "road" directing the metrical shape of the poem in much the same way as do the sawmills or Washington shore.

Whereas Barnard developed the balanced line as a means of governing her free verse, Williams put forward the "variable foot" as a means of governing his. Although different in name, their measures worked to similar principles; they sought a single, reliable rule for counting free verse "shape[s] in time." Williams's concept of the variable foot crystallized when he was writing *Paterson* in the 1940s, although it is clear from his early poems that he had experimented with the measure before he was conscious of it, just as Barnard had with her balanced line. Characterized by a triadic, step-down line that Williams perfected in late poems like "The Descent" and "Asphodel, That Greeny Flower," Williams treated each line as a single foot, its end coincident with the pause in breath that Williams claimed dictated his line divisions. "The lines must be capable of being counted," Williams explained to the poet Richard Eberhart, giving as an example the following lines and placing a number before each line or "foot":

(1) The smell of the heat is boxwood
    (2) when rousing us
        (3) a movement of the air
(4) stirs our thoughts
    (5) that had no life in them
        (6) to a life, a life in which[63]

The way to count this kind of verse, Williams told Eberhart, was by counting each line as it appeared in the overall rhythmic shape. "Count a single beat to each numeral. You may not agree with my ear, but that is the way I count the line. Over the whole poem it gives a pattern to the meter that can be felt as a new measure," Williams explained.[64] So whereas Barnard's lines were balanced with attention to the weighted *syllable* and how it moved in time, Williams's lines were balanced with attention to the *line* and how that moved in time. Both were after a set of rhythmic shapes of equal duration: Barnard achieved this *within* the line, so that each line divided into dimeters (or two measures) that had roughly the same length; Williams achieved this *between* lines, each stepped line approximating the length of the one that preceded it.

Between them, then, Barnard and Williams worked almost simultaneously at the formulation of a truly distinctive brand of American free verse. Their "new way of measuring verse according to the expanded requirements of the age," as Williams put it, more than fulfilled the criteria that fellow American Amy Lowell had set out for the Anglo-Americanization of "vers libre" back in 1914. Writing in the preface of her collection *Sword Blades and Poppy Seed*, Lowell explained just how crucial balance and time were to the process, foreshadowing the ways in which Barnard and Williams would work out the details of their respective measures:

> Many of the poems in this volume are written in what the French call "vers libre," a nomenclature more suited to the French use and to French versification than ours. I prefer to call them poems in "unrhymed cadence," for that conveys their exact meaning to an English ear. They are built upon "organic rhythm," or the rhythm of the speaking voice with its necessity for breathing, rather than upon a strict metrical system. . . . These poems, built upon cadence, are more subtle, but the laws they follow are not less fixed. Merely chopping prose lines into lengths does not produce cadence, it is constructed upon mathematical and absolute laws of balance and time.[65]

Neither Barnard nor Williams employed a "strict metrical system"—although Barnard did try with Sapphics—but they both formed idiosyncratic "fixed" counting systems based upon the "laws of balance and time" that came about through the attention they paid to "the rhythm of the speaking voice with its necessity for breathing." Perhaps such deviation in method, but not in principle, was to be expected, given that both poets favored a measure made for a variable national language—Williams and his "yawping speakers" in New Jersey, Barnard and her "yawping speakers" among the skunk cabbages and swamps in the Northwest—for a strong element of intuition and feel for the "amurikan langwidge" informed them. Williams denied ever consciously counting when in the process of composition; instead, he claimed that measurable lines were the result of a semiconscious sense of the line's rhythmic shape as a spoken utterance, as he further explained to Richard Eberhart: "not that I ever count when writing but . . . I may, half-consciously . . . count the measure under my breath as I write,"[66] echoing Lowell's observation of the character of vers libre. Barnard's work with Sapphics may have exhausted her, but it gave her a solid command of how time affected the American utterance as she heard it. "I don't think I have composed any good Sapphics in my sleep," Barnard declared to Pound after a couple of years of "chawin'" at Sapphics, "but I have got to the place where I measure off the quantities of words spoken in my dreams."[67] And this kind of instinct for rhythm was to serve her well; she was mindful, as she wrote much later, that "metric is a very slippery subject. I often wonder whether I am doing what I think I am doing."[68]

As Barnard further explored the "roots" of her local, metrics and the external world came to complement, indeed, nurture one another, much as Imagist techniques, sawmills, and shorelines had seemed natural bedfellows—American poetic forms lay in American physical forms, "physical" in the very broadest of senses (geographical, social, linguistic, and so on). It had been much the same for Williams. "How do we know reality?" Williams had rhetorically asked in a lecture given at the University of Washington in 1948. "The only reality that we can know is MEASURE," he answered.[69] In Barnard's "Road to Xanadu," submitted, unsuccessfully, via the "Pound connection" to *Furioso* in 1939, she takes another road as a metaphor for her practice. The road of the poetic imagination, she implies, is one that takes in the local and its models of time:

> The pea pods are cool, firm,
> And easily popped under the thumb;
> The naked peas roll into the pan.
>
> On the backsteps the sun
> Comes crimson between low branches.
> Taps of clothespins back of the lilacs.
> Crunch of gravel at the garage door. Evening.
>
> (And it happens—the sudden
> Freshening of spring water over
> Dry stones from a source in shadow
> The bright-tongued water spilling
> Its syllables, I chosen, hushed channel to
> Its extravagance—)
> Peas dropping
> Make a small evening sound.
> The clouds flush slowly.[70]

Images of food and music operate in concentrated tandem. Peas are "popped" like a percussion instrument, in anticipation of the clothespins that "tap," building up a gentle music highlighted in the closing image of dropping peas that "make a small evening sound." Meals, music—both are the products of time-orchestrated movements, a motif enhanced by the local weather imagery that drapes the scene: "On the backsteps the sun / Comes crimson," which is later replaced by "the clouds flush slowly."

Intriguingly, there is no explicit "road" in this poem; there is the "crunch of gravel," a metonym for the road, but any visible "road to Xanadu" is markedly absent. As such, Barnard suggests that the imagination is in the immediate environment: the road "out" is irrelevant, because the imagination begins "at the garage door," at "the backsteps," in the most local of spaces—the grounds of one's house. This is perhaps where the purest kind of "contact" with local materials, as Williams advocated, following Whitman, is to be had, in the minor everyday details of "clothespins" tapping out a "small . . . sound" at the "back of the lilacs" in a backyard. Such "contact," the poem reasons, triggers an energy that rejuvenates—here, the "sudden / Freshening of spring water over / Dry stones," coming from a "source in shadow," the poet, perhaps, effacing herself in favor of the land, which trumps all.

It is perhaps a small coincidence that both Barnard and Williams use images of spring and river water to plot a common poetic course that draws on the textures of the American terrain like water flowing over rocks. Just as Williams's Dr. Paterson draws "substance from the noise of the pouring river" in book 1 of *Paterson*[71]—under conception, in Williams's mind, around the same time Barnard was writing "Road to Xanadu"—so does Barnard's "I chosen" derive power from channeling "the bright-tongued water spilling / Its syllables," transforming the syllables of spring water emitted from American land into poetry. Barnard thus makes poetry from the "stuff" of the land, believing that her land is the provider of all the sound and substance that she needs as material for poetry. In the "Creed" that she had written as a preface to her college thesis, Barnard declared: "I BELIEVE in the sound of the words. By that I mean words that sound as if they grew together, although they may be common and not particularly beautiful in themselves."[72]

This interaction between time, place and poem is evident in "Dick," one of the poems that Williams admired in *A Few Poems*. Images of food are again at the forefront, alongside images of cultivation:

Dick

In the morning, early, sitting
Eating our loaves on weedgrown milestones
At the edge of the city, we hear the bells
Swinging, challenging the attentive air.

The four-leaved pattern of a quarter hour
Unfolds its conundrum; oh what
Will the day bring? What, when the bells
Ring evening, will we remember?
Of hours and quarter hours, which
Will be honey-tongued? Which echo
In the stroke of all hours forever?

At twilight the sphinx in the bell tower
Answers her riddle, ringing: Remember?
Remember wondering: oh what will the day bring?[73]

Barnard said in a radio interview in 1975 that "Dick" was inspired by the central courtyard at the University of Buffalo where she had worked as

Poetry Curator in the early 1940s, but in many ways it had its roots in the Northwest landscape poems she began writing in the 1930s. In the images of "weedgrown milestones" and "the four-leaved pattern of a quarter hour" (a reference to the shadow cast by a clock overlooking the university courtyard), Barnard synthesizes measures of time and space with local vegetation. This makes for a larger metaphor, which suggests that the "measures" of her poetry are both rhythmic (they have "pattern," like the clover) and also rough and variable (they are "weedgrown"). "Weedgrown" is particularly apt, conveying a desire for a measure that, like weeds, is "native," eternally sprung from the local earth just as weeds push through the same ground year upon year.

By the time Barnard came to print "Dick" in 1952, her American free verse line had considerably matured. She may have begun working with quantity some twenty years after Pound and may have seized the American local as a resource for measure some time after Williams, but by the early 1950s it appeared that she had made up some of the experimental distance between her and her mentors. The education supplied by the chapter on Greek metric from the *Encyclopédie de la Musique* had been pivotal to her innovations. Pound claimed that he had never really studied the chapter he had recommended—"I don't know how much real use it wd / be," he had commented in a postcard to Barnard in 1934, confessing "I have never worked on it / or with it / but it contains intelligent remarks."[74] But Barnard did work on it and was quickly rewarded; much of her poetry in the 1930s and 1940s could be seen to be working successfully with Greek cadences and principles of balance, even if Barnard did not feel fully confident of her technique until she came to compile *A Few Poems*. It was then that Williams declared that Barnard's poetry signaled a breakthrough for American free verse. It was, he told her in his letter of December 31, 1952, an example of "what we have been about all these years":

> These poems in A FEW POEMS are distinguished, by far the best you have ever done. I was thrilled at reading them . . .
>
> It is all there; the new is all there. I have only this to say. Not yet has it been recognized for what it is: a recognition that what we have been about for all these years is a change from, away from, accented verse to a verse that takes as its unit elapsed time. When this is recognized, all the experiments in free verse, such beautiful verses as your present ones with their regularity, will be recognized for what they are: a new way of measuring verse according to the expanded requirements of the age.
>
> But we require, what free verse has never had, regularity. Without a means of MEASURING THE MEASURE, we

> are lost. I have found one means of measuring the measure which may not be satisfactory to you but which if worked with can serve.[75]

"What we have been about for all these years" was no casual statement; for Williams, Barnard had steered a mean course between himself and Pound, incorporating their instructions into a path that was as much her own as it was identifiably American and modernist. Williams might not have liked Pound's deference to the classics, but he appreciated the effort toward musical rhythm that classical meters had perfected. Indeed, perhaps Barnard had something to do with this, for in 1948 Williams's contempt for classical adaptation appeared to have mellowed:

> It is next to impossible to bring over the quantitative Greek and Latin texts into our language. But does anyone ever ask *why* a Latin line in translation tends to break in half in our language? *Why* it cannot be maintained in its character, its quantitative character as against our accented verse? Have *all* the equivalents been exhausted or even tried? I doubt it.[76]

Williams himself went on to publicize his "means of measuring the measure"—the variable foot—in various essays, perhaps most emphatically in "On Measure: Statement for Cid Corman" in 1954. However, Barnard is strangely absent in name from his essays, despite their obvious common ground and the praise he heaped upon her. Perhaps he was a little *too* indebted to her, or feared that Barnard might steal his thunder. After all, under the heading "W.C.W" in her notes for her memoir, Barnard had written, "The paragraph on poetic rhythm + the musical ear—taken from my conversation,"[77] almost certainly referring to Williams's paragraph on the musician's ear in his statement for Cid Corman.[78] All this suggests that there was some polite rivalry on the subject, although Barnard did not publish her feelings on the perceived slight. Or perhaps Williams could not quite reconcile Barnard's classical influences to his idea of what American poetry should be, even though both poets were really after the same things. Reflecting upon her differences with Williams at the time that *A Few Poems* was published in 1952, Barnard wrote:

> I was still convinced that Greek cadences were not so alien as Bill thought. I had once heard a dining car waiter chanting in perfectly recognizable dactylic hexameter:

Luncheon is now bein' served / in the dining car five cars
forward.
Please take your seat checks with you![79]

Some American critics were not agreeable to Barnard's poetry, let alone her metrics, but perhaps this was a testament to the strength of her achievement. Allen Tate delivered a vicious attack on *Cool Country* (1940) in the pages of the *Partisan Review* that, in retrospect, seems wholly naive:

> Miss Barnard sets out to say nothing and, with a great deal of propriety, succeeds. . . . I think Miss Barnard might be more interesting if she applied the same finical anxiety to the development of a prosody that she applies now to avoiding one.[80]

That Tate thought Barnard's work had no prosody after decades of "strict exercise" *and* "loopin' the loop" is indicative of just how accomplished it actually was. She did not want meter that was affected in any way, evocative of the "English poets . . . posed like mannikins" that she had condemned in *The Faber Book of Modern Verse*; she wanted "the sound of the speaking voice that was native to me." Her lines did not provide the reassurance of a recognizably emphatic meter modeled on the English system. Moreover, Barnard's lines were perhaps *too* natural-seeming, too easy on the ear, too close to speech and ordinary, everyday colloquial rhythms, so that they did not seem "poetic" at all, at least not to Tate.

4.4 "An Idiom AND a Swing": *Sappho: A New Translation*

In *Sappho: A New Translation*, Barnard's experiments with Greek cadences in her free verse paid off, as they freed her to try for a translation that was much more thoughtfully modern *and* American without shifting too far away from the musical rhythms typical to the Melic order. As Anita Helle explains:

> The most important part of Barnard's "new translation" . . . is its meter. Wanting to come as close as possible to the sound of the speaking voice, Barnard considered the convention of the Japanese haiku, as well as strictly quantitative metrics—which some scholars felt were impossible to convey in English. Her solution was a looser adaptation, balancing the number of weighted syllables from line to line. Consequently Sappho's colloquies with friends, as well as her wedding songs and passionate soliloquys, read as though they have form,

but one which resembles conversational stresses instead of humdrum repetition:

> You may forget but
>
> let me tell you
> this: someone in
> some future time
> will think of us.[81]

This process of "balancing the number of weighted syllables from line to line" in search of the conversational was something that Barnard herself generously illustrated in detail in her essay "A Communication on Greek Metric, Ezra Pound and Sappho," giving numerous examples, such as the following, as Barnard scanned them:

> – –
> 58. Tell me
> – ᴗ –
> Out of all
> – – –
> mankind, whom
> ᴗ ᴗ –
> do you love
> – ᴗ ᴗ
> Better than
> – – –
> you love me?
>
> ᴗ – – ᴗ
> 59. I said, Sappho
> ᴗ – –
> Enough! Why
> – ᴗ –
> try to move
> ᴗ – –
> a hard heart?[82]

"Naturally, I did not work out the scansion first, and fit the words to it, but I worked back and forth, scanning when a line sounded wrong, to see where it needed adjustment,"[83] Barnard recounted, her "conversation" with the fragments themselves an aid toward finding the kind of conversational emphases that Helle alludes to. Take, for instance, one of the longer passionate soliloquies that Barnard bound into a series, in part 3 of her translation. In the University of California Press edition, Barnard's fragment number 42 reads:

I have had not one word from her

Frankly I wish I were dead.
When she left, she wept

a great deal; she said to
me, "This parting must be
endured, Sappho. I go unwillingly."

I said, "Go, and be happy
but remember (you know
well) whom you leave shackled by love

"If you forget me, think
of our gifts to Aphrodite
and all the loveliness that we shared

"all the violet tiaras,
braided rosebuds, dill and
crocus twined around your young neck

"myrrh poured on your head
and on soft mats girls with
all that they most wished for beside them

"while no voices chanted
choruses without ours,
no woodlot bloomed in spring with-
out song. . . ."[84]

Balanced lines are immediately discernible, as in this scansion of the opening lines:

ᴗ ᴗ – – / – – ᴗ ᴗ
I have had not one word from her

– ᴗ ᴗ – /ᴗ ᴗ –
Frankly I wish I were dead.

– ᴗ – / ᴗ –
When she left, she wept
ᴗ – – / ᴗ – ᴗ
a great deal; she said to
ᴗ – – / ᴗ – ᴗ
me, "This parting must be
ᴗ – – ᴗ ᴗ/ – ᴗ – – ᴗ
endured, Sappho. I go unwillingly."

As with so many of her fragments, the first line balances the weights of its syllables both *exactly* and *symmetrically*, in contrast to Barnard's usual use of approximate balance in the main body of the poem. From the beginning, then, the voice of the poem exudes a cool verbal control, evocative of Barnard's own metrical competence. Barnard's trademark set-off first line, in this instance, has the effect of implied conversation, as if we are hearing an answer to the question "Have you heard from her, then?" Other poems and fragments follow suit, creating a frame around themselves in which one participant in the conversation is placed within (the speaker), and her partner in conversation placed outside. Some fragments begin with an explicit address to the conversation partner (for example, Barnard's fragment number 21—"Cyprian, in my dream" and fragment number 50—"But you, monkey face"), others begin mid-conversation (fragment number 37—"You know the place: then / Leave Crete"; fragment number 40—"Yes, Atthis, you may be sure"), and the opening arrangement of fragments in part 1 brings forth set-off lines that cumulatively suggest a conversation between two partners, between the self-absorbed Sappho (fragment number 4—"I asked myself"; fragment number 5—"And I said"; fragment number 6—"I confess") and one of her partners (fragment number 15—"You are the herdsman of the evening"; fragment number 17—"Sleep, darling"; fragment number 19—"Tomorrow you had better"). This is just one of the ways in which Barnard endows her translation with "high art," that rare complement to the "exact translation" that Dudley Fitts came to praise, as we saw at the end of chapter 3: she makes "conversation" a muscle in the overall articulation of Sappho's corpus.

Of course, the metrical balance in Barnard's translation was in part informed by the decisions Barnard made about which words to choose, and in this her efforts were meticulously informed by her Imagist training. If we turn to one of her drafts of fragment number 42, written as her ear worked "back and forth," what is striking is the extent to which Barnard's revisions toward "maximum abruptness" almost always ensure greater "movement" of the kind she had admired in Sappho and Homer in the original, not to mention that advocated by the Imagists in the campaign for a directness of presentation composed strictly in "the sequence of the musical phrase." This she had sent to Pound for comment, which he obliged by return (see figure 7).

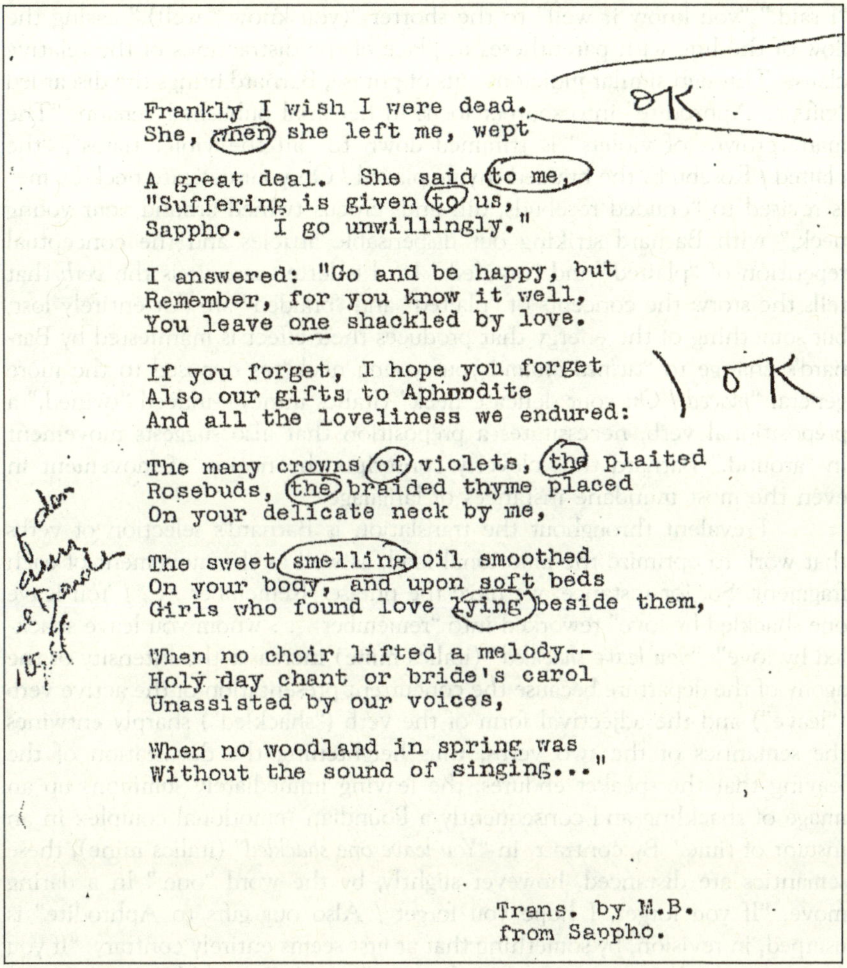

Frankly I wish I were dead.
She, when she left me, wept

A great deal. She said to me,
"Suffering is given to us,
Sappho. I go unwillingly."

I answered: "Go and be happy, but
Remember, for you know it well,
You leave one shackled by love.

If you forget, I hope you forget
Also our gifts to Aphrodite
And all the loveliness we endured:

The many crowns of violets, the plaited
Rosebuds, the braided thyme placed
On your delicate neck by me,

The sweet smelling oil smoothed
On your body, and upon soft beds
Girls who found love lying beside them,

When no choir lifted a melody--
Holy day chant or bride's carol
Unassisted by our voices,

When no woodland in spring was
Without the sound of singing..."

Trans. by M.B.
from Sappho.

FIGURE 7. Facsimile draft of Mary Barnard's fragment no. 42, with ink annotations by Ezra Pound. Mary Barnard Papers. Courtesy of Elizabeth J. Bell and New Directions Publishing Corp.

In the published version, Barnard changes "Suffering is given to us, / Sappho," from above, to "This parting must be / endured, Sappho," shifting from the abstract and almost proverbial to the very specific ("*This* parting," italics mine). Although still offering us a noun in "parting," at least this noun suggests movement in itself—"suffering" could be static, intangible, but not "parting," which entails an observable move away of one person from another. In the third stanza, she changes "I answered" to the more concise

"I said," "you know it well" to the shorter "(you know / well)," easing the flow of the line with parentheses in place of the distractions of the relative clause. Through similar judicious cuts of phrase, Barnard brings the discarded "gifts to Aphrodite" into sharper focus in her final published version. "The many crowns of violets" is trimmed down to "all the violet tiaras"; "the plaited / Rosebuds, the braided thyme placed / On your delicate neck by me" is revised to "braided rosebuds, dill and/ crocus twined around your young neck," with Barnard striking out dispensable articles and the conceptual repetition of "plaited" and "braided." In this latter case, it is the *verb* that tells the story: the concepts of "plaited" and "braided" are not entirely lost, but something of the energy that produces their effect is manifested by Barnard's change to "*twined around* your young neck" as opposed to the more general "*placed* / On your delicate neck" (italics mine)—indeed "twined," a prepositional verb, necessitates a preposition that also suggests movement in "around." Barnard thus cleverly conscripts the notion of movement in even the most mundane instances of language.

Prevalent throughout the translation is Barnard's selection of verbs that work to optimize the emotional load, as well as the movement of each fragment. So, for instance, we have the phrase "Remember . . . / You leave one shackled by love" reworked into "remember . . . whom you leave shackled by love": "*you leave shackled*" (italics mine) increases the intensity of the agony of the departure because the concurrent presentation of the active verb ("leave") and the adjectival form of the verb ("shackled") sharply entwines the semantics of the two verbs, thus heightening the devastation of the leaving that the speaker endures: the leaving immediately summons up an image of shackling and consequently a Poundian "emotional complex in an instant of time." By contrast, in "*You leave one shackled*" (italics mine), these semantics are distanced, however slightly, by the word "one." In a daring move, "If you forget, I hope you forget / Also our gifts to Aphrodite" is usurped, in revision, by something that at first seems entirely contrary: "If you forget me, think / of our gifts to Aphrodite," which Barnard later went on to publish. But the added imperative "think," here, works cohesively with the other imperatives in the poem that come quickly before it ("Go," "remember"), cranking up the kinetic energy of the poem. Simultaneously, "think" emboldens our picture of the gifts as Sappho prompts both the listener and *us* to "think" of these gifts—she does not merely lament them but asks *us* to visualize the gifts as much as Sappho's departing lover is asked to memorialize them. Other verb choices deepen this induction into the poem, selected for the story their *sounds* can tell as much as for the story their semantics tell. The soothing sibilance of "The sweet-smelling oil *smoothed* / On your body," for instance, is replaced by the abrasive rhythm of "myrrh *poured* on your head," yielding a sound unsettlingly commensurate with the jagged and droning consonance that spikes the presentation of Aphrodite's gifts in the interplay between "tiaras/twined," "braided rosebuds, dill," "crocus/neck." It would have been easy for Barnard to have retained "The sweet-smelling oil smoothed / On your body" or even to have cut it down to "The sweet oil / smoothed on your body." But in selecting "myrrh" and "poured" she subtly admits a vengeful element to the poem's drama (in that "poured on your head" has an aggressive subtext) and thus extends the emotional reach of the poem—to return to Longinus, she compacts the "extremes of love's history" within the poem in a deft verbal move that assuredly, here, "embrace[s] the post-Tennysonian mode," as she herself later described her translation.[85]

If there is one distinction of *Sappho: A New Translation*, then, it must be the way in which *movement* is intrinsic to the composition at every level, from the level of the word, as can be seen in the verb choices, to the level of prosody, through to the level of design in the arrangement and sequencing of the fragments. The translation does not begin with the well-known Fragment One, the prayer to Aphrodite, but with a tiny fragment that, in its use of the imperative and appeal to the "now," immediately draws the reader into a specific moment:

> Tell everyone
>
> Now, today, I shall
> sing beautifully for
> my friends' pleasure[86]

The much-anthologized Fragment One resurfaces as number 37 in Barnard's translation, as she slots it into a moving narrative that begins in part 1 with fragments about youthfulness and leisurely courtships (as in the above example), through to part 2, whose *epithalamia* (wedding songs) offer timely sequels, with the laments and woes of Fragment One and several other longer poems (as in Barnard's fragment number 42) collected in part 3 in poems that voice the highs and lows of the matured relationships that follow the weddings, particularly those that register departures. Part 4 counterbalances this, rather like musical counterpoint, with very short fragments that speak of returns, both imagined and real, and parts 5 and 6 are punctuated by reminiscences, stories of aging, a summing up of knowledge, acceptances of death. In this, Barnard presents fragments that move within themselves, in time, and with each other, in a narrative that engenders a loose but discernible chronology across a life. They are, with respect to Pound's prescription to Barnard back in 1934, "shapes" that are "cut . . . in time."

By the time Barnard was sending out drafts of her translation in 1953, in Pound's eyes, Barnard's key strength was her ability to write classically derived modern poetry with "an idiom AND a swing," as she reflected in *Assault on Mount Helicon*:

Ezra's response [to *Sappho*], which was dated March 3 [1953], six weeks before his release from St. Elizabeth's, began abruptly:

> It is now to be pointed out that there is no decent translation of Callimachus "Delos" or of the old bogie Bion "Adonis" / both of which give something to get one's teeth into and a sustained body of verse, that needs an idiom AND a swing etc.

In other words, no pat on the head, no pat on the back, certainly no raptures, just a crack of the whip![87]

Surely a "pat on the back" was due for her concept of the "weighted syllable" as a solution to the problem of finding enough syllables to approximate the cadences of the Melic poets in American verse, cadences she felt were natural to American speech patterns? Or for her use of the "balanced line" as a solution to the problem of finding a means of regulating free verse "according to the expanded requirements of the age"? Williams supplied plenty of pats on the back without fully understanding what he was complimenting her on (he sees her moving "away from . . . accented verse to a verse that takes as its unit elapsed time" when she does not completely disregard accent). Pound, on the other hand, gave little praise but appeared to appreciate what Barnard was doing—and she certainly preferred that to the praise that "gushed forth as easily and indiscriminately as it did in Bill's case. Ezra's brusque admonition to get on with it, although momentarily frustrating, probably meant more to me in the end."[88]

It is now the turn of scholars to do what Williams and Pound strove to do between them: recognize *and* articulate the terms of Barnard's achievement. The musical world certainly has, as Bell points out in her biography on the Mary Barnard website www.marybarnard.com:

> It is no surprise that composers have found her poems easily adaptable to musical settings. In Pound's earliest letters to Mary, he stressed the importance of the musical line and rhythm, elements which had attracted Mary to poetry as a young child. Her poem "Lai" was set to music in the 30's by the New York composer Edwin Gerschefski, whom she met at Yaddo. "Sappho" has appeared at least twice in musical settings: one was composed by Sheila Silver for soprano and piano and performed at Wheaton College; the other, *Fragments from Sappho* for piano, clarinet, flute and soprano, was composed by David Ward-Steinman and recorded with Phyllis

> Curtin on CRI records. Tibor Serly, a friend of Pound in Paris and Rapallo, and a resident of Longview, Washington in his later years, composed the *Pleiades*, a cantata for chorus and orchestra, which was performed in Portland in 1978. Tomas Svoboda, composer in residence at Portland State University, wrote the cantata *Journey* for mezzo-soprano and baritone solo, choir, and orchestra, Op. 127, which was performed in Portland on February 13, 1987.[89]

But the academy needs to act, too, for Barnard's significant achievement is that she gave to American free verse poetry a line that was not only flexible *and* regular, as suited the "yawping speakers" of the new nation, but also historically aware—hers was not a hashed, hit-and-miss prosody, as is occasionally said of Williams's efforts, but one well-informed in tradition and thus well-placed to transcend it in the interests of creating an autonomous American verse. Just as she transmuted Sappho from a source to emulate into a cultural force to compete with in her explorations of image and voice, so, too, did Barnard make the nature and principles of Sapphics and related Greek meters work *for* her as she created an American metric, as Emerson had implored, to suit an "ample geography [that] dazzles the imagination." It was one, Emerson had said, that would "not wait long for metres." Barnard delivered in abundance.

Chapter Five

"A Bright Particular Excellence"

The Achievement of Mary Barnard

"Perhaps it is impolite to the guest to leave him with the feeling that there is more in the kitchen than I have put on the table," Mary Barnard told the editor of her memoir, August Fruge, in justification of the exclusion of some of her letters to her modernist friends, "but I prefer it that way."[1] Such demand for privacy during one's lifetime is entirely understandable. Yet the undeniable fact is that the kitchen was kept immaculately ordered, as if Barnard knew, someday, that the guest might try the door. Examining Barnard's poems in the light of this new archival evidence, intensively mapping their contours of influence and exchanges with Pound, H.D., and Williams for the first time, it is clear that Mary Barnard was far from an incidental figure languishing at the tail end of modernism, as some critics would have us believe. She was as "Roman" as the Romans, so to speak, however "Late," to quote her own poem. So much for the "digit in many footnotes." Energetically engaged with the aesthetics of American poetry in the wake of the modernist revolution during her years in New York from the Depression through to the postwar period, Barnard received "one of my nicest compliments"[2] from Williams in 1948, and it is not hard to see why. "Both Floss and I love you very much and admire you tremendously for the way you have battled through in that God forsaken city without bitterness," Williams wrote; "we find you to be a distinguished person of great gentleness in a world not very much to be admired."[3] For Williams, more than anyone else—even Pound—had enduring faith in Barnard, right from the moment the "awkward young woman with sawdust in her hair" first started sending poems to him from the opposite coast. Although typically encouraging in his early letters to her, Pound had had some early doubts about her competence to be part of "the NEXT 'movement'"—unsmeared by "Lowells and people who WON'T work"—as he told James Laughlin:

"The Barnard kid has took'd a prize, an I spose that is about that, and that she will procede along the normal coive of young lady riters. i.e. no worse, and in 7% of the quadrant about 3% bettern the men that don't count," Pound wrote after hearing of *Poetry's* award of the Levinson Prize, but he was careful to have Laughlin keep a silence, "no need to broadcast discouragement," Pound added in parentheses.[4] Just as well, too, for it is perhaps unlikely that Barnard would ever have hammered down New York's many "inhospitable looking doors," as Victor Chittick saw them,[5] without the help of either Pound or Laughlin, for "trying to get poetry books published" during the fractious social and economic climate of the late American 1930s was, as Babette Deutsch warned Barnard, "a discouraging affair,"[6] regardless of what the men of modernism thought about the talents of writers who happened to be women.

Always among the first to read her new work, Pound changed his mind, of course. "Gawd yu are fit to associate only with people like Marianne and the Possum's ghost," he wrote to Barnard in his later years.[7] But Williams was with her from the start. His response to her Levinson success was almost the reverse of Pound's, as Paul Mariani told her in private correspondence in preparation for his Williams biography. Where Pound was trying to help Barnard place a manuscript with Laughlin, Williams was trying to interest Ronald Lane Latimer, editor at Alcestis Press, and saw the Levinson Prize as a defining mark of her caliber. "Williams did write to Latimer as he said he would," Mariani told Barnard, "and you might be interested to see the cameo he shot off in the letter dated April 21 [1936]":

> If you care to do so you might look up Mary Barnard just in from Portland, Oregon. She recently won Poetry's Levinson Prize. She has a script to be looked at and is a nice girl besides tho' tall and thin and chaste and I think intellectual. But she's nice and we ought to make her welcome. She doesn't drink. . . . Her verse is well above the ordinary.[8]

Although Williams exaggerated some of Barnard's personal qualities—she was no teetotalling killjoy, for one—the Rutherford doctor, who quickly welcomed Barnard into his circle of family and friends, was well positioned to judge her artistically, and consistently registered her achievement as much as he believed in her potential as the years of their friendship passed by. "If, as it appears, you are made of the things that these poems suggest," he had told her in his first letter to her of January 30, 1935, "there is reason to salute you seriously."[9]

And so I hope this book has. I had begun it with the intention of neatly placing Barnard as a "late Imagist" descending from the "perfect Imagist," H.D., seeing Barnard's work, as Pound had done, as a continuation and transcendence of "what H.D. . . . said in 1913," just as much equipped, if not better so, in her knowledge of Greek language and meter, to pull off "straight as the Greek" modern poetry for an American audience and with a penchant for a poetry based on exacting observation, of a "hurting fineness," as Florence Codman, one of Barnard's early readers, applauded,[10] of the same aesthetic stature as H.D.'s "accurate mystery." This was perhaps no naïve enterprise, for their common interest in Sappho suggested a different path was being taken by modernism's female poets, that there *did* exist an easily separable body of "lady riters," as Pound saw them, within the rush and fury of modernism's many voices, but one that defied any "normal coive." After all, the H.D. critic Diana Collecott based an entire book around such distinctions, following Susan Gubar's seminal essay "Sapphistries," and reflected in her introduction to *H.D. and Sapphic Modernism* that as Pound and Eliot took Homer and Dante, respectively, as gurus, H.D. and other female modernists (Bryher, Lowell, Woolf) took Sappho as theirs—the implication being that as emergent modern writers searched frantically for figures of cultural authority amid the chaos of war, their quests were played out along specifically gendered lines.[11]

But Barnard did not hold much truck with such polemics. For one, she knew that Sappho had been a solid example to male poets, including Pound and Aldington, who she followed on from, as well as to those over the centuries often accused of "doing up [Sappho] in ribbons and feathers and artificial flowers and anointing her with marshmallow sauce,"[12] as Deutsch quipped in a letter shortly after reading the first printing of Barnard's translation, which did anything but. Barnard also thought that Sappho's distinction and influence had been overplayed by feminist critics. "Recently I found in one periodical whose women editors should hide their heads in shame, the statement that Sappho was considered the greatest Greek poet," Barnard wrote in *Assault on Mount Helicon*. "Nobody in his (or even her) right mind ever said such a thing. She was always, I believe, considered the greatest Greek woman poet; and some have called her the greatest Greek lyric poet; but no one ever suggested she was a greater poet than Homer or Sophocles."[13]

It would also be a mistake to think that Barnard translated Sappho because she was a role model for women poets. Homer was important too. In fact, Barnard had every intention of following up *Sappho: A New Translation* with a translation of the *Iliad*, and she got as far as translating the first five books before *The Mythmakers* became a more pressing priority in the 1960s, followed by the need to care for her ailing parents over the "eight years" (1969–1977) she was "trying to forget," as she confided in Fruge,[14] until James Anderson entered her life in the late 1970s wanting to do *Collected Poems* and then her *Time and the White Tigress* in the 1980s. The *Iliad* project went on the back burner until it simply became too late; there was no other "catastrophe," as she had first seen her illness of 1951, that would, perversely, generate some pure, protected time from the demands of the everyday, as had been the case with her Sappho project, with which "the thing to do was what I would never do if I were up and leading a normal life," as she had told Williams.[15] But Homer was a catalyst to her Sappho translation—after all, it was the *Iliad* and the *Odyssey* that she was reading while confined to bed for weeks at a time during that miserable midcentury winter, until D. D. Paige sent her a volume containing some Sappho and her mind turned back to those old experiments in the 1930s with Pound. The "Would-Be Sappho" was also, we must remember, a "Would-Be Homer."

Indeed, Barnard had scant interest in being "gendered" in any way, in being set apart as a female modernist, as the ambiguous gender politics of her sand poetics reveal—in the end, they seem to be more about Imagist practice, and American writing, than they are about gender difference. As Williams was to say in *In the American Grain*, "The particles of language [in American writing] must be clear as sand," and it is this ideological model toward which Barnard tended to gravitate.[16] Feminism was useful only in so far as it enabled her to get on with the business of writing, which was where she thought her energy best placed:

> When I read Virginia Woolf's *A Room of One's Own*, which was published during my second or third year in college, I thought it a wonderful book and took to heart her advice to women writers: do not, like Charlotte Brontë, mount the soap-box and harangue your audience on women's rights when you should be getting on with the story; do not waste time and energy railing against men; abandon any consciousness of your sex when you write, and write simply as a human being.[17]

Although she had grown up "thinking that women were already liberated" because "we have the vote; we wore clothing that allowed freedom of movement; we were welcomed at co-educational colleges and universities; we could travel alone, and pursue our careers in whatever city we chose . . . we could choose to marry or not marry," Barnard was not wholly naïve about implicit gender biases in the structures of modern society. "In college . . . I began to sense that some (but not all) the professors regarded the education of a female as of secondary importance," she recalled. But she felt, as she did with the proletariat circles in 1930s New York, that "I never at any time needed my 'consciousness raised.'"[18] Nor did she think that such politicking was the purpose of her writing, or ought to be the default purpose of writing by women. As she remonstrated with Carolyn Kizer, who took Barnard to task over such views expressed on feminist polemics in *Assault on Mount Helicon*, she felt that:

> It's all right to resent the exclusion, so long as we don't become too vocal about it and use it as an excuse for falling short of our goals. Better to turn it into an advantage—I'm inclined to think that almost any limitation or exclusion can be turned to an advantage if we stop whining and *try*. I don't read Japanese, but my understanding is that Japanese women have written excellent poetry in the past as well as in this century, and if Japanese women could do it with *their* limitations. . . .[19]

It is easy to see why Barnard politely refused Germaine Greer's request to serve as a guest professor at the Tulsa Center for the Study of Women's Literature in the early 1980s, even if she did accept an invitation to join the inaugural advisory board to *Tulsa Studies in Women's Literature*—this was only following Greer's reassurance, however, that "you'd be rubbing shoulders with Dame Rebecca West, Professor M. C. Bradbrook and Mary Ellman—none of them sabre-toothed feminists"[20] and her stiff defense that the Tulsa journal existed "to develop appropriate criteria for women's work, not to pretend that women have made a contribution to literature which has never been recognized."[21] But Barnard was resolute, her willingness to be one of those who would "work," to quote Pound, unshakeable. "I dislike the idea of being segregated as a writer," she told Greer; "I would rather finish fifteenth in the Derby than first in a race for fillies only."[22]

And so Barnard was no H.D. remodel, no willing inheritor of a "gendered Imagism," and she would probably have objected loudly to any attempt to present her as such. Perhaps this is why Barnard's correspondence with H.D. failed to get off the ground—for all of H.D.'s supposed jealousy, maybe Barnard shunned H.D. too, Pound's stinging jibe from 1936 that her work was a makeover of *Sea Garden* a hurt from which she never quite recovered. Not that Barnard entirely spurned contact, mind—she became acquainted with H.D.'s daughter Perdita Schnaffer when she relocated to the United States in the late 1940s through their mutual friend, that relentless go-between for the American modernists, Viola Baxter Jordan, and Barnard was close enough to Schnaffer to place her on her publisher's gift list for a copy of *Collected Poems* in the late 1970s. Through all of this, Pound's "dryad" and "gazelle" were likely to have been stirred up in each other's thoughts from time to time.

But despite all their intertextual links, it was not with H.D. that Barnard reshaped American poetry via a "sabre-toothed" "Sapphic Modernism," however tempting it is to finalize an enquiry along these lines. Although the idea of the "school" was anathema to her, there was one program I think she happily supported, albeit in her own inimitable style.

She may have felt that "Elizabeth Bishop [was] the one of my contemporaries with whom I felt the most rapport, as far as her work was concerned,"[23] but the one poet whom these new archives show Barnard was *really* closer to, aesthetically, was Williams—and her work was every bit as important as his in creating free verse American poetry "in the American grain." She may have started out, in Williams's eyes, as "one of Ezra's string of ponies" that Pound wanted him to steer through his New York circles, but in time that changed, and the reality is that in time they assisted and encouraged each other as peers more than playing out a Poundian master/apprentice dynamic. For Barnard was not afraid to take Williams to task over his ideas. "There you go again, I held my tongue last time, but now listen" one of her letters begins, hectoring Williams on his views on women, before turning the scientific tables on the doctor: "You are interested in women as a variant of the male impetus, and a complement to it, enabling it to show off 'at its maximum.' Biologically it would be much sounder to say that the male impetus is a variant of and complementary to the female, enabling *it* to show off etc. Ain't?"[24] Nor was she so deferential that she could not pick holes in Williams's achievements—for instance, she anticipated some of the skepticism that surrounds his claims for his variable foot when she privately noted that she thought that Williams did not really know what he was aiming at.[25] And she was protective, too, of his legacy, wanting his poetry to live on beyond the incessant gossip about his supposed philandering, which he did not do much to play down. Williams should have burned some of the letters he donated to Buffalo, she told her parents in a letter home in 1943 when she was curating his archive, including one the tactful archivist "surreptiously buried . . . in the unidentifiables where I hope it remains for a long time."[26]

So to the New Jersey doctor writing his edgy pastorals in search of American poetic form, Barnard was an important West Coast counterpoint mapping the "cool country" of the northwestern corner of the "new world naked" as both poets textured the timbre of modernist poetry with the speech cadences of the "amurikan langwidge." But there were some creative differences, too, making theirs a complementary partnership that ultimately broadened the scope of American poetry in the twentieth century. Where Williams's measure had, in some respects, the same kind of loose improvisation as jazz, Barnard's had its origins in scholarship and the hard, technical graft of Poundian "strict exercise," even if she ultimately arrived at a "free version" (or, rather *freer* version) of American rhythm over the "studied version" Williams had urged. It had backbone. Where Williams demanded a turn away from Europe, Barnard came to see that her youthful "shriek of defiance" against European influence was perhaps a touch naïve. Knowledge of Greek meter did not *have* to undermine the attempt to articulate the "sound of the speaking voice that was native," she concluded, nor was it desirable, for it was perhaps foolish to conceive of the "amurikan langwidge" as generically pure. New, yes, and formally distinct from the English, as Williams and H. L. Mencken, among others, had been at pains to point out to the likes of Yvor Winters, but not wholly unrelated to the languages that originated in Europe.

Barnard's perceptiveness was perhaps due in no small part to the fact that she benefitted handsomely from the dual input of Pound *and* Williams, as had other "ponies," Laughlin and Zukofsky. "Williams viewed any European influence as pollution, while Ezra viewed it as a pollenization," Barnard surmised at the end of her memoir.[27] Her special contribution was to show that it was possible to cut a third path, that it was entirely workable for an American poet to write the American poem *in* America with *some* "pollenization" from Europe without "polluting" or obscuring the American grain—indeed, to fulfill Williams's prophecy in "The American Background" (1934) that "the two great bands of effort" that had hitherto dogged American art (one "looking toward Europe, necessitous but retrograde . . . the other forward-looking but under a shadow from the first") would "take a Titan to bring together and weld into one again."[28] Barnard was that Titan. As she was to put it in the tellingly titled "Prometheus Loved Us," European ideas could warmly assist with the creation of the autonomous American self in poetry, however seeming a paradox that conception was:

Prometheus Loved Us

I walk in a twilight half-drawn
Along the edge of town,
Walk with rain on my coatsleeves,
Drops clinging upon the prongs of the wool.
Should I record anything?

Runnel of rain at the curb will
Drop down to the river. Vacant lots
Spill grass on the sidewalk
And I walk nowhere in particular.
Nothing.

Except the merest match-wing
Of fire pricks through the rain
And the street is stung to life.
Heart leaps, like a fish striking.[29]

The American poem, the poet-like figure contends as she walks the streets for something to "record" (playing up old stereotypes of America-as-empty-space), certainly lies in the "runnels of rain at the curb," in the minute details of the American local, as Williams would approve, but it could steal, too, as Prometheus did, from the "gods" of Europe. And perhaps this is why the trickster-creator Prometheus is so approving of the American "us," for the sheer nerve of such a raid. Barnard's message is clear. America *can* ignite its *own* cultural life from raw, even basic materials (the "merest match-wing") in even the most unpromising circumstances (among the rain-sodden "vacant lots") without any need for the godlike authority of "the European" that menaced in "Provincial II." But perhaps America ought to maintain some connection, too, as Barnard does here by using Greek myth to furnish a suggestive (but not fixed) frame around a scene from small-town American life. The myth does not intrude upon the poem, or even enable it, as the poem would work perfectly well without the Greek reference in the title—indeed, it could easily bear the same name as another poem about the riches of slight places, "Encounter in Buffalo," and be rid of any European "pollution," without losing any significant effects, I think.

The inclusion of Prometheus nevertheless widens the antennae of the poem, enabling Barnard to speak to those Americans who revere European influence, such as Winters; to those expatriated, such as Pound and Eliot; as well, of course, as to "the European." It is a masterful act of "pollenization," only without a resultant hybridization—as that early reader at Arrow had said of the "statements" of Barnard's poetry, the use of the Greek myth here combined with American elements is in "a particularly open, detached sequence," having "the effect of particles reflectively dropped to make a pattern." The particles do not take root. Skunk cabbages and Johnny-jump-ups live on. And the matter-of-fact tone of the poem—which sounds as if it might have slipped out of a Marianne Moore poem—suggests that Barnard's American Prometheus might just get away with it. There is no sinister undertone here, no hinting of punishing eagles to come. Barnard rewrites the myth and in so doing frees the American poem, as well as her Prometheus, from the "torture" of cultural servitude to Europe. The "street" of her America is thus "stung to life," as is her Promethean poet, whose "heart leaps," liver intact. Perhaps, in all this, Barnard was further blessed by the "little-known landscape" that she thought her "luckiest chance," for when Williams took his first major tour of the West in 1950—including a stop at Reed College, where he gave a talk and looked at student manuscripts—he was struck by the effect of space on the Western imagination. "But the outstanding thing that I was aware of among all the West Coast cities," Williams wrote in his autobiography, "was that they faced the Orient; that Europe had no more than a legendary hold on them." Given Barnard's ability to distance her speaker in "Provincial" from the "quilted legends" of

Europe, Williams probably had a point, although this ability did not mean, as Williams went on to say, that she was ever among "the young in the colleges [who] yearn for France, for New York, Boston, for 'that' culture and look (through the eyes of New England teachers) to a past, feeling themselves yokels."[30] Barnard was far too advanced, and well-schooled, for that.

Williams stole too, of course, where it suited him, even translating Sappho's Fragment Two in book 5 of his own "shriek of defiance" against European models, *Paterson*, "a reply to Greek and Latin," he said, "with the bare hands."[31] No doubt he was inspired by Barnard, who had the distinction of being the first American modernist who *really* knew Greek to stay in the United States and make good with it, whose Sappho translation, as Babette Deutsch described it, was as fine a blend of Poundian Imagism by an American as could be had. "I know no other englishing that is at once so economical and so lyrical," the New Yorker glowed over *Sappho: A New Translation*.[32] Or, to quote a bona fide Poundian, it was "clean, hard poetry in our natural language, no frills and no squishiness," as Mary de Rachewiltz put it.[33] Williams had not thought such precision and rhythm possible in the "natural language" when he first mentored Barnard, even sending her a cheeky send-up of a Sappho fragment in 1940 scotching her experiments with Sapphics. Inscribed "Mary Barnard—WCW," annotated "writing time 40 seconds," and written in New Jersey vernacular, Williams put Barnard's Sappho down in nonsense rhyme:

> Sappho was a lady
> who taught young gals
> but what she
>   thought
> and never taught
> lay hidden there as pearls[34]

But Barnard was no derivative "gal," nor did she become a "lady" leading any school of female poets, be they American, modernist, or whatever. Barnard was an example of the "vigorously individuated" voice singled out by the editors of the Library of America's landmark survey in several volumes, *American Poetry: The Twentieth Century*, which they began publishing at the century's close. If Barnard's era was "the era of the Harlem Renaissance, the Objectivists, the Fugitive poets, the proletarian poets," then the editors issued a reminder long overdue. "It was also an era of vigorously individuated voices—knotty, defiant, sometimes eccentric."[35] More direct and "clearer than clear air" than "knotty," more measured than "defiant," and less given to "modernist pyrotechnics" than some of her peers in order to attain her "spare but musical style," Barnard was one such voice. It is lamentable that during her own lifetime such individualism occasionally caused others to mistake her as irrelevant, as Allen Tate did, or to place brackets around her achievement, as others did, however honorable their intentions. Fellow northwestern poet William Stafford got her wrong in his introduction to *Collected Poems*, as Barnard was quick to chide her editor. "I don't like it at all," Barnard opened a letter curtly to James Anderson on November 4, 1978. "It seems to me that that he quotes only my slightest or earliest poems. On the first page he says 'quietly'; on the second he says 'silently'; on the second, 'quiet' again; on the fourth, 'quiet' again. Oh, come now," Barnard seethed, "surely there is some toughness of fiber there?" "None of this would matter except that reviewers are so apt to take their cue from an Introduction, I would say, better not have an Introduction," she snipped, before appending an abrupt footnote. "Dammit, Stafford's introduction isn't an affirmation, it's an apology. . . . if the best he can find to say is that the poems have virtues that the reader will probably miss, he had better to stick to biographical material."[36] Stafford's introduction was approved, but only after much wrangling. Some five years later, Malcolm Cowley was misreading her too, despite having known her from those early years in New York. As one of Barnard's old friends from Buffalo, Anne Ludlow, opined in a letter to her of March 29, 1984, Cowley's review of *Assault on Mount Helicon* in *The New York Times* was "nice" enough but had missed the point: "I . . . wish that Cowley hadn't called you *peaceable*, since that was not what your work stood for in the craft." Though Barnard did not subscribe to the kind of Red literary politics of which Cowley approved, despite allowing him to publish an early version of "Roots" in *New Republic*, she was still, Ludlow noted, "decidedly trying to break patterns and let a new voice be heard."[37]

And so she did. If, as Williams noted early on in a letter to another one of his protégés-soon-turned-collaborator, Zukofsky, Barnard's work contained a "more or less conventional surface,"[38] beneath it she was "loopin' the loop," to remember Pound's words, with rhythm, experimenting vigorously with the possibilities of Greek metric in order to create "new patterns" for American verse. No wonder she thought herself "much more fun than . . . the bearded Beatniks of S.F.," as Babette Deutsch recalled her saying,[39] even if she was quite content to be overlooked in the company of Ferlinghetti, to recall that dual appearance together in the late 1950s. It was not a frivolity she ever wanted attached to her persona, her life next to the poetry—she was not given to doing a metaphorical "strip-tease in a local tavern" for anybody, she told Anderson.[40]

But there is undoubtedly a potent blend of metrical and imagistic "pyrotechnics" simmering beneath the cool surface of poems like "Shoreline," "North Window," "The Trestle," "Roots," and so on, indicating that Barnard surely set as many precedents for the open form poets as, say, Lorine Niedecker, another poet influenced by the Imagists and hung up on Williams's ideas for the American poem. Although not actively correspondent with these later Poundian "ponies," it is not without some significance that Corman, one of Niedecker's correspondents, found the "maximum abruptness" of Barnard's *Sappho: A New Translation* a suitable model for his crystalline poetics in the small chapbook he produced of tightly hewn fragments following Barnard's example, entitled *Sappho: Wee Ones*.[41] And if Gary Snyder is widely credited with reestablishing contact with an Emersonian model of "nature" coincident with the environmentalist movement in the American twentieth century, then Barnard, as with Niedecker, was ahead of him by a couple of decades at least, for her "verbal landscaping,"[42] as Muriel Rukeyser once described her poetry, depended on a deep awareness and profound respect of the natural world around her—an awareness she had once thought made her stand at a peculiar tangent to the engine room of midcentury poetry skippered by those who had found favor with Allen Tate et al. Asked how she would have situated herself among the modernists in an interview in 1982, Barnard told Anita Helle that

> I thought I had sort of fallen down through the cracks. I was too late for the Imagists, and I was too early for the Lowell, Berryman, Jarrell wave. I was formed by the 20s . . . . and then in the 30s there were all the social poets, and then there was the war, the war poets, and none of this was really my line, and finally it seemed to me that my work was so antiquated, that there was not going to be enough interest in it to warrant publication [of *Collected Poems*].[43]

By "antiquated," Barnard meant her interests in nature and mythology, deemed "utterly out of fashion from 1930 onwards for almost forty years," she told Molly O'Hara Ewing in 1992.[44] But these interests had come very much back into fashion by the time that Snyder, a self-confessed "Forest Beatnik,"[45] came on the scene, his poems merging mind and place in exacting diction very much anticipated by Barnard, his *Riprap* poems, in which "each rock" is "a word / a creek-washed stone / Granite . . . / Crystal and sediment linked hot"[46] following on, as if intuitively, from Barnard's sand poetics and Williams's attempt to merge the people with the stones. Just as Snyder and his friend Lew Welch internalized the northwestern forest canopy following their stints as forest fire lookouts in the 1950s, so too had Barnard internalized what lay beneath the canopy when she took the sawmill as a model. Just as Snyder, Welch, Michael McClure, and Jack Kerouac, as Rod Phillips has argued,[47] developed an unusual strand within Beat literature in their devising of a nonurban Beat aesthetic, so too had Barnard set an example in her nonmetropolitan modernism, which eschewed the city as a subject and took the desolate spaces of the green "cool country" of the Northwest as a valid—and necessary—site for literary enquiry. If anything, this was entirely appropriate, for her contrastive "spare but musical" aesthetic was not ever going to be found in the bustling metropolis. Williams and his Dadaist friends, "restless" and looking for "the immediate image,"[48] found new forms for the new art in the geometry, speed, and movement of the city; Barnard found their counterparts in the spare, abandoned spaces of the Pacific Northwest, in the logging trestle, in the flat, reflective shoreline, in the quiet stream under the highway bridge, in the bloodless stones by a lake beach, in the trail roads "spongy with sawdust." "I think that [landscape] the luckiest chance of my life," Barnard said of the "little-known landscape" that she had come from when she arrived in New York with sawdust in her hair. It was the "luckiest" of landscapes partly because of the opportunity it offered her to understand the literary past and find ways of scoring smooth lines forward. For one of the reasons Barnard did not seek the kind of rupture from modernism like some of peers did, such as Randall Jarrell, was that she felt that her regional background gave her a particular and unique perspective on modern poetry: a "space-perspective." As she explained to Pound in 1937, as his letters signaled growing enthusiasm for her work, "Perhaps the reason I show so much discernment in the case of my own generation is that I have the space-perspective as a substitute for the time-perspective."[49] Jarrell might have felt the "rails terminate" in modernism, yet the rails of such a project had not yet extended to the Pacific Northwest by the time Barnard first began writing in the late 1920s. The largely uncharted Northwest had a different kind of "newness" to it than the technological "new" of the city; this, too, demanded its place in poetry. It was no less than what Precisionist painter Louis Lozowick called for in America's artists in the year Barnard wrote the earliest poems to appear in her archives, demanding that they locate the nation's art in "the grain elevators of Minneapolis, the steel mills of Pittsburgh, the oil wells of Oklahoma" as much as in "the skyscrapers of New York" in an essay for the catalogue of the Machine-Age Show held in New York in 1927.[50] Barnard added, in poetry, the sawmills of Washington; its forests; its mountains; its rivers, streams, and creeks; its clearings; its coastline; its roads; its railroads. "You see," Barnard told a local newspaper in 1979, "I came along post-Imagism, but I didn't know it. I grew up in what Pound called a 'half savage country out of date,' and it would take a while for the ground swell to get here. I was living in an era of social poetry, but I wasn't writing social poetry, so people would dismiss what I was doing as 'nature poetry.' It wasn't."[51]

In such attention to the fine particulars of place, Barnard anticipated the kind of "hyper-local" Imagism (as I interpret it) that Charles Olson was to put forward in the postwar years. In her operation of a "space-perspective as a substitute for the time-perspective," Barnard provided a vital link between Poundian-Williamsian modernism and the open form of Olson, who declared in 1964 that any literary enquiry into the condition of "America" should pursue space as much as time: "the *locus* is now both place & time."[52] In her tenacious pursuit of what was personal and local to her, Barnard's aesthetic stretched the boundaries of what the Imagist sought to give "direct presentation" of, from the "thing itself" (*any* thing, regardless of time and place) to particularly American things, in their place of encounter. By the 1960s, Olson was redrawing the boundaries of Imagism in his criticism as Barnard had done in her poetry. As he told Ed Dorn:

> but that the process of the imagination is from 1) a place person
> thing event—to—2) the naming of it—to—3) the reenactment
> or representation of it, in other words
> object name image or
> story[53]

Here, "thing" is placed in a continuous string of words, "place person thing event"; all four concepts are important and integral to the imagination. Although there thus seems to be no hierarchy of materials for the imagination to "name" and "reenact" or "represent," Olson's positioning of "place" ahead of any other word and "event" last is telling; he seems, like Barnard, to privilege the "space-perspective" over one shaped by chronology. From the "more or less conventional surface" of Barnard's poems "loopin' the loop" with metrics of the 1930s to the broken surfaces of Olson's "projective verse" of the 1950s, both, in their own way, answered the question that Pound had asked of Harriet Monroe as she was starting up *Poetry* back in 1912: "Can you teach the American poet that poetry *is* an *art*, an art with a technique, with media, an art that must be in constant flux, a constant change of manner, if it is to live?" Pound had heckled the Chicago editor. "Can you teach him that it is not a pentametric echo of the sociological dogma printed in last year's magazines?"[54] Pound's ponies delivered a resounding "yes."

Barnard's poetry of her emergent years, from the poems she first sent to Pound in 1933 through to the collection that had Williams buzzing with excitement about the "new" being "all there" in 1952, was, to steal a phrase from Babette Deutsch, of "a bright particular excellence."[55] And it seems that Barnard had taken another phrase from Deutsch when she gestured toward her achievement in her conclusion to *Assault on Mount Helicon*. "To scale the heights, one must be born with eagle wings and lion haunches," she speculates in her very last sentence, "but genuine griffons are as rare as unicorns."[56] Although never one to blast her own trumpet, Barnard knew what kind of griffon (the Reed mascot, no less) she was, for she told Deutsch over and over in letters that she possessed certain convictions about poetry. Such convictions, Deutsch told Barnard in 1937, "are almost as rare as unicorns."[57] I doubt the repetition was lost on Barnard, always the exacting archivist who almost certainly had all her letters to hand as she embarked upon her memoir, always determined, if not delighted, to find the precise source of important ideas where she could, as her extensive research papers into ethnobotany and archeoastronomy for *The Mythmakers* and *Time and the White Tigress* testify. I would like to think she might be pleased at my attempt to go to the source, here, as well as the incorporation, throughout this book, of material from the substantial and tantalizing archives that have recently come to light. For Barnard said that the 1880s was "a great decade for the hatching of griffons: Williams born in 1883, Pound in 1885, Marianne in 1887. Add Eliot, 1888; H.D., 1886," concluding that "there must have been some conjunction of planets presaging the birth of American poets."[58] It is a conjunction that stretched beyond that time, of course, including Barnard's own "great decade" of "griffons" born in the 1900s and those that followed after. If, in economics and politics, the twentieth century was seen as the American century, then the same was true in poetry. Barnard was no mere footnote in all of this, and this book is no routine addition to the field of recovery studies, which some think are flooded. Barnard's achievement was, like her poetry, of "a bright particular excellence," her firm and enduring contribution to the later stages of American modernism as "hard" and "substantial" as the "colors" she wanted for her writing, "*on* something, not transparent," and it is high time she was recognized for this and, to quote Williams, saluted seriously. So to steal a phrase from Barnard: here be griffons.[59]

Epilogue

The Mary Barnard Papers

A Note

The Mary Barnard Papers were transferred from the archives of Elizabeth J. Bell, literary executor to Mary Barnard's estate, in Vancouver, Washington, to the Yale Collection of American Literature at the Beinecke Rare Book and Manuscript Library in January 2005. I consulted some of these papers (some originals, some copies) in Vancouver during visits to Elizabeth J. Bell in 2003, 2006, 2009, and 2011. I also consulted some of these papers at the Beinecke during my tenure as H.D. Fellow 2007–2008. For reasons of transparency, I have thus referenced materials according to the source I personally consulted during the preparation of this book—either "Mary Barnard Papers, provided by Elizabeth J. Bell, literary executor to the estate of Mary Barnard, Vancouver, Washington," or "Mary Barnard Papers, Yale Collection of American Literature, Beinecke Rare Book and Manuscript Library, Yale University."

Notes

Chapter One. "Spare but Musical": The Poetry of Mary Barnard

1. Mary Barnard, journal, 1932, marked in pencil "Mary Ethel Barnard, Reed," one of two sets (manufacturer: Chief. Student's Note Book No. 639), Mary Barnard Papers, provided by Elizabeth J. Bell, literary executor to the estate of Mary Barnard, Vancouver, Washington.

2. Barnard, *Assault on Mount Helicon*, 15.

3. Mary Barnard to Ezra Pound, letter, October 11, 1933, Ezra Pound Papers, Yale Collection of American Literature, Beinecke Rare Book and Manuscript Library, Yale University, New Haven, Conn.

4. Ezra Pound, "In a Station of the Metro," in *Personae*, 111.

5. Mary Barnard to Emily Grosholz, letter, January 8, 1989, Mary Barnard Papers, provided by Elizabeth J. Bell. Grosholz was a poet and advisory editor at *The Hudson Review* at the time this letter was written.

6. Ezra Pound to Mary Barnard, second letter of two, August 13, 1934, Mary Barnard Papers, provided by Elizabeth J. Bell.

7. Ezra Pound to Mary Barnard, letter, November 28, 1934, Mary Barnard Papers, provided by Elizabeth J. Bell.

8. Barnard, *Assault on Mount Helicon*, 27.

9. Barnard, poetry reading. Recording provided by Thomas J. Donovan, Latin professor at the University of Portland and long-term friend of Barnard.

10. Barnard, *Assault on Mount Helicon*, 280.

11. Ibid. Italics Barnard's.

12. Ibid., 282.

13. Ibid.

14. Ibid.

15. Flint, "Imagisme," 199. Ezra Pound's essay "A Few Don'ts by an Imagiste" appeared immediately after Flint's essay, 200–206.

16. Mary Barnard, "Shoreline," 255. Subsequent references to "Shoreline" are to the version as it was first published in this particular volume of *Poetry*; Barnard later omitted "The smudged odor/ . . . Stains as with color the salt stench of the sea," increasing the staccato rhythm, I think. In her early poems, Barnard used capital letters to start every line, a practice she had dropped by the time she published *Collected Poems* in 1979.

17. Ezra Pound, "A Few Don'ts by an Imagiste," *Poetry* 1, no. 6 (March 1913), 200–206: p. 200.

18. Barnard, "North Window," dated February 4, 1936, in Barnard's hand, Mary Barnard Papers, provided by Elizabeth J. Bell.

19. H.D., *Sea Garden*, 41.

20. Ibid., 20.

21. Ibid., 1.

22. Aldington, "A Young American Poet," 23.

23. Flint, "The Poetry of H.D.," 72.

24. For this insight I am indebted to Dr. Eric White, Oxford Brookes University.

25. Viola Baxter Jordan to Mary Barnard, letter, April 8, 1948, Mary Barnard Papers, provided by Elizabeth J. Bell.

26. Williams, "Spring and All," *Selected Poems*, 45.

27. Wilson, "American Writing: 1941."

28. Barnard, journal, 1932.

29. Barnard, "Creed," preface to "The Horae of Mary Ethel Barnard."

30. Williams, "Against the Weather," 1939, in *Selected Essays*, 212.

31. Mary Barnard quoted by Jane Van Cleve, "Hearing Sappho," copy courtesy of the Mary Barnard Papers, Yale Collection of American Literature, Beinecke Rare Book and Manuscript Library.

32. Carlson, *Contemporary Northwest Writing*, 3.

33. William Carlos Williams to Louis Zukofsky, letter, April 21, 1936, in Ahearn, *The Correspondence of William Carlos Williams and Louis Zukofsky*, 232.

34. James Laughlin to Mary Barnard, letter, July 27, 1978, Mary Barnard Papers, Yale Collection of American Literature.

35. Until this book, the only published criticism that placed Barnard at the center was the Spring 1994 special edition of *Paideuma* and my own essays in *Paideuma* and *Western American Literature*.

36. O'Hara Ewing, "The Poetry of Mary Barnard,"—67. O'Hara Ewing is reiterating an observation made by Valerie Trueblood in 1982. See Trueblood, review of *Collected Poems* by Mary Barnard, 10–11.

37. The newly catalogued Mary Barnard Papers include manuscripts of poetry, prose, and nonfiction (both unpublished and published), correspondence with editors and poets (including James Laughlin, Marianne Moore, Ezra and Dorothy Pound, May Sarton, and William Carlos Williams), travel journals, and photographs, as well as first editions of many of her works. For more information, visit http://beineckepoetry.wordpress.com/2006/10/23/mary-barnard-papers/.

38. D. D. Paige to Mary Barnard, letter, November 3, 1950, Mary Barnard Papers, Yale Collection of American Literature.

39. John Crowe Ransom to Mary Barnard, letter, September 3, 1941, Mary Barnard Papers, Yale Collection of American Literature.

40. Theodore Purdy to Mary Barnard, letter, September 27, 1938, Mary Barnard Papers, Yale Collection of American Literature.

41. Ibid.

42. William Carlos Williams to Mary Barnard, letter, January 30, 1935, in Barnard, *Assault on Mount Helicon*, 64.

43. Barnard, *Assault on Mount Helicon*, 86.

44. Florence Codman to Mary Barnard, letter, May 25, 1937, Mary Barnard Papers, Yale Collection of American Literature.

45. Reader's report for Arrow Editions on an unpublished collection by Mary Barnard, enclosed in a letter from Florence Codman to Mary Barnard, May 8, 1936, Mary Barnard Papers, Yale Collection of American Literature.

46. Monro, "The Imagists Discussed," 79.

47. Flint, "The Poetry of H.D.," 72.

48. Barnard, *Assault on Mount Helicon*, 97.

49. James Laughlin to Mary Barnard, letter, September 17, 1937, Mary Barnard Papers, Yale Collection of American Literature.

50. Barnard, *Assault on Mount Helicon*, 194.

51. Ibid., 190.

52. Pound is cited thus by D. D. Paige in a letter to Mary Barnard, November 3, 1950, Mary Barnard Papers, Yale Collection of American Literature.

53. Babette Deutsch to Mary Barnard, letter, February 13, 1941, Mary Barnard Papers, provided by Elizabeth J. Bell.

54. Babette Deutsch to Mary Barnard, letter, May 30, 1941, Mary Barnard Papers, provided by Elizabeth J. Bell.

55. William Carlos Williams to Mary Barnard, letter, March 26, 1937, Mary Barnard Papers, provided by Elizabeth J. Bell.

56. Barnard, *Assault on Mount Helicon*, 94.

57. Barnard, "A Note on Poetry," 5.

58. Barnard, *Assault on Mount Helicon*, 105.

59. Babette Deutsch to Mary Barnard, letter, July 8, 1938, Mary Barnard Papers, provided by Elizabeth J. Bell.

60. Babette Deutsch to Mary Barnard, letter, November 30, 1937, Mary Barnard Papers, provided by Elizabeth J. Bell.

61. Babette Deutsch to Mary Barnard, letter, February 13, 1941, Mary Barnard Papers, provided by Elizabeth J. Bell.

62. Barnard, *Assault on Mount Helicon*, 21.

63. Ibid., 20.

64. Ibid., 98.

65. Mary Barnard to her cousin Suzanne Ila Gray, letter, May 2, 1986, Mary Barnard Papers, provided by Elizabeth J. Bell.

66. Barnard, *Assault on Mount Helicon*, 31.

67. Mary Barnard to Ezra Pound, letter, February 10, 1937, Ezra Pound Papers.

68. Mary Barnard to Ezra Pound, letter, December 26, 1934, Ezra Pound Papers.

69. Mary Barnard, quoted in Helle, "Dialogue with Mary Barnard," 29.

70. See Randall Jarrell's essay of 1942, "The End of the Line," in his *Kipling, Auden & Co.*, 76–83.

71. Jarrell, "A Note on Poetry," 88.

72. Barnard, *Assault on Mount Helicon*, 123.

73. Babette Deutsch to Mary Barnard, letter, April 2, 1938, Mary Barnard Papers, provided by Elizabeth J. Bell.

74. William Carlos Williams to Mary Barnard, letter, March 26, 1937, Mary Barnard Papers, provided by Elizabeth J. Bell.

75. Marianne Moore to Ezra Pound, letter, November 24, 1936, in Costello, Goodridge, and Miller, *Selected Letters of Marianne Moore*, 371.

76. Barnard, *Assault on Mount Helicon*, 276. Pound is referring to Barnard's Greenwich Village apartment in a building on Minetta Street.

77. Barnard, *Assault on Mount Helicon*, 61.

78. Ibid., 106.

79. Ibid.

80. Ibid., 112.

81. Mary Barnard to Ezra Pound, letter, April 1, 1934, Ezra Pound Papers.

82. Mary Barnard to Samuel and Bertha Hoard Barnard, letter, April 22, 1939, Mary Barnard Papers, Yale Collection of American Literature.

83. Mary Barnard to Molly O'Hara Ewing, letter, January 9, 1992, cited in O'Hara Ewing, "The Poetry of Mary Barnard—," 67.

84. Barnard, *Assault on Mount Helicon*, 88.

85. William Carlos Williams to Louis Zukofsky, letter, April 21, 1936, in Ahearn, *Correspondence of William Carlos Williams*, 232.

86. Robert Bertholf to Mary Barnard, letter August 16, 1983, Mary Barnard Papers, Yale Collection of American Literature.

87. Mary Barnard to William Carlos Williams, letter, March 24, ca. 1958, William Carlos Williams Papers.

88. For this aspect of Barnard's attitude regarding the preservation of her work, I am indebted to Elizabeth J. Bell, literary executor to Mary Barnard's literary estate.

89. Elizabeth Bishop to Mary Barnard, letter, May 6, 1973, Mary Barnard Papers, provided by Elizabeth J. Bell.

90. Hamilton, *Against Oblivion*, 182.

91. Barnard, *Assault on Mount Helicon*, 60.

92. Hamilton, *Against Oblivion*, 182.

93. Barnard, *Assault on Mount Helicon*, 214.

94. Ibid., xvii–xviii.

95. James Laughlin to Mary Barnard, letter, August 8, 1940. Mary Barnard Papers, Yale Collection of American Literature.

96. James Laughlin to Mary Barnard, letter, August 9, 1940, Mary Barnard Papers, Yale Collection of American Literature.

97. Jarrell, "A Note on Poetry," 85.

98. Barnard, "A Note on Poetry," 5.

99. William Carlos Williams to John Riordan, letter, January 26, 1926, in Mariani, *William Carlos Williams*, 251.

100. Mary Barnard to William Carlos Williams, letter, undated (begins "You don't need to tell me to keep writing, for pity's sake"), William Carlos Williams Papers.

101. Mary Barnard to William Carlos Williams, letter, December 22, 1959, William Carlos Williams Papers.

102. Barnard, *Assault on Mount Helicon*, xvii.

103. Babette Deutsch to Mary Barnard, letter, May 31, 1939, Mary Barnard Papers, provided by Elizabeth J. Bell.

104. Review cited in a letter from Mary Barnard to August Fruge, August 31, 1988, Mary Barnard Papers, Yale Collection of American Literature.

105. May Sarton to Mary Barnard, letter, May 4, 1984, Mary Barnard Papers, Yale Collection of American Literature.

106 Mary Barnard to James Anderson, letter, November 8, 1978, Mary Barnard Papers, Yale Collection of American Literature.

107. Mary Barnard to the president of the New England Poetry Club, letter, December 29, 1987, Mary Barnard Papers, Yale Collection of American Literature.

108. Ezra Pound to Mary Barnard, letter, winter 1939 (precise date unknown), in Barnard, *Assault on Mount Helicon*, 152.

109. Barnard, *Assault on Mount Helicon*, 153.

110. Ibid.

111. Barnard, *Collected Poems*, 66.

Chapter Two: Late Imagism

1. Barnard, *Assault on Mount Helicon*, 35–36.

2. Barnard, "The Carver."

3. Barnard, "Disillusionment."

4. Barnard, "Over the Hill with the Moon."

5. The last line of "The Carver" can be scanned for stressed/unstressed syllables as follows:

o o / / /o o o / / /
With the hard, bright chisel of the thin-edged moon

6. Barnard, *Assault on Mount Helicon*, 36.

7. Until, that is, the launch of publishing house New Directions in the mid-1930s, which was to do much to enlarge Williams's reputation with the American public.

8. Barnard, *Assault on Mount Helicon*, 38.

9. Ibid., 39.

10. Barnard, "The Horae."

11. Barnard, *Assault on Mount Helicon*, 51.

12. Ibid., 52.

13. Mary Barnard, quoted by Van Cleve, "Hearing Sappho."

14. Ezra Pound, quoted by William Stafford in his introduction to Barnard's *Collected Poems*.

15. Ezra Pound to Mary Barnard, postcard, February 23, 1934, in Paige, *The Letters of Ezra Pound*, 254.

16. Barnard, *Assault on Mount Helicon*, 77–78.

17. H.D., *End to Torment*, 18.

18. Barnard, *Assault on Mount Helicon*, 69–70.

19. From the unsubmitted portion of Barnard, "The Horae of Mary Ethel Barnard," Mary Barnard Papers, provided by Elizabeth J. Bell.

20. Barnard, *Assault on Mount Helicon*, 14.

21. Ibid., 16; italics Barnard's.

22. Ibid., 14.

23. Ibid., 14–15.

24. James Anderson, address, memorial service for Mary Barnard, Vancouver, Washington, transcript, September 4, 2001, Special Collections, Reed College Library.

25. Barnard, *Assault on Mount Helicon*, 14.

26. Barnard, *Collected Poems*, 11–12.

27. Barnard, *Cool Country*, 9.

28. Mary Barnard to August Fruge, letter, April 6, 1982, Mary Barnard Papers, Yale Collection of American Literature.

29. Ezra Pound to Mary Barnard, letter, Spring 1938 (precise date unknown), in Barnard, *Assault on Mount Helicon*, 118.

30. William Carlos Williams to Mary Barnard, letter, October 6, 1938 (precise date unknown), in Barnard, *Assault on Mount Helicon*, 136.

31. Ibid., 13.

32. Ibid., 19.

33. David Wagoner, cited in Nicholas O'Connell, *At the Field's End*, 40.

34. Barnard, "Faun in Exile.."

35. Barnard, *Assault on Mount Helicon*, 19.

36. Mary Barnard to H.D., letter, March 10, 1943, H.D. Papers, Yale Collection of American Literature, Beinecke Rare Book and Manuscript Library, Yale University, New Haven, Conn.

37. Barnard, *Assault on Mount Helicon*, 18.

38. In H.D.'s *Sea Garden*, see the following poems: "Hermes of the Ways," "Pursuit," "Sea Gods," "Sea Iris," "Sea Poppies," "Sea Lily," "Sea Rose," "Sea Violet," "The Gift," "The Shrine," and "The Wind Sleepers." In Mary Barnard's *Cool Country*, see "Lethe," "Note to a Neapolitan," "Shoreline," and "Wine Ship." Unpublished Barnard poems featuring sand include "An Evening by the Sea," "Chapter 1," "Commerce," "Fire," "Forest Fire," "For Jane," "For Those Who Dwell on the Marches," "The Invitation," "Moonstone," and "The Sound to which the Sea Is Stirred." Mary Barnard Papers, provided by Elizabeth J. Bell. Sand also appears in "Ondine," published in *Poetry* in 1935, and "The Silk Leaf," published in *American Prefaces* in January 1936; neither were collected into *Cool Country*.

39. H.D., *End to Torment*, 35.

40. See, for example, Gregory, *H.D. and Hellenism*, which calls attention to the influence of Walter Pater's aesthetics of crystal on H.D.'s poetry (p. 85). See also Ostriker, "No Rule of Procedure" and Pondrom, "H.D. and the Origins of Imagism."

41. Barnard had many regionally inspired nicknames with which she signed correspondence to her family, including "Sand Flea" and "The Splinter," the former a reference to days spent roaming the sands of Ocean Park, Washington, the latter

a reference to being a lumber merchant's daughter. See Barnard's extensive family correspondence, Mary Barnard Papers, Yale Collection of American Literature.

42. H.D., *Sea Garden*, 41.

43. Ibid.

44. Ibid., 9.

45. Pound, "A Few Don'ts," 200.

46. H.D., *Sea Garden*, 20.

47. Ibid., 29.

48. Mary Barnard, "For Jane," possibly 1934, Mary Barnard Papers, provided by Elizabeth J. Bell.

49. Barnard, *Assault on Mount Helicon*, 15.

50. H.D., *Sea Garden*, 1.

51. Ibid., 12.

52. Mary Barnard, "An Evening by the Sea," Mary Barnard Papers, provided by Elizabeth J. Bell; H.D., *Sea Garden*, 31.

53. Mary Barnard to Ezra Pound, letter, April 15, 1938, Ezra Pound Papers.

54. Emily Dickinson, *Complete Poems of Emily Dickinson*, 180.

55. Barnard, "For Those Who Dwell Among the Marches," Mary Barnard Papers, provided by Elizabeth J. Bell.

56. See respectively, H.D.'s *Sea Garden*, 25, 31, 8.

57. See, respectively, H.D., *Sea Garden*, 20, 12, 40; Pound, *Personae*, 110–113. Alternatively, Pound's poems can be read as explorations of psychological notions of "the complex"—in the extensive references to water and fluids, it is possible that Pound was in part drawing upon his reading of Bernard Hart's formulation of the subconscious as "a sea of unconscious emotions" ("The Conception of the Subconscious," 129). I am grateful to Helen Carr for bringing Hart's influence to my attention.

58. Barnard, *Assault on Mount Helicon*, 53.

59. Ibid., 56.

60. Ibid., 282.

61. See, respectively, "Lai," first published in *Poetry* in April 1935; "Planks," "Provincial," and "Playroom," first published in *New Democracy* in February 1936 in a sequence titled "Eleven Poems"; "Adversity and the Generations," first published in James Laughlin's *New Directions 2* in 1937; "The Rapids," published in *Furioso* in 1940; and "Note to a Neapolitan," published in *Cool Country* in 1940.

62. Barnard, *Cool Country*, 14. "Roots" was first published under the title "Northwest Anchorage" in *New Republic*, 368.

63. Barnard, *Cool Country*, 10.

64. Ibid.

65. In a letter of 1938, Pound advised Barnard that "you better get a language and an author / greek, latin or chinese / the latter being less occupied ground . . . as to the AUTHOR; you will want a SUBJECT by the time you are 40 / may as well pick it NOW so that you will then know something about it." Quoted in Barnard, *Assault on Mount Helicon*, 116–117.

66. Ezra Pound, "A Retrospect," *Literary Essays of Ezra Pound*, 12.

67. Ezra Pound, cited in Reck, *Ezra Pound*, 14–15.

68. Pettijohn, Potter, and Siever, *Sand and Sandstone*, 1.

69. Barnard, *Assault on Mount Helicon*, 283.

70. Ezra Pound to Harriet Monroe, letter, October 1912, in Paige, *The Letters of Ezra Pound*, 11.

71. William Carlos Williams quoted in MacGowan, *The Letters of Denise Levertov*, 11.

72. Marianne Moore to Mary Barnard, letter, September 11, 1934, Mary Barnard Papers, provided by Elizabeth J. Bell.

73. Pound, "A Few Don'ts," 204.

74. Ibid., 200–201.

75. H.D. primarily uses this figure to describe the image her protagonist sees when looking at the other characters. See H.D., *Bid Me to Live*, 89.

76. Monro, "The Imagists Discussed," 77.

77. Pound, "A Few Don'ts," 205.

78. Lowell in Lawrence, Lowell, et al, *Some Imagist Poets*, vi.

79. Pettijohn et al., *Sand and Sandstone*, 2.

80. Pound, *Gaudier-Brzeska*, 92.

81. Pound, "A Few Don'ts," 200.

82. Barnard, *Collected Poems*, 91.

83. Barnard, "The Invitation," Mary Barnard Papers provided by Elizabeth J. Bell.

84. O'Connell, *At the Field's End*, ix.

85. Mary Barnard to Ezra Pound, letter, July 15, 1935, Ezra Pound Papers.

86. Barnard, *Cool Country*, 10, 40.

87. Mary Barnard to Ezra Pound, letter, February 10, 1937, Ezra Pound Papers.

88. From Barnard, *A Few Poems*, which has no page numbers. A copy of this poem can be found in Barnard, *Collected Poems*, on page 29.

89. Whitman, *Leaves of Grass*, 532.

90. Barnard, "The Trestle," 7.

91. Barnard, "Provincial II," 258.

92. Emerson, "The Poet," 281.

93. Barnard, "Shriek of Defiance (in the manner of Ezra Pound)," unpublished poem, 1932, Mary Barnard Papers, provided by Elizabeth J. Bell. A "Johnny-jump-up" is a small yellow and violet flower; native to Spain, it has flourished in the United States, particularly along roadsides and waste areas.

94. Mary Barnard to Ezra Pound, letter, October 11, 1933, Ezra Pound Papers.

95. Williams, prologue to *Kora in Hell*, 14.

Chapter Three: "A Would-Be Sappho"

1. Gordon, "Ezra Pound to Mary Barnard," 159.

2. Mary Barnard to her mother, letter, October 27, 1930, Mary Barnard Papers, provided by Elizabeth J. Bell.

3. H.D., *End to Torment*, 41.

4. For a detailed overview of the emergence of modern Sappho translations in Europe, see DeJean, *Fictions of Sappho*.

5. Vivien, *Sapho*.

6. See Edmonds, "Three Fragments of Sappho" and "More Fragments of Sappho."

7. This is the title that Aldington gave the poem for its first publication in *The New Freewoman* in September 1913 (see footnote 195). However, in *Des Imagistes*, Aldington changed the title to reflect its preliminary acquisition by Germany: "To Atthis (After the Manuscript of Sappho Now in Berlin)"—see Pound, *Des Imagistes*, 19.

8. See H.D.'s account in *End to Torment*, p. 40. Richard Aldington recounts this incident slightly differently; he thought it possible that H.D. might have in fact mailed it to Pound—see Aldington, *Life for Life's Sake*, 122.

9. Dorothy Shakespear to Ezra Pound, letter, September 14, 1911, in Omar Pound and Litz, *Ezra Pound and Dorothy Shakespear*, 58.

10. Pound, "The Return" and "Apparuit," 343–44.

11. Ezra Pound to Harriet Monroe, letter, October 1912, in Paige, *Selected Letters of Ezra Pound*, 11.

12. This version was entitled "To Atthis (From the Rather Recently Discovered Papyrus of Sappho Now in the British Museum)."

13. H.D., "The Poems of Sappho," 596.

14. *The Love of Myrrhine and Konallis and Other Prose Poems* was first published in Cleveland by Clerk's Press in 1917; very few copies of this first printing remain. A limited edition of one hundred and fifty signed copies was published in 1926 in Chicago by Pascal Covici.

15. See, for example, the first of this series—*The Poems of Anyte of Tegea*, translated by Richard Aldington, 7. There were six editions in this series, including *Poems and Fragments of Sappho*, translated by Edward Storer. Aldington and Storer's translations were later reprinted in one volume, entitled *The Poems of Anyte of Tegea and Poems and Fragments of Sappho*.

16. Reynolds, *The Sappho Companion*, 314.

17. Rohrbach, "H.D. and Sappho," 187.

18. Pound, *Personae*, 115.

19. Witemeyer, "Early Poetry," 50.

20. Paton, *The Greek Anthology*.

21. Pound, "A Few Don'ts," 205.

22. See, respectively, "Apples of Hesperides," in Lowell, *A Dome of Many-Coloured Glass*, 9–10; "The Captured Goddess," in Lowell, *Sword Blades and Poppy Seed*, 31–33; and "Madonna of the Evening Flowers," in Bradshaw and Munich, *Selected Poems of Amy Lowell*, 68–69.

23. Lowell, "The Sisters,"' in Bradshaw and Munich, *Selected Poems*, 22.

24. Longinus, *A Treatise on the Sublime*, 48.

25. H.D., "The Wise Sappho,"' in *Notes on Thought and Vision*, 58.

26. Ibid., 57.

27. Ibid., 58.

28. Collecott, *H.D. and Sapphic Modernism*, 161.

29. H.D., "The Wise Sappho," 58.

30. H.D., *Sea Garden*, 29.

31. Florence Codman to Mary Barnard, letter, May 25, 1937, Mary Barnard Papers, Yale Collection of American Literature.

32. Mary Barnard to Samuel and Bertha Hoard Barnard, letter, October 27, 1930, Mary Barnard Papers, Yale Collection of American Literature.

33. Barnard, "The Fool's Serenade," Mary Barnard Papers, provided by Elizabeth J. Bell.

34. Barnard, "Two Songs for Rosamond," Mary Barnard Papers, provided by Elizabeth J. Bell.

35. Barnard, "Blanchefleur," Mary Barnard Papers, provided by Elizabeth J. Bell.

36. Marianne Moore to Mary Barnard, letter, September 11, 1934, Mary Barnard Papers, provided by Elizabeth J. Bell.

37. Barnard, "Love Poem," Mary Barnard Papers, provided by Elizabeth J. Bell.

38. Mary Barnard to Samuel and Bertha Hoard Barnard, letter, October 27, 1930, Mary Barnard Papers, Yale Collection of American Literature.

39. Ibid.

40. Mary Barnard, "Cupbearer" and untitled poem that begins "Fire, snow, and the night," Mary Barnard Papers, provided by Elizabeth J. Bell.

41. Pound, "A Few Don'ts," 201.

42. See Barnard's fragment number 37 in *Sappho*.

43. See Barnard's fragment number 42 in *Sappho*.

44. See Barnard's fragment number 21 in *Sappho*.

45. "Leucas" derives from "leukos," which means "white." Leucas is an island in the Ionian sea, named after the whiteness of its rocks.

46. Barnard, "Departure," unpublished poem, 1935, Mary Barnard Papers, provided by Elizabeth J. Bell.

47. See Barnard's "A Footnote to These Translations" in *Sappho*, 102.

48. Bowra, *Greek Lyric Poetry*, 193.

49. Pound, *Personae*, 93.

50. Ricou, *The Arbutus/Madrone Files*, 16–17. Italics Ricou's.

51. Prins, *Victorian Sappho*, 5. Italics Prins's.

52. Mary Barnard, journal, 1932.

53. Gregory, *H.D. and Hellenism*, 154. The "pre-verbal level" that Gregory cites is a quotation from Carne-Ross's essay "Translation and Transposition," 8. Carne-Ross uses the term "pre-verbal level" to describe the point to which H.D. broke down Euripides's *Ion* before reconstituting it on her own terms. Gregory is somewhat misquoting Carne-Ross here, but creatively so, using the term to describe the extent to which H.D. had *absorbed* Sappho into her mind. Margaret Reynolds concurs with Gregory's usage and quotes it in *The Sappho History*: "Sappho's vocabulary, and her imagery, are everywhere in H.D. absorbed, as Gregory says . . . 'at the pre-verbal level.'" See Reynolds, *The Sappho History*, 219.

54. For this observation I am indebted to Bert G. Brehm, professor of biology emeritus at Reed College. On June 3, 2005, I attended one of Brehm's field

trips to the Columbia River Gorge, where Brehm emphasized the unique biology of the region.

55. For this example, and subsequent references to this poem, see Barnard, *Collected Poems*, 21–23. Although Barnard did not publish "The River Under Different Lights" in the mid-century period I am examining, her unpublished manuscripts show that she made several drafts of it during this time. When it was finished, it was significant enough for Barnard to set amid her *Collected Poems* in 1979.

56. Mary Barnard, "September," possibly 1932, Mary Barnard Papers, provided by Elizabeth J. Bell.

57. Barnard, *Collected Poems*, 23.

58. Williams, "A Sort of Song," in *Selected Poems*, 133.

59. Barnard, *Collected Poems*, 56. First published in *Poetry*, 262–63.

60. Williams, "The Red Wheelbarrow," in *Collected Poems*, 224.

61. William Carlos Williams to Ford Madox Ford, letter, 1931, cited in Mariani, *William Carlos Williams*, 330.

62. Williams, author's note to *Paterson*.

63. Ibid.

64. Williams, "The Red Wheelbarrow," in *Collected Poems*, 224.

65. Williams, author's note to *Paterson*.

66. Barnard, "Remarks on Poetry and the Physical World," 6.

67. Mary Barnard to William Carlos Williams, letter, September 16, 1939, William Carlos Williams Papers.

68. William Carlos Williams to Mary Barnard, letter, September 29, 1938, Mary Barnard Papers, provided by Elizabeth J. Bell. Williams is referring to the poem as it appeared in the *New York Herald Tribune* on September 25, 1938.

69. William Carlos Williams to Mary Barnard, letter, June 8, 1940, Mary Barnard Papers, provided by Elizabeth J. Bell.

70. William Carlos Williams to Mary Barnard, letter, October 6, 1938, Mary Barnard Papers, provided by Elizabeth J. Bell.

71. Williams, "Notes from a Talk on Poetry," 213.

72. Mary Barnard quoted in Van Cleve, "Hearing Sappho."

73. Barnard, *Cool Country*, 7.

74. For the geographical references in "The Rapids," I am indebted to Elizabeth J. Bell. Bell suggests that Beacon Rock is also the setting for one of Barnard's fables in *Three Fables*, "Ascent with Chorus."

75. See, respectively, Barnard's fragment numbers 1, 4, 5, 6, and 8, in *Sappho*.

76. See, respectively, Barnard's fragment numbers 11, 13, 41, and 43, in *Sappho*.

77. For further discussion of this, see Williamson, *Sappho's Immortal Daughters*, 75–84.

78. Prins, *Victorian Sappho*, 38.

79. See Barnard's translation of Sappho's Fragment Thirty-One (fragment number 39 in Barnard's translation), in which passion overwhelms the speaker so much that she reports "I can't / speak—my tongue is broken."

80. Barnard, fragment number 63 in *Sappho*.

81. Williams, "The Poem as a Field of Action" (1948), in *Selected Essays of William Carlos Williams*, 286. Italics mine.

82. For all references to "Shoreline" discussed in this section, see Barnard, "Shoreline," 254–56.

83. Reynolds, *The Sappho History*, 4. See, also, Yopie Prins's discussion of how Sappho permits the "I" into existence in *Victorian Sappho*, 38–39.

84. Mary Barnard, untitled poem that begins "The slenderly poised clean shaft of your fir," possibly 1937, Mary Barnard Papers, provided by Elizabeth J. Bell.

85. William Carlos Williams, quoted in Paul Mariani, *William Carlos Williams*, 490.

86. Emerson, "The Poet," 281.

87. Barnard, "A Footnote to These Translations" in *Sappho*, 95.

88. Barnard, *Cool Country*, 17.

89. Barnard, *Cool Country*, 28.

90. Babette Deutsch to Mary Barnard, letter, September 15, 1937, Mary Barnard Papers, provided by Elizabeth J. Bell.

91. Barnard, *Cool Country*, 13.

92. Williams, *Collected Poems*, 183.

93. Williams, "Caviar and Bread Again" (ca. 1930), in *Selected Essays*, 103.

94. See Mariani, *William Carlos Williams*.

95. Williams, "The Poem as a Field of Action" (1948), in *Selected Essays*, 290. Italics Williams's.

96. Williams, "Notes from a Talk on Poetry," 216.

97. Wilson, "American Writing."

98. Mariani, *William Carlos Williams*, 450.

99. Barnard, *Assault on Mount Helicon*, 289.

100. See Lattimore, *Greek Lyrics*; Groden, *Sappho*; Barnstone, *Sappho*; O'Connell, *Sappho*; and Davenport, *Archilochos, Sappho, Alkman*.

101. Fitts, foreword to *Sappho*, ix–x.

102. Guy Davenport to Mary Barnard, letter, January 18, 1981, Mary Barnard Papers, provided by Elizabeth J. Bell.

103. Barnard, fragment number 64 in *Sappho*.

104. Williams, "Marianne Moore" (1931), in *Selected Essays*, 123.

105. Barnard, "Further Notes on Metric," 153. Italics Barnard's.

106. Gordon, "Ezra Pound to Mary Barnard," 171.

Chapter Four: "A New Way of Measuring Verse"

1. Mary Barnard to Ezra Pound, letter, June 14, 1937, Ezra Pound Papers; Roberts, *The Faber Book of Modern Verse*.

2. Barnard, "A Communication on Greek Metric," 148.

3. Elizabeth J. Bell, letter to the editor, *Reed Magazine*, June 2010, accessed March 17, 2013, http://www.reed.edu/reed_magazine/june2010/columns/letters/index.html.

4. Eliot, "Reflections on Vers Libre," 518–19.

5. Williams, "America, Whitman, and the Art of Poetry," 2.

6. William Carlos Williams to Mary Barnard, letter, December 31, 1952, Mary Barnard Papers, provided by Elizabeth J. Bell.

7. Barnard, *Assault on Mount Helicon*, 24.

8. Ibid., 3. Riley was no stranger to Barnard's parents, who were married in Riley's hometown of Greenfield, Indiana, in 1907, when Riley was at the height of his fame, before they headed west on a one-way homesteader's ticket. Barnard's mother had worked for a brief time with Riley's brother, and her mother's great-uncle had known Riley at school.

9. Ibid., 12.

10. Ibid., 25.

11. Ibid., 29–30. Italics mine.

12. Ibid., 39.

13. Ibid., 39.

14. Barnard, "Lethe," 354.

15. Ezra Pound to Mary Barnard, postcard, October 29, 1933, cited in Barnard, *Assault on Mount Helicon*, 53.

16. Flint, "Imagisme," 199.

17. Barnard, *Assault on Mount Helicon*, 12.

18. Mary Barnard to Ezra Pound, letter, November 15, 1933, Ezra Pound Papers.

19. Ezra Pound to Mary Barnard, letter, December 2, 1933, in Barnard, *Assault on Mount Helicon*, 54.

20. Quoted in Barnard, *Assault on Mount Helicon*, 55. Layout is duplicated from Barnard's transcriptions of Pound's communications, of which Barnard says: "I have retained his own spelling, spacing, capitalization and punctuation except for a few typographical errors which I have corrected. Marginalia are incorporated in the text. Wherever a word is followed by a series of dots, these dots are Pound's own punctuation and do not indicate omissions from the original text." Barnard, *Assault on Mount Helicon*, 52–53.

21. Pound, "The Tradition," 140.

22. Mary Barnard to Ezra Pound, letter, January 2, 1934, Ezra Pound Papers.

23. Barnard, "Lai," 28–29.

24. I am using the terms "long" and "short" as they were used by classical metrical theorists in scansion of quantitative verse, whose practice is defined in Preminger and Brogan, *New Princeton Encyclopedia*, 1009–10.

25. As Barnard did in her quantitative scansions, I am following here the traditional practice for scanning quantitative verse for long/short syllables using breves (–) and macrons (◡), respectively, with "×" for indeterminate quantity.

26. Such deviation is evident in the first, second, third, fifth, and thirteenth syllables.

27. These include "A Defence of the Poet's Method," "Commerce," "Departure," and one untitled poem whose first line begins "Tranquil and shallow, spread across the flat stones." Mary Barnard Papers, provided by Elizabeth J. Bell.

28. Quotations are taken from the poem which begins with the words "Tranquil and shallow." Mary Barnard Papers, provided by Elizabeth J. Bell.

29. This poem is dated "Nov. 21 1935?" in Barnard's typeface, probably a copy of an original from 1935. "A Defence of the Poet's Method" was subsequently published in *New Democracy* in February 1936 in a sequence of eleven poems.

30. Pound, *Personae*, 64–65.

31. Mary Barnard to Ezra Pound, letter, April 20, 1935, Ezra Pound Papers.

32. Barnard, *Assault on Mount Helicon*, 80.

33. Ibid., 81. Longfellow's poem *Evangeline* is in accentual hexameter.

34. Mary Barnard, "Rouse," notes in Mary Barnard's typescript, Mary Barnard Papers, Yale Collection of American Literature. In a letter to August Fruge of April 25, 1982, Barnard writes: "I got out the Rouse letter last night and went over it. It is eight pages of what I've heard described as 'Oxford squiggle.' . . . I think the whole letter deserves to be published somewhere, in Terrell's *Sagetrieb*, perhaps."

35. Mary Barnard to Ezra Pound, letter, July 15, 1935, Ezra Pound Papers.

36. Barnard, "A Communication on Greek Metric," 150.

37. This poem is as it appears in a version in an unpublished book of poems sent to Barnard's friend Mildred Cline sometime during their college years (1928–1932). A later version of "Commerce" was subsequently published in 1935 in *The Westminster Quarterly*, a short-lived modernist journal edited by Pound, John Drummond, and T. C. Wilson.

38. Mary Barnard, "Rouse," Mary Barnard Papers, Yale Collection of American Literature. Scansion marks Barnard's (possibly after Rouse).

39. Barnard, *Assault on Mount Helicon*, 57.

40. Victor Chittick to Mary Barnard, letter, March 30, 1955, Mary Barnard Papers, provided by Elizabeth J. Bell.

41. Barnard, "Faun in Exile," 25–26.

42. Barnard, *Assault on Mount Helicon*, 284.

43. Ibid., 54.

44. Barnard, "A Communication on Greek Metric," 147–48. Scansion marks are Barnard's, which she marks beneath the line, as I have reproduced here. My own scansion marks, in other parts of this chapter, appear above the line.

45. According to *The New Princeton Encyclopedia of Poetry and Poetics*, Glyconics can be scanned as follows: × × – ◡ ◡ – ◡ –. See *The New Encyclopedia of Poetry and Poetics*, 9 and 479.

46. Barnard's epitrites here are interesting, for they have nothing in common with the definition offered by *The New Princeton Encyclopedia of Poetry and Poetics* except for their composure from four syllables. Typically, the definition explains, epitrites are composed of two longs to a long and short and usually take any one of four possible combinations ("respectively ◡ – – –, – ◡ – –, – – ◡ –, – – – ◡"). I have not been able to trace the source of Barnard's usage. See *The New Encyclopedia of Poetry and Poetics*, 379.

47. Barnard, *Cool Country*, 7.

48. Ibid., 19.

49. "There is . . . in the best verse a sort of residue of sound which remains in the ear of the hearer and acts more or less like an organ-base," commented Pound in "A Few Don'ts by an Imagiste" (p. 205).

50. See Gordon, "Ezra Pound to Mary Barnard."

51. William Carlos Williams quoted in Thirlwall, *Selected Letters of William Carlos Williams*, 129.

52. Williams, *Selected Essays*, 286.

53. William Carlos Williams, quoted in Thirlwall, *Selected Letters*, 136.

54. Barnard, "A Communication on Greek Metric," 148.

55. Ibid., 148–49.

56. Ibid., 149.

57. Barnard, "The Silk Leaf," 61.

58. "Cassandra" was published alongside "Lethe" in *New English Weekly*; this too can be scanned for balanced lines, as in the following excerpt:

– ∪ ∪ ∪ – / ∪ – – ∪ –
Write of her if you / will, but never try
∪ – ∪ ∪ ∪ – ∪ / ∪ – ∪ – – – ∪
To speak of her as though in / her person "I, Cassandra—"
– ∪ ∪ ∪ ∪ / – ∪ ∪ – ∪
Speak of her as the / least of the Trojan
– ∪ – / ∪ – ∪
Women might / have spoken

59. William Carlos Williams to Mary Barnard, letter, March 19, 1935, Mary Barnard Papers, provided by Elizabeth J. Bell.

60. Ibid.

61. Ezra Pound to Mary Barnard, letter, December 18, 1934, Mary Barnard Papers, provided by Elizabeth J. Bell.

62. Barnard, "Roots," 6. Brackets around the scansion marks correspond to the meter identified in the smaller brackets at the end of the line.

63. William Carlos Williams to Richard Eberhart, letter, May 23, 1954, in Thirlwall, *Selected Letters*, 326.

64. Ibid., 327.

65. Lowell, preface to *Sword Blades and Poppy Seed*, x–xi.

66. William Carlos Williams, quoted in Thirlwall, *Selected Letters*, 326.

67. Mary Barnard to Ezra Pound, letter, January 19, 1936, Ezra Pound Papers.

68. Barnard, "Further Notes on Metric," 156.

69. Williams, *Selected Essays*, 283.

70. Mary Barnard, "Road to Xanadu," unpublished poem, 1939, Furioso Papers.

71. Williams, *Paterson*, book 1, 6.

72. Barnard, "The Horae of Mary Ethel Barnard."

73. Barnard, *A Few Poems*.

74. Ezra Pound to Mary Barnard, postcard, February 23, 1934, in Barnard, *Assault on Mount Helicon*, 57.

75. William Carlos Williams to Mary Barnard, letter, December 31, 1952, Mary Barnard Papers, provided by Elizabeth J. Bell.

76. Williams, *Selected Essays*, 280. Italics Williams's.

77. Mary Barnard, folder marked "Red Notebook used in organizing Mount Helicon," box 1, Mary Barnard Papers, Yale Collection of American Literature.

78. See the paragraph that begins "It's not only a question of daring," in which Williams goes on to exclaim "Thank God we're not musicians, with our lack of structural invention we'd be ashamed to look ourselves in the face otherwise.

There is nothing interesting in the construction of our poems, nothing that can jog the ear out of its boredom." Williams, "On Measure," 338.

79. Barnard, *Assault on Mount Helicon*, 287.

80. Tate, "The Last Omnibus," 241–44.

81. Helle, "The Odysseys of Mary Barnard," 8. Sappho fragment taken from Barnard, *Sappho*.

82. Barnard, "A Communication on Greek Metric," 150.

83. Ibid., 152.

84. Barnard, fragment number 42 in *Sappho*.

85. Barnard, *Assault on Mount Helicon*, 290.

86. Barnard, fragment number 1 in *Sappho*.

87. Barnard, *Assault on Mount Helicon*, 293.

88. Barnard, *Assault on Mount Helicon*, 293.

89. Bell, "Mary Barnard."

Chapter Five: "A Bright Particular Excellence": The Achievement of Mary Barnard

1. Mary Barnard to August Fruge, letter, April 25, 1982, Mary Barnard Papers, Yale Collection of American Literature.

2. Mary Barnard to James Anderson, letter, November 4, 1978. Private correspondence given to the author by James Anderson in August 2009, to be deposited with the Mary Barnard Papers at the Beinecke.

3. William Carlos Williams to Mary Barnard, letter, June 1, 1948 (marked "1948?" by Barnard in ink), Mary Barnard Papers, provided by Elizabeth J Bell. With thanks to Elizabeth J. Bell for double-checking the date and wording of this source.

4. Ezra Pound to James Laughlin, letter, in Gordon, *Ezra Pound and James Laughlin*, 37.

5. Victor Chittick to Mary Barnard, letter, October 4, 1938, Mary Barnard Papers, provided by Elizabeth J. Bell.

6. Babette Deutsch to Mary Barnard, letter, September 15, 1937, Mary Barnard Papers, provided by Elizabeth J. Bell.

7. Ezra Pound to Mary Barnard, letter, undated, Mary Barnard Papers, provided by Elizabeth J. Bell.

8. Paul Mariani to Mary Barnard, letter, February 1, 1979, Mary Barnard Papers, Yale Collection of American Literature.

9. William Carlos Williams to Mary Barnard, letter, January 30, 1935, in Barnard, *Assault on Mount Helicon*, 65.

10. Florence Codman to Mary Barnard, letter, May 25, 1937, Mary Barnard Papers, Yale Collection of American Literature.

11. See Collecott, *H.D. and Sapphic Modernism*, 2–5; Gubar, "Sapphistries," 43–62.

12. Babette Deutsch to Mary Barnard, letter, September 29, 1958, Mary Barnard Papers, provided by Elizabeth J. Bell.

13. Barnard, *Assault on Mount Helicon*, 316–17.

14. Mary Barnard to August Fruge, letter, May 3, 1982, Mary Barnard Papers, Yale Collection of American Literature.

15. Mary Barnard to William Carlos Williams, letter, March 10, 1953, William Carlos Williams Papers. Yale Collection of American Literature.

16. Williams, *In the American Grain*, 221.

17. Barnard, *Assault on Mount Helicon*, 313.

18. All quotations in this paragraph are from Barnard, *Assault on Mount Helicon*, 313.

19. Mary Barnard to Carolyn Kizer, letter, July 18, 1984, Mary Barnard Papers, Yale Collection of American Literature. Empasis Barnard's.

20. Germaine Greer to Mary Barnard, letter, November 5, 1981, Mary Barnard Papers, Yale Collection of American Literature.

21. Germaine Greer to Mary Barnard, letter, December 2, 1981, Mary Barnard Papers, Yale Collection of American Literature.

22. Mary Barnard to Germaine Greer, letter, November 10, 1981, Mary Barnard Papers, Yale Collection of American Literature.

23. Mary Barnard to William Stafford, letter, October 15, 1978, Mary Barnard Papers, Yale Collection of American Literature.

24. Mary Barnard to William Carlos Williams, letter, March 24, ca. 1958, William Carlos Williams Papers.

25. See folder 2 of file marked "August Fruge (mainly regarding Mt. Helicon)," box 11, Mary Barnard Papers, Yale Collection of American Literature. For an excellent treatment of Williams's use of measure (and the intriguing inconsistencies with his theory), see Cushman, *William Carlos Williams and the Meanings of Measure*. Cushman attests that "exploring Williams's theory of measure entails a certain amount of deciphering, translating, and filling in of blanks. Here is what Williams says his verse is doing, and here is what it actually does" (p. 93). Noting that Williams falls short of a purely *technical* application of his theory that his verse was organized into units, as in music, that could be timed and counted, Cushman directs the reader toward the ways in which Williams more likely tended toward a *visual* application of his theory, in his use of enjambment and typography, and his use of the term "measure" as an aesthetic term.

26. Mary Barnard to Samuel and Bertha Hoard Barnard, letter, January 8, 1943, Mary Barnard Papers, Yale Collection of American Literature. Barnard dates this letter as 1942, but this is most probably an error, given the newness of the year and its relation to surrounding letters; I date it as 1943.

27. Barnard, *Assault on Mount Helicon*, 311.

28. Williams, "The American Background" (1934), in *Selected Essays*, 135.

29. Barnard, *Cool Country*, 16.

30. Williams, *Autobiography*, 383.

31. Williams, *Paterson*, book 5, 2.

32. Babette Deutsch to Mary Barnard, letter, October 4, 1958, Mary Barnard Papers, provided by Elizabeth J. Bell.

33. de Rachewiltz, "Dove St Memora," 8.

34. William Carlos Williams to Mary Barnard, handwritten poem enclosed with letter, January 19, 1940, Mary Barnard Papers, provided by Elizabeth J. Bell.

35. See jacket flap, Literary Classics of the United States, Inc., New York, N.Y. *American Poetry: The Twentieth Century*.

36. Mary Barnard to James Anderson, letter, November 4, 1978. Private correspondence given to the author by James Anderson.

37. Anne Ludlow to Mary Barnard, letter, March 29, 1984, in folder marked "Helicon correspondence," box 13, Mary Barnard Papers, Yale Collection of American Literature.

38. William Carlos Williams to Louis Zukofsky, letter, April 21, 1936, in Ahearn, *Correspondence of William Carlos Williams*, 232.

39. Babette Deutsch to Mary Barnard, letter, October 4, 1958, Mary Barnard Papers, provided by Elizabeth J. Bell.

40. Mary Barnard to James Anderson, letter, November 4, 1978. Private correspondence given to the author by James Anderson.

41. Corman, *Sappho*. Contains a slip of paper enclosed from the publisher with the following words: "*Sappho* drawn out of Mary Barnard's versions by Cid Corman." In one of the copies that Elizabeth J. Bell bought, there is a note regarding the chapbook's origins. In an email to me of May 4, 2010, Bell reports: "As near as I can make out, [the note] says 'Dear E. B.—I am Cid's long time friend and literary executor of his estate. We were fellow poets and friends together—also published under an imprint "Longhase [sic]—origin." The Wee Ones just evolved as Cid worked—he sent directly to us to publish. They have been no where else—Best wishes, BA [for Bob Arnold].'"

42. Muriel Rukeyser, quoted in letter from Babette Deutsch to Mary Barnard, July 8, 1938, Mary Barnard Papers, provided by Elizabeth J. Bell.

43. Helle, "Dialogue with Mary Barnard," 29.

44. O'Hara Ewing, "The Poetry of Mary Barnard," 67.

45. Snyder, *Earth House Hold*, 96.

46. Gary Snyder, "Riprap," in *Riprap*, 36.

47. Phillips, *Forest Beatniks*.

48. Williams, *Autobiography*, 148.

49. Mary Barnard to Ezra Pound, letter, June 14, 1937, Ezra Pound Papers.

50. Lozowick, "The Americanization of Art," 18.

51. Mary Barnard, quoted in Van Cleve, "Hearing Sappho."

52. Olson, *Bibliography on America*, 14. Emphasis Olson's.

53. Olson, *Bibliography*, 10.

54. Ezra Pound to Harriet Monroe, letter, August 18, 1912, in Paige, *Selected Letters*, 9.

55. Babette Deutsch to Mary Barnard, letter, September 29, 1958, Mary Barnard Papers, provided by Elizabeth J. Bell.

56. Barnard, *Assault on Mount Helicon*, 318.

57. Babette Deutsch to Mary Barnard, letter, September 15, 1937, Mary Barnard Papers, provided by Elizabeth J. Bell.

58. Barnard, *Assault on Mount Helicon*, 318.

59. Ibid., xviii.

Bibliography

Ahearn, Barry, ed. *The Correspondence of William Carlos Williams and Louis Zukofsky*. Middletown, Conn.: Wesleyan University Press, 2003.

Aldington, Richard. *Life for Life's Sake: A Book of Reminiscences*. London: Cassell, 1968.

———, trans. *The Poems of Anyte of Tegea*. Poet's Translation Series 1. London: The Egoist, 1915.

———. *The Love of Myrrhine and Konallis and Other Prose Poems*. Cleveland, Ohio: Clerk's Press, 1917.

———. "To Atthis (From the Rather Recently Discovered Papyrus of Sappho Now in the British Museum)." *The New Freewoman* 6, no. 1 (September 1, 1913): 114.

———. "A Young American Poet." *The Little Review* 2, no. 1 (March 1915): 22–25.

———, and Edward Storer, trans. *The Poems of Anyte of Tegea and Poems and Fragments of Sappho*. London: The Egoist, 1919.

Allen, Donald, ed. *The New American Poetry: 1945–1960*. New York: Grove Press, 1960.

Barnard, Mary. *Assault on Mount Helicon*. Berkeley: University of California Press, 1984.

———. "The Carver." *Gawdawfulers Anthology 1928–1929*. Portland, Ore.: Reed College, 1929.

———. "Cassandra." *New English Weekly* (February 7, 1935): 354.

———. "The Cat." *Today's Woman* (March 1947): 18.

———. *Collected Poems*. Portland, Ore.: Breitenbush, 1979.

———. "A Communication on Greek Metric, Ezra Pound, and Sappho." *Paideuma* 23, no. 1 (Spring 1994): 147–152.

———. *Cool Country*. In *Five Young American Poets*. Edited by James Laughlin, 3–40. Norfolk, Conn.: New Directions, 1940.

———. "Crossroads." *Poetry* 63, no. 5 (February 1944): 262–63.

———. "Disillusionment." *Gawdawfulers Anthology 1929–1930*. Portland, Ore.: Reed College, 1930.

———. "Eleven Poems." *New Democracy* (February 15, 1936): 193–94.
———. "Faun in Exile." *Poetry* 46, no. 1 (April 1935): 25–26.
———. *A Few Poems*. Portland, Ore.: Graphics Arts Workshop, Reed College, 1952.
———. "Further Notes on Metric." *Paideuma* 23, no. 1 (Spring 1994): 153–57.
———. "The Horae of Mary Ethel Barnard." PhD diss., Reed College, 1932.
———. "Lai." *Poetry* 46, no. 1 (April 1935): 28–29.
———. "Lethe." *New English Weekly* (February 7, 1935): 354.
———. *Nantucket Genesis: The Tale of My Tribe*. Portland, Ore.: Breitenbush Books, 1988.
———. "Northwest Anchorage." *New Republic* 91, no. 1183 (August 4, 1937): 368.
———. "A Note on Poetry." Preface to *Cool Country*. In *Five Young American Poets*. Edited by James Laughlin, 3. Norfolk, Conn.: New Directions, 1940.
———. "Ondine." *Poetry* 46, no. 1 (April 1935): 27–28.
———. "Over the Hill with the Moon." *Gawdawfulers Anthology 1929–1930*. Portland, Ore.: Reed College, 1930.
———. Papers. In the possession of Elizabeth J. Bell, literary executor to the estate of Mary Barnard, Vancouver, Washington.
———. Papers. Yale Collection of American Literature. Beinecke Rare Book and Manuscript Library. Yale University, New Haven, Conn.
———. Poetry reading. On KBOO Community Radio, Portland, Ore. Broadcast April 1, 1975. Recording provided by Thomas J. Donovan.
———. "Provincial II." *Poetry* 52, no. 5 (August 1938): 258.
———. "The Rapids." *Furioso* 1, no. 3 (Spring 1940): 23.
———. "Remarks on Poetry and the Physical World." *Townsman: A Quarterly Review* 1, no. 4 (October 1938): 6.
———. "Roots." *Townsman: A Quarterly Review* 1, no. 4 (October 1938): 6.
———. *Sappho: A New Translation*. Berkeley: University of California Press, 1958.
———. "Shoreline." *Poetry* 45, no. 5 (February 1935): 254–56.
———. "The Silk Leaf." *American Prefaces* 1, no. 4 (January 1936): 61.
Three Fables. Portland, Ore.: Breitenbush Books, 1983.
———. "The Trestle." *Townsman* 1, no. 4 (October 1938): 7.
Barnsley, Sarah. "Mary Barnard's 'North Window': Imagism and the Pacific Northwest." *Western American Literature* 44, no. 3 (Fall 2009): 251–74.
———. "Sand Is the Beginning and the End of Our Dominion: Mary Barnard, H.D. and Imagism." *Paideuma* 36 (2010): 47–74.
Barnstone, Willis. *Sappho: Lyrics in the Original Greek*. New York: Anchor Books, 1965.
Bell, Elizabeth J. "Mary Barnard: December 6, 1909–August 25, 2001." Barnardworks. 2004. Last accessed January 8, 2013. http://www.marybarnard.com/biolong.html.
———. Letter to the editor. *Reed Magazine* (June 2010). Last accessed January 8, 2013. http://www.reed.edu/reed_magazine/june2010/columns/letters/index.html.
Bowra, C. M. *Greek Lyric Poetry: From Alcman to Simonides*. Oxford: Clarendon Press, 1936.
Bradshaw, Melissa, and Adrienne Munich, eds. *Selected Poems of Amy Lowell*. New Brunswick, N.J.: Rutgers University Press, 2002.

Carlson, Roy, ed. *Contemporary Northwest Writing: A Collection of Poetry and Fiction*. Corvallis: Oregon State University Press, 1979.

Carne-Ross, D. S. "Translation and Transposition." In *The Craft and Context of Translation*. Edited by William Arrowsmith and Roger Shattuck, 3–21. Austin: University of Texas Press, 1961.

Corman, Cid. *Sappho: Wee Ones*. Green River, Vt.: Longhouse Publishers and Booksellers, 2004.

Collecott, Diana. *H.D. and Sapphic Modernism*. Cambridge: Cambridge University Press, 1999.

Costello, Bonnie, Celeste Goodridge, and Cristanne Miller, eds. *The Selected Letters of Marianne Moore*. London: Faber and Faber, 1998.

Cushman, Stephen. *William Carlos Williams and the Meanings of Measure*. New Haven, Conn.: Yale University Press, 1985.

Davenport, Guy. *Archilochos, Sappho, Alkman*. Berkeley: University of California Press, 1980.

de Rachewiltz, Mary. "Dove St Memora." *Paideuma* 23, no. 1 (Spring 1994): 7–9.

DeJean, Joan. *Fictions of Sappho, 1546–1937*. Chicago: University of Chicago Press, 1989.

Dickinson, Emily. *The Complete Poems of Emily Dickinson*, edited by Thomas H. Johnson. London: Faber and Faber, 1975.

Duval, Hanson R. *Aldous Huxley: A Bibliography*. New York: Arrow Editions, 1939.

Edmonds, J. M. "More Fragments of Sappho." *Classical Review* 23, no. 5 (August 1909): 156–58.

———. "Three Fragments of Sappho." *Classical Review* 23, no. 4 (June 1909): 99–104.

Eliot, T. S. "Reflections on Vers Libre." *New Statesman* (March 3, 1917): 518–19.

Emerson, Ralph Waldo. "The Poet." In *Selected Essays, ed.* Larzer Ziff. London: Penguin, 1985.

Esenwein, J. Berg, and Mary Roberts, eds. *The Art of Versification*. Springfield, Mass.: The Home Correspondence School, 1913.

Fitts, Dudley. Introduction to *Sappho: A New Translation*. Translated by Mary Barnard, vii–x. Berkeley: University of California Press, 1958.

Flint, F. S. "Imagisme." *Poetry* 1, no. 6 (March 1913): 198–200.

———. "The Poetry of H.D." *The Egoist* (May 1, 1915): 72–73.

Furioso Papers. Yale Collection of American Literature. Beinecke Rare Book and Manuscript Library. Yale University, New Haven, Conn

Gawdawfulers Anthology, vol. 2 (1928–1929). Portland, Ore.: Reed College, 1929.

Gawdawfulers Anthology, vol. 3 (1929–1930). Portland, Ore.: Reed College, 1930.

Gordon, David, ed. *Ezra Pound and James Laughlin: Selected Letters*. New York: W. W. Norton & Company, 1994.

———. "Ezra Pound to Mary Barnard: An ABC of Metrics." *Paideuma* 23, no. 1 (Spring 1994): 159–79.

Gregory, Eileen. *H.D. and Hellenism: Classic Lines*. Cambridge: Cambridge University Press, 1997.

Groden, Suzy Q. *Sappho*. Indianapolis, Ind.: Bobbs-Merrill Educational Publishing, 1964.

Gubar, Susan. "Sapphistries." *Signs* 10, no. 1 (1984): 43–62.

Hamilton, Ian. *Against Oblivion: Some Lives of the Twentieth-Century Poets*. London: Penguin, 2003.

Hart, Bernard. "The Conception of the Subconscious." In *Subconscious Phenomena*. Edited by Hugo Munsterberg, Theodore Ribot, Pierre Janet, Joseph Jastrow, Bernard Hart, and Morton Prince, 102–141. London: Rebman Limited, 1911.

H.D. *Bid Me to Live*. London: Virago, 1984.

———. *End to Torment*. New York: New Directions, 1979.

———. *Notes on Thought and Vision and the Wise Sappho*. London: Peter Owen, 1988.

———. Papers. Yale Collection of American Literature. Beinecke Rare Book and Manuscript Library. Yale University, New Haven, Conn.

———. "The Poems of Sappho." *Saturday Review of Literature* (March 14, 1925): 596.

———. *Sea Garden*. London: Constable, 1916.

Helle, Anita. "Dialogue with Mary Barnard." In *Homespun: A Tribute to Mary Barnard. Edited by* Douglas Spangle and Brian Hamilton, 25–32. Portland, Ore.: Quiet Lion Press, 1994.

———. "The Odysseys of Mary Barnard." *Encore* (February–March 1978): 6–9.

Hughes, Glenn. *Imagism and the Imagists: A Study in Modern Poetry. Stanford*, Calif.: Stanford University Press, 1931.

Hulme, T. E. "A Lecture on Modern Poetry." Paper presented to Poets' Club, London, November 1908.

Jarrell, Randall. *Kipling, Auden & Co.: Essays and Reviews 1935–1964*. Manchester, England: Carcanet, 1981.

———. "A Note on Poetry." In *Five Young American Poets*. Edited by James Laughlin, 3. Norfolk, Conn.: New Directions, 1940.

Johnson, Thomas H., ed. *The Complete Poems of Emily Dickinson*. London: Faber and Faber, 1975.

Lattimore, Richard. *Greek Lyrics*. Chicago: University of Chicago Press, 1960.

Laughlin, James, ed. *New Directions 2*. Norfolk, Conn.: New Directions, 1937.

Lavignac, Albert, and Lionel de la Laurencie, eds. *Encylopédie De La Musique et Dictionnaire du conservatoire*. Paris: Delgrave, 1920.

Lawrence, D. H., Amy Lowell, et al., eds. *Some Imagist Poets: An Anthology*. Boston: Houghton Mifflin, 1915.

Literary Classics of the United States, Inc., New York, N.Y. *American Poetry: The Twentieth Century*. Volume 2. New York: Library of America, 2000.

Longinus. *A Treatise on the Sublime*, translated by Frank Granger. London: Stanley Nott, 1935.

Lowell, Amy. *A Dome of Many-Coloured Glass*. Boston: Houghton Mifflin, 1912.

———. *Sword Blades and Poppy Seed*. London: Macmillan, 1914.

Lozowick, Louis. "The Americanization of Art." In *The Prints of Louis Lozowick: A Catalogue Raisonné*. Edited by Janet Flint, 18–19. New York: Hudson Hills Press. First published in *The Machine-Age Exposition*. New York: Little Review, 1927.

MacGowan, Christopher, ed. *The Letters of Denise Levertov and William Carlos Williams*. New York: New Directions, 1998.

Mariani, Paul. *William Carlos Williams: A New World Naked*. New York: McGraw-Hill, 1981.

Monro, Harold. "The Imagists Discussed." *The Egoist* (May 1, 1915): 77–80.
O'Connell, Nicholas. *At the Field's End: 20 Pacific Northwest Writers*. Seattle, Wash.: Madrona Publishers, 1987.
O'Connell, Richard. *Sappho*. Philadelphia, Penn.: Atlantis Editions, 1975.
O'Hara Ewing, Molly. "The Poetry of Mary Barnard: A Study in Voice and Verse." *Paideuma* 23, no. 1 (Spring 1994): 65–108.
Olson, Charles. *A Bibliography on America for Ed Dorn*. San Francisco: Four Seasons Foundation, 1964.
Ostriker, Alicia. "No Rule of Procedure: The Open Poetics of H.D." In *Signets: Reading H.D.* Vol. 4. Edited by Susan Stanford Friedman and Rachel Blau DuPlessis, 336–51. First published in *Agenda* 25 (Autumn/Winter 1987–1988): 145–54.
Paige, D. D., ed. *The Selected Letters of Ezra Pound, 1907–1941*. New York: New Directions, 1971. First published by Harcourt, 1950.
Paton, W. R., trans. *The Greek Anthology*. Vol. 1. London: Heinemann, 1916.
Pettijohn, F. J., P. E. Potter, and R. Siever, eds. *Sand and Sandstone*. New York: Springer-Verlag, 1987.
Phillips, Rod. *"Forest Beatniks" and "Urban Thoreaus": Gary Snyder, Jack Kerouac, Lew Welch, and Michael McClure*. New York: Peter Lang, 2000.
Pondrom, Cyrena. "H.D. and the Origins of Imagism." In *Signets: Reading H.D.* Edited by Susan Stanford Friedman and Rachel Blau DuPlessis, 85–109. Madison: University of Wisconsin Press, 1990.
Pound, Ezra. "Apparuit." *The English Review* (June 1912): 343–44.
———. *The Cantos*. London: Faber and Faber, 1968.———, ed. *Des Imagistes: An Anthology*. London: The Poetry Bookshop, 1914.
———. "A Few Don'ts by an Imagiste." *Poetry* 1, no. 6 (March 1913): 200–206.
———. *Gaudier-Brzeska: A Memoir*. New York: New Directions, 1974.
———. *Instigations*. New York: Boni and Liveright, 1920.
———. *Literary Essays of Ezra Pound*. New York: New Directions, 1968.
———. *Lustra*. London: Elkin Mathews, 1916.
———. Papers. Yale Collection of American Literature. Beinecke Rare Book and Manuscript Library. Yale University, New Haven, Conn.
———. *Pavannes and Divisions*. New York: Alfred Knopf, 1918.
———. *Personae*. New York: New Directions, 1990.
———. "The Return." *The English Review* (June 1912): 343–44.
———. "The Tradition." *Poetry* 3, no. 3 (December 1913): 137–41.
Pound, Omar, and A. Walton Litz, eds. *Ezra Pound and Dorothy Shakespear*. London: Faber and Faber, 1984.
Preminger, Alex, and T. V. F. Brogan, eds. *The New Encyclopedia of Poetry and Poetics*. Princeton, N.J.: Princeton University Press, 1993.
Prins, Yopie. *Victorian Sappho*. Princeton, N.J.: Princeton University Press, 1999.
Reck, Michael. *Ezra Pound: A Close-Up*. London: Rupert Hart David, 1968.
Reynolds, Margaret. *The Sappho Companion*. London: Vintage, 2001.
———. *The Sappho History*. Basingstoke, England: Palgrave Macmillan, 2003.
Ricou, Laurie. *The Arbutus/Madrone Files: Reading the Pacific Northwest*. Edmonton, Alberta: NeWest Press, 2002.

Roberts, Michael, ed. *The Faber Book of Modern Verse*. London: Faber and Faber, 1936.

Rohrbach, Erika. "H.D. and Sappho: A Precious Inch of Palimpsest." In *Re-reading Sappho: Reception and Transmission*. Edited by Ellen Greene, 184–198. Berkeley: University of California Press, 1996.

Snyder, Gary. *Earth House Hold: Technical Notes and Queries to Follow Dharma Revolutionaries*. New York: New Directions, 1969.

———. *Riprap*. San Francisco: Four Seasons Foundation, 1965.

Special Collections. Reed College Library, Portland, Ore.

Stafford, William. Introduction to *The Collected Poems of Mary Barnard*. Portland, Ore.: Breitenbush, 1979.

Storer, Edward, trans. *Poems and Fragments of Sappho*. Poet's Translation Series 2. London: The Egoist, 1915.

Tate, Allen. "The Last Omnibus." *Partisan Review* 8, no. 3 (May–June 1941): 241–44.

Thirlwall, John, ed. *The Selected Letters of William Carlos Williams*. New York: McDowell, Obolensky, 1957.

Trueblood, Valerie. Review of *Collected Poems*, by Mary Barnard. *American Poetry Review* 9, no. 6 (November–December 1980): 10–11.

Van Cleve, Jane. "Hearing Sappho." *Willamette Weekly*, October 16–22, 1979.

Vivien, Renée. *Sapho: Traduction nouvelle avec le texte grec*. Paris: [n.pub.], 1913.

Wharton, Henry Thornton. *Sappho: Memoir, Text, Selected Renderings and a Literal Translation*. London: David Stott, 1885.

Whitman, Walt. *Leaves of Grass (1891–92)*. In *Complete Poetry and Collected Prose*. Edited by Justin Kaplan. New York: Library of America, 1982.

Williams, William Carlos. "America, Whitman, and the Art of Poetry." *William Carlos Williams Review* 13, no. 1 (Spring 1987): 1–4. First published in *The Poetry Journal* 8, no. 1 (November 1917): 27–36.

———. *The Autobiography of William Carlos Williams*. New York: Random House, 1951.

———. *Collected Poems*. Vol. 1. New York: New Directions, 1986.

———. *In the American Grain*. Norfolk, Conn.: New Directions, 1925.

———. *Kora in Hell*. In *Imaginations*. New York: New Directions, 1970. First published privately in limited edition, 1917.

———. "Notes from a Talk on Poetry." *Poetry* 14, no. 4 (July 1919): 211–16.

———. "On Measure: Statement for Cid Corman." In *Selected Essays of William Carlos Williams*. New York: Random House, 1954.

———. Papers. Yale Collection of American Literature. Beinecke Rare Book and Manuscript Library. Yale University, New Haven, Conn.

———. *Paterson*. New York: New Directions, 1963.

———. *Selected Essays of William Carlos Williams*. New York: Random House, 1954.

———. *Selected Poems*. Edited by Charles Tomlinson. London: Penguin, 2000.

Williamson, Margaret. *Sappho's Immortal Daughters*. Cambridge, Mass.: Harvard University Press, 1995.

Wilson, Edmund. "American Writing: 1941." Editorial. *The New Republic* 104, no. 16 (April 21, 1941).

Witemeyer, Hugh. "Early Poetry 1908–1920." In *The Cambridge Companion to Ezra Pound*. Edited by Ira B. Nadel, 43–58. Cambridge: Cambridge University Press, 1999.

Index